THE WAR ON THE UYGHURS

PRINCETON STUDIES IN MUSLIM POLITICS

Dale F. Eickelman and Augustus Richard Norton, *Series Editors*

A list of titles in this series can be found at the back of the book

THE WAR ON THE UYGHURS

China's Internal Campaign against a Muslim Minority

SEAN R. ROBERTS

Princeton University Press
Princeton and Oxford

Published in the United States and Canada in 2020 by Princeton University Press
41 William Street, Princeton, New Jersey 08540
press.princeton.edu

First published in the United Kingdom in 2020 by Manchester University Press
Altrincham Street, Manchester M1 7JA
www.manchesteruniversitypress.co.uk

Library of Congress Control Number 2020934178
First paperback printing, 2022
Paperback ISBN 978-0-691-23449-6
Cloth ISBN 978-0-691-20218-1
ISBN (e-book) 978-0-691-20221-1

Jacket/Cover image: Two ethnic Uyghur women pass Chinese paramilitary policemen
standing guard outside the Grand Bazaar in the Uyghur district of the city of Urumqi
in China's Xinjiang region, July 14, 2009. Peter Parks/AFP/Getty Images

Typeset by Servis Filmsetting Ltd, Stockport, Cheshire, UK

For my 'A-team' at home: Asel and Aideen Roberts

ABOUT THE AUTHOR

Sean R. Roberts is the Director of the International Development Studies program at the George Washington University's Elliott School of International Affairs. He has a Master's degree in Visual Anthropology and a PhD in Cultural Anthropology from the University of Southern California. He has been studying the Uyghur people for thirty years, ever since his first trip to the Uyghur homeland in 1990. Roberts made a documentary on the Uyghurs of the China-Kazakhstan borderlands for his MA thesis in 1996 and completed his PhD dissertation on this community in 2003. He has been conducting ongoing field research with Uyghurs around the world ever since, and he reads and speaks the Uyghur language. This book is the product of this long-term research and employs a wide range of Uyghur language sources, including interviews with Uyghurs as well as Uyghur language documents and videos, which have previously not been analyzed in academic works.

CONTENTS

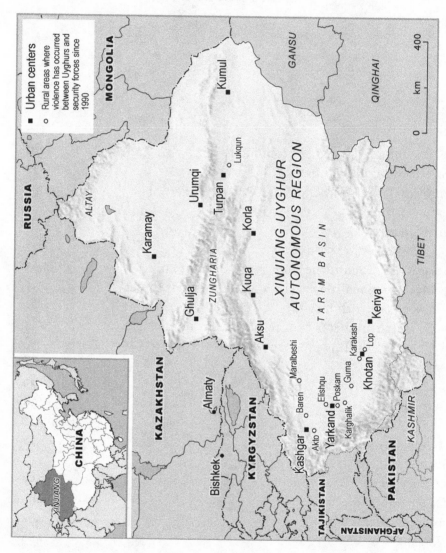

Xinjiang Uyghur Autonomous Region

PREFACE

This book's release was delayed due to the COVID-19 pandemic, which was quickly sweeping the world as the book was being prepared for publication. However, this delay offers me an important opportunity to contextualize the book's content in our present moment of global crisis and provide related updates on the situation of Uyghurs in China. This is particularly important given the book's thesis that the fate of the Uyghurs inside China has been facilitated by the intersection of local and global political processes. While the book focuses on the ways that the Global War on Terror (GWOT) has intertwined with the story of the Uyghur cultural genocide, one can expect that the COVID-19 global pandemic will serve as an equally important watershed moment in global political processes that will inevitably also impact the fate of Uyghurs inside China.

It is first important to note that the full extent of the impact of the public health crisis created by COVID-19 on Uyghurs inside China remains unknown. From the appearance of the disease in Wuhan in December 2019 until May 2020 when I wrote this preface, there has been very little reliable information coming out of the Uyghur homeland. There are multiple reasons for this. First, the entire People's Republic of China (PRC) remained mostly in lockdown during this time, making accurate information from far-flung regions even scarcer than usual. Second, the PRC expelled from China the best international journalists covering the Uyghur cultural genocide from *The New York Times*, *The Wall Street Journal*, and *Washington Post* during Spring 2020. While this was done largely in retaliation for

for the international community to take urgent action. A group of mainly western states has recently condemned the persecution of the Uyghurs at the UN level. The US Secretary of State has also taken up the issue on a bilateral level, and efforts are afoot to impose sanctions on Chinese officials through so-called Magnitsky legislation in the US. Other countries with Magnitsky legislation (including the UK) need to follow suit urgently.

Sean Roberts' account of China's war on the Uyghurs provides a vital resource for those wishing to understand the background to this human rights atrocity. It traces the history of Uyghur nationalism, and objectively examines the evidence exposing the myths perpetrated by the Chinese Communist Party to justify this atrocity in the making. This book should act as a wake-up call for policy-makers worldwide. Armed with the piercing and detailed analysis of the recent past in East Turkistan, and the graphic accounts of the present, no one has any further excuse for failing to grasp the full reality of the human tragedy that is taking place. Roberts de-mystifies the background, debunks the false excuses of the Chinese state, and presents the reality of the persecution unfolding before our eyes. None of us can afford to look away.

Ben Emmerson QC
Former UN Special Rapporteur on Counter-Terrorism, and former Judge of the United Nations International Criminal Tribunals for Rwanda and the Former Yugoslavia.

kind is, in itself, a fundamental human rights violation on a mass scale. Strategies that inflict deep psychological wounds on an entire community never succeed. They are invariably counter-productive and nurse the very grievances that cause people to turn to extreme ideologies.

The Chinese Communist Party is using counterterrorism as a fig-leaf for cultural genocide. Inside the camps, the regime is regulated by directives that are designed to break the will of those who have been imprisoned. That is the first step in a classic program of brainwashing. The individual's autonomy is completely eliminated. Every tiny aspect of their daily lives, from where they sit, to when they can speak, is controlled with vicious attention to detail. Any deviation is met with severe forms of punishment. Prisoners are forbidden from using their own language, from practicing their religion, or manifesting their cultural identity in any way. They are held incommunicado, cut off from the outside world, and are only eligible for release after incarceration for months or years. In order to have any chance of being considered for release, they must prove that they have absorbed the official Han Chinese orthodoxy, and have abandoned their independent identity altogether.

The camps are only part of the state apparatus that has been mobilised against the Uyghurs. There have been widespread and credible reports of torture, disappearances, forced sterilisation, and organ harvesting. Traditional Uyghur burial sites and other sites of cultural heritage have been bulldozed and are being built upon as this book goes to press. These are the hallmarks of cultural genocide – a policy that aims at the destruction of the separate identity of a distinct ethnic, cultural, or religious group.

China has, so far, eluded effective international action against it. That is because it is not party to any of the international human rights treaties that would enable other states to enforce the basic rules of human rights and humanitarian law. But there is no doubt whatsoever that the actions of the Chinese authorities amount to crimes against humanity. They constitute a widespread and systematic attack on the civilian population, and they may be pointers towards the commission of the crime of genocide. It is vital

FOREWORD

Over the past two years, the international community has become increasingly aware of the relentless persecution of the Uyghurs in East Turkistan (Xinjiang Uyghur Autonomous Region) by the authoritarian Chinese Communist Party. This ancient community has become stigmatised as enemies of the monolithic Chinese state that occupies its homeland. They have been subjected to collective punishment in the form of mass incarceration in concentration camps, aimed at their so-called 're-education'. Between one million and three million Uyghurs have disappeared into this dystopian prison estate. The Chinese government claims these institutions are voluntary re-education camps, designed to eradicate extremism among the Muslim population of East Turkistan. The reality is that they are part of a much wider strategy aimed at eliminating the separate ethnocultural identity of the Uyghurs, and effectively wiping them off the map as a separate ethnic group.

In my role as United Nations Special Rapporteur on Human Rights and Counter-Terrorism, I spent six years examining the various means used by different states to prevent the spread of violent extremism and to counter the appeal of extremist narratives. I examined various programs from Europe to the Middle East, from Sweden to Saudi Arabia. None of them have involved a wholesale attack on an entire community, or the mass incarceration of entirely innocent people solely on the basis of their ethnicity or religion. What is happening in Xinjiang province is not, in any sense, a legitimate counterterrorism strategy. On the contrary, collective punishment of this restrictions on Chinese journalists in the US, it also served to stall ongoing investigations into PRC actions against Uyghurs. Finally, the attention of the world writ large, and thus of journalists, has been diverted from the plight of the Uyghurs and focused squarely on the global response to the pandemic.

Fortunately, initial impressions suggest that the worst-case scenario of the disease spreading among the likely over one million Uyghurs still in some form of internment or incarceration appears to have not come to pass. Officially, the numbers of those infected and killed by the virus in the Uyghur region of China remained low at the time of writing this preface, with the number of cases under 100 and the number of deaths below five. Of course, given the PRC's track record of blatant misinformation about this region since 2017, there is no reason to believe these statistics, and, given the unprecedented numbers of Uyghurs in overcrowded penal institutions, it remains possible that the virus did serious physical damage to this population about which we may never know. However, no reliable evidence had emerged as of this preface's writing of the mass illness and/or deaths of Uyghurs in internment and incarceration, and, given China's apparent containment of the virus, it is likely that the spread of COVID-19 in the Uyghur homeland, even if greater than official statistics assert, has been limited, at least into May 2020.

If it appears that this worst-case scenario had not transpired, available information does suggest that the global pandemic was already creating a situation by May 2020 where PRC actions facilitating the Uyghur cultural genocide were being consolidated and normalized. In particular, the processes described in Chapter 6 and the conclusion of this book that point to a transition from mass internment to a system of coerced and segregated residential labor, including family separation and population transfers, appear to have accelerated during the first months of the pandemic. This also seems to have been accompanied by increased assimilation measures, particularly targeting children, and perhaps even efforts to encourage Han settlement in the region. While the details of these actions remain sparse, they may point to a new phase in the campaign to destroy Uyghur identity and transform their homeland that could render the region unrecognizable to international observers once they are able to return there after the pandemic is under control globally. In this sense, the legacy of the COVID-19 pandemic for the Uyghurs may be its role as a smoke-screen that obscures the measures that were taken against them as a people since 2017, and helps to erase the memory of both Uyghur culture in China and the Uyghur homeland as they existed before 2017.

The first signs of these actions to consolidate and normalize what is happening to Uyghurs inside China were apparent already in late February 2020 as the various coerced residential labor programs for rural Uyghurs, both inside their homeland and in inner China, were resumed if not increased.[1] Taking place while China was generally in lockdown to contain the pandemic, this green light given to Uyghur factory workers raised speculation that this already marginalized population might also be among the 'expendable' workers used to re-start the country's economy while most Chinese people were kept safely isolated. Uyghurs in exile appeared to further confirm this mass mobilization of rural Uyghur laborers through the re-posting of videos from the Uyghur region on social media showing large labor brigades, with suitcases and wearing pandemic-mandated masks, presumably being transported to work in factories. While such programs are officially framed as voluntary, in the context of the mass internment and incarceration of Uyghurs that has been ongoing since 2017, it is assumed that not participating would be viewed as subversive and punishable by imprisonment or internment.

As described in Chapter 6 of this book, these labor programs, while less violent and more palatable to outside observers than the mass internment camps, play a critical role in the control and 'trans-formation' of China's rural Uyghur population. Inside the home-land, the state is mobilizing thousands of rural Uyghurs, both former internees and others, to work in scores of new residential factories throughout the region, helping to depopulate rural towns that were once overwhelmingly Uyghur and destroying the bonds of family and community that make up Uyghur culture. Additionally, these programs also seek to 'transform' these new factory workers by man-dating that they take political 're-education' and Chinese-language classes while removing them from a Uyghur linguistic and cultural further the destruction of the world's tenuous 'rules-based order' that has been deteriorating since GWOT was declared, bringing us increasingly into the post-privacy, post-rights, and anti-diversity global environment I describe in the book's conclusion. However, it is also possible that this moment of global upheaval could facilitate a reversal of these trends, as common global suffering highlights the need for more international oversight and humanitarianism as well as for the empowerment of non-state actors to hold states and other sources of international power accountable both within and across borders. Whichever of these trajectories evolves in the aftermath of this global crisis, one can expect the world to be even more contentious than it has become during the pandemic. While likely not to be at the top of the post-pandemic global agenda, how the story of the Uyghur cultural genocide told in this book further develops may be indicative of which way a new post-2020 world order is headed.

Sean R. Roberts
15 May 2020
Washington, DC

the Uyghur region if they settle in new under-populated cities in the traditionally Uyghur-majority south.[5] While the extent of this program is unknown, combined with the deliberate displacement of Uyghurs in the region through labor programs, this appears to mark a new stage of state-sponsored settler colonization by the Han majority population of China. Concurrently, it is assumed that the transformation of the landscape of the Uyghur homeland described in Chapter 6 is also continuing unabetted during the pandemic to make way for this settlement.

All of these actions make sense in the context of the overall goals of the state in its campaign to destroy the Uyghur identity. As this book suggests, the state campaign against the Uyghurs in China, while couched in terms of 'counterterrorism,' has really been driven by settler colonialism, ultimately seeking to make the Uyghur homeland indistinguishable, with the exception of physical geography, from the rest of China both in appearance and demographics. In the book's conclusion, I suggest that the present trajectory in the region is successfully facilitating such a colonization, but I also argue that this process would take several years of sustained and unchallenged repression to become irreversible. Unfortunately, the signs of accelerated colonization evident during the early months of the COVID-19 pandemic could facilitate the entrenchment of this process by the time the pandemic has passed, making the ultimate transformation of the Uyghur homeland into a Han-dominated part of the PRC a *fait accompli*. Furthermore, in the process, the Chinese state may be able to erase much of the physical evidence of the violent mass internment of Uyghurs since 2017 that helped propel the final chapter of this colonization.

In this context, the call to grassroots activism on the issue of the Uyghur cultural genocide that I articulate in the book's conclusion is all the more urgent today. However, now, any activism on the Uyghur issue will also need to contend with a changing geopolitical context. While the impact of the COVID-19 pandemic on global political and economic processes remains one of the largest unknowns for the future, it seems clear that the present crisis will seriously alter geopolitics. It may be that this critical juncture in world history will land as it increasingly releases former internees into these controlled labor programs. Already in December 2019, the ethnic Uyghur chairman of the regional government, Shohrat Zakir, suggested that most residents in these camps, which he calls 'vocational training centers,' had 'graduated' and were now being placed in employment, presumably in the above-mentioned factory labor programs. As a result, he also suggested that these camps would be open to the broader Uyghur public who could pursue 'vocational training' in them prior to job placement.[3] While the information black-out from the Uyghur region since January 2020 has made it impossible to know what steps have been taken towards this end, it is possible that the smokescreen of COVID-19 could allow for such a normalization of the mass internment camps, turning them into less violent, but still coercive and indoctrinating intake points for the expanding coercive labor programs. As such, the Chinese government might even open up these centers to international observers after the pandemic has passed in an attempt to hide and deny the extra-judicial, violent, and involuntary nature of the internment that took place in these camps starting in 2017.

Other actions by the state also suggest that the government of China is consolidating its destruction of Uyghur identity during the global pandemic. While the state is relegating large numbers of adults to residential factories, it is also stepping up the construction of boarding schools in Uyghur-populated areas, including for preschool-aged children, where Uyghur students are taught in Chinese language and culture while being separated from their families and communities. In Khotan's Karakash region, the local government has even allegedly issued an order requiring that all preschools in the region require live-in boarding for the 2020–2021 school year.[4] If these reports are accurate, they may signal the early stages of a mandatory boarding school program for all Uyghur children. If that were to happen, the next generation of Uyghurs would be brought up in blatantly assimilationist institutions with little access to the cultural markers of their identity as Uyghurs.

Finally, reports since the pandemic began have also suggested that the Chinese state is now providing subsidies for outside settlers to milieu. Even more insidious are the related labor programs that bring rural Uyghur laborers to factories in inner China, where they are segregated in special dormitories, not allowed to leave factory grounds, and subjected to 're-education' after work hours. In addition to attempting to 'transform' those rural Uyghurs participating, these programs inside China proper also ostensibly help to depopulate the Uyghur homeland of Uyghurs, perhaps establishing a limited form of ethnic cleansing.

While programs transferring Uyghurs to work in inner China have been operational since at least 2006, the *South China Morning Post* revealed in May 2020 that the numbers of such coerced Uyghur migrant laborers are now being increased in line with quotas assigned to 19 different provinces and municipalities of the PRC, likely the same regions involved in the controversial 'Pairing Assistance Program' (PAP) that has driven the development of the Uyghur homeland since 2010.[2] With the quota assigned to Shenzhen alone alleged to be 50,000 laborers, one can assume that the total numbers scheduled to be transferred from the Uyghur homeland through this program over the next several years will be in the hundreds of thousands, seriously altering the demographics of the region.

As Chapter 6 of this book suggests, these labor programs appear to present an endgame for the mass internment camps that have been at the center of China's campaign against its Uyghur population since 2017. The system of mass internment, imprisonment, and surveillance that has been in place in the Uyghur homeland has effectively neutralized resistance from the Uyghur people in China and has served to destroy their social capital and break their spirits. Now, with most intellectuals still interned or incarcerated, the majority of the rural population are being marginalized and controlled through relegation to an underclass of factory labor where they are targeted for political indoctrination and assimilationist measures. Furthermore, a significant portion of this new Uyghur underclass are being transferred to inner China and separated from their homeland entirely.

In this context, it appears that the regional government has started to reimagine the role of mass internment camps in the Uyghur home-

INTRODUCTION

During the second half of 2017, most international scholars studying Uyghurs and/or the Xinjiang Uyghur Autonomous Region (XUAR) recognized that something was seriously wrong as our Uyghur colleagues and friends in the region began disappearing. Many Uyghur students studying abroad were called back to their homeland by the government at this time, and Uyghurs in diaspora were told by relatives inside China to stop contacting them.[1] This coincided with a time when western scholars and journalists were reporting on an unprecedented securitization of the XUAR under recently appointed regional Party Secretary Chen Quanguo, who was turning the region into an Orwellian surveillance state.[2] Although Chen had implemented similar securitization tactics in Tibet, where he had previously served, in the XUAR it was bolstered by a new massive system of electronic surveillance, which included an extensive database on Uyghur residents' habits, relations, religiosity, and other traits that could be used to assess their 'loyalty' to the state.[3]

These measures appeared to represent yet another intensification of repressive policies in a region where securitization and suspicions about Uyghurs' loyalty to the state had been increasing for decades. Nonetheless, these trends towards increased repression in the XUAR did not prepare people for the shocking revelations in late 2017 that the People's Republic of China (PRC) had created extrajudicial mass internment camps for Uyghurs and other indigenous Muslims throughout the region.[4] By 2018, estimates of the number of Uyghurs and other local Muslims in these camps had been set around 1 million, with some suggesting that it could be closer to 2 million.[5] These camps' ethnic and religious profiling of Uyghurs and other indigenous Turkic groups has raised fears that the world is witnessing the preamble to yet another genocide.

While the use of the term 'genocide' to describe what is happening to the Uyghurs inside the XUAR, like any use of this word, is controversial, with time it has become clear that the PRC is at the very least committing acts of 'cultural genocide' against the Uyghurs. In effect, the Chinese state has launched a campaign to destroy Uyghur identity as we know it. This is being accomplished through a complex of policies, which work together to attack the cultural products and practices, religious beliefs, and social capital that define Uyghurs, while simultaneously transforming the landscape of the XUAR, which Uyghurs consider to be their homeland. The internment camps, in which a significant portion of the Uyghur population has been detained indefinitely and without due process, are at the center of this complex of policies.

Inside these camps, the internees are subjected to prison-like conditions, forced to study the Chinese language for hours on end, followed by additional hours of being force-fed Communist Party propaganda, much of which targets Islam and related Uyghur cultural practices as a dangerous ideology.[6] Some accounts suggest that internees are prevented from speaking their native languages and even from casually communicating with each other, and there are numerous reports of severe torture plus multiple claims by former detainees of having been forced to take unidentified drugs.[7] While there are reportedly criteria for being put into the camps, which are designated for suspected 'terrorists,' 'extremists,' and 'separatists,' detention appears to be quota-based and largely arbitrary, leading to the internment of Uyghurs and other indigenous Muslims from all walks of life.[8]

While these internment camps, which have been compared both to Nazi concentration camps and Stalin's gulags, are the most headline-grabbing aspect of the surge in PRC repression of Uyghurs since 2017, they are only part of a larger system of control and coercion that has been unleashed on all Uyghurs inside the XUAR. The largely arbitrary criteria for detention in the camps creates an omni-

present fear of internment throughout the local indigenous population. Uyghurs who have not been interned have reported that they wait every evening for a 'knock on the door' from authorities who might take them to the camps, and that they fear talking about the camps with even their closest friends and families, since being overheard doing so is likely to end in one's internment.[9] Additionally, there is a growing distrust, even within the Uyghur community, as people live in fear that co-workers or neighbors on the basis of petty personal grudges might report them as 'terrorists,' 'extremists,' or 'separatists,' categories of population which the PRC has framed collectively as the 'three evils' and one of the most existential internal security threats to state and society.

Furthermore, this fear is reinforced by a widespread system of surveillance, which was put in place just prior to mass internment and serves to track virtually every Uyghur in the region – their movements, their interactions, and their thoughts. The backbone of this surveillance focuses on public spaces that are closely watched by frequent check-points, omnipresent small police stations, and a massive network of CCTV cameras equipped with facial recognition software. However, this surveillance network reaches even beyond public space and also invades the private lives of Uyghurs.[10] Spyware that is forcibly installed on the smart phones of Uyghurs is able to track their whereabouts via GPS, surveil their communications, and observe any media held on their devices. Uyghurs are also subjected to constant evaluations of loyalty to the Party conducted at their workplaces and in their neighborhoods by authorities.[11] Finally, in perhaps the most surreal part of this system of mass surveillance, upwards of a million Party cadres have been tasked with visiting and temporarily living with Uyghur families throughout the region, allowing them to report on their household décor, their private discussions, their personal habits, and their spirituality as potential signs of the 'three evils.'[12] All of these data points are incorporated into a massive database, which provides security organs with vast information on individual Uyghurs and can determine their fate, whether they are interned, imprisoned, or allowed to continue their lives for the time being.[13]

In effect, this network of surveillance, indoctrination, and internment is serving to destroy Uyghur identity by breaking the linkages of social capital, discouraging Uyghur language use, and dismantling any aspects of Uyghur cultural practices the state deems threatening. At the same time, it serves as a potent force to coerce compliance with other policies promoting Uyghur assimilation and the transformation of the landscape of the XUAR in an attempt to strip it of signs of indigenous culture, except when packaged in a sanitized form for tourists. The Uyghur language is gradually being removed from public spaces, there is a campaign to destroy mosques and Muslim graveyards throughout the XUAR, and neighborhoods of traditional Uyghur housing are being demolished.[14] Many of those Uyghurs and other indigenous Muslims who remain outside of the mass internment system and prisons, especially those in rural areas, are being pushed into either working within the security system or taking part in new large residential industrial brigades detached from their families and communities.[15] Additionally, they are encouraged to engage in ethnically mixed marriages with Han citizens, and their children are being sent to boarding schools where they are taught Chinese language and culture without the socialization into Uyghur culture offered by parents.[16] If they do not take advantage of such opportunities when offered, they inevitably come under suspicion and consideration for either imprisonment or internment.

This campaign to destroy Uyghur identity will be discussed in much more detail in the book's final chapter, which will also elaborate on its nature as a form of cultural genocide, but it is important to convey to the reader at least the extent and scale of this campaign's atrocities at the book's outset. The book seeks to explain how this repressive campaign evolved, why it is being undertaken, and how it is being justified to both Chinese citizens and the world. Overall, the book argues that the campaign's intent is to once and for all forcibly integrate and assimilate the territory of the XUAR and its people into the PRC's vision of a modern China, something Uyghurs have long resisted. In this sense, the campaign is reminiscent of settler colonial projects from the last three centuries, which sought to break the will and destroy the communities of indigenous populations, quarantine

and decimate large portions of their populations, and marginalize the remainder while subjecting them to forced assimilation.

Modern China has a long history of colonial relations with Uyghurs and their homeland. While this region has nominally been part of modern China since the mid-eighteenth century, the Qing Empire and Republican China largely failed in their efforts to integrate its territory and people into a modern Chinese polity. Since 1949, the PRC has been more forceful in this goal, significantly changing the demographics of the region and subjecting its population to state-wide policies, but as late as 1990, the region remained marginal to the politics and economy of the PRC and its population resistant to assimilation into PRC-led Chinese society. The present campaign of cultural genocide has its roots in the 1990s when the PRC first began developing this region as part of its economic reforms, recognizing that its geographic location on the borders of the former Soviet Union could be an asset to China's growing export-oriented economy. However, after almost three decades of increased development and incentivized assimilation measures, the PRC found that the region's people remained resistant to its attempts to integrate and assimilate this territory and its population into the state's vision for the future of its polity and society. It is in this context that the state, emboldened by the authoritarian turn of Xi Jinping and his vision of a unified and uniform PRC, has resorted to the tactics of forcible assimilation and cultural genocide.

While during the nineteenth and early twentieth centuries, such a fate befell countless Indigenous Peoples around the world, including the Native Americans of both North and South America and the Aboriginals of Australia and New Zealand, since the late twentieth century, global norms have generally recognized that the excesses of cultural genocide were unjustified in the name of 'modernization' and 'development' and should not be repeated. UN Conventions and Declarations on Genocide, the rights of Indigenous Peoples, and the rights of ethnic minorities, while not necessarily preventing such acts, have flagged them as unacceptable and open to condemnation. Nonetheless, we now appear to be witnessing cultural genocide's return in the twenty-first century, aided by all of the information

technologies of this century that were once imagined to serve as a democratizing force in the world.

A central argument of this book is that this return of cultural genocide in the twenty-first century is largely facilitated by a particular ideology that is unique to this century – that of the 'Global War on Terror' (GWOT). As will be further argued below, GWOT has allowed the use of the 'terrorist' label to justify the blatant suspension of human rights for entire populations, based on their racial, religious, and/or ethnic profile, conveniently lending itself to genocidal strategies. In the context of GWOT, the 'terrorist' label marks an existential threat that has been used to justify a variety of atrocities against those whom become branded with this label. Furthermore, since what constitutes a 'terrorist' is not clearly defined, but is assumed to refer to a threat that is hidden within a larger population, the identification of a 'terrorist threat' within any given group of Muslims can quickly justify the suspension of human rights for, and perhaps genocidal acts against, an entire category of people.

Therefore, it is not surprising that the PRC, after initially denying the existence of its mass internment and related repressive policies in the XUAR, has justified all of these measures by claiming that those being subjected to them have become adherents of Islamic 'extremist' ideologies and, thus, pose a grave 'terrorist threat' to Chinese society.[17] In this context, the Chinese state suggests that its policies are not seeking to destroy Uyghur culture, but merely to eradicate an 'extremist' ideology it claims has infected that culture. In making this argument, the PRC readily deflects international criticism of its actions vis-à-vis Uyghurs as being little different than the actions taken by western states against alleged 'terrorists' since 2001. Likewise, it has employed this narrative extensively in the domestic sphere, ensuring that most Chinese citizens, including state officials, understand what is happening in the XUAR to be an appropriate response to an existential 'terrorist threat,' not a blatant attempt to forcibly assimilate Uyghurs and colonize their homeland.

In this context, the book demonstrates how the intersection of GWOT with a history of colonial relations between modern China

and Uyghurs has created the unprecedented repression we are witnessing in the Uyghur homeland today. In doing so, it places blame for this situation at the feet of both the PRC and the international community. While the repressive measures presently being carried out against the Uyghurs are undoubtedly the initiative of the Chinese government, which should be held accountable for them, it has been the international obsession with combating a vaguely defined 'terrorist' enemy that has allowed the PRC to implement these measures with impunity and that, at least in part, has inspired their excessively brutal and genocidal nature.

WHO ARE THE UYGHURS?

The Uyghurs are a mostly Muslim people speaking a language from the Turkic linguistic family, and they primarily inhabit the northwest region of China presently known officially as the XUAR, but often referred to by Uyghurs as 'Eastern Turkistan.' In this region, which Uyghurs consider their homeland, the group's population is over 11,300,000.[18] Additionally, an estimated 500,000 Uyghurs live around the world, with particularly large populations in Kazakhstan, Kyrgyzstan, and Turkey. Culturally, linguistically, and historically, they share much more with the peoples of former Soviet Central Asia than they do with the Han ethnic group of China. Within the greater Central Asian cultural region, they are primarily identified with the settled traditions as opposed to those of the nomadic Kazakhs, Kyrgyz, and Turkmen, and their language is mostly mutually intelligible with that of the Uzbeks, who likewise have a long history of settled agriculture, urbanism, and trade.[19]

Islam has a long history among the Uyghurs, and today most Uyghurs identify as Muslims. While Islam in the Uyghur homeland is usually depicted as being affiliated with the Hanafi School of Sunni Islam, local practices are very diverse and syncretic, drawing from a long history of mystical Sufi traditions and indigenous religious practices.[20] While Uyghurs have long made the *Haj* pilgrimage to Mecca, the distance of their homeland from the Islamic centers of the Middle East has always left them on the margins of the Muslim world and global Islamic movements. Furthermore, in their homeland today, there are numerous Uyghurs who are not religious at all, but adopt various Muslim practices as part of their cultural traditions. However, Islam has played an important role in the development of Uyghur identity and, during the modern period, has served as a means for this population to differentiate itself from the dominant Han people of China.

While modern Uyghurs generally draw their lineage from an ancient Uyghur empire that ruled much of their homeland in the eighth and ninth centuries, like most modern ethnic groups, they are actually an amalgamation of different peoples who have inhabited this region at different times historically.[21] In particular, the Uyghurs developed from a combination of different Turkic peoples, who entered the region first in the sixth century, and various Indo-European peoples, who are assumed to be the earliest inhabitants of their homeland.[22] As a result, the physical appearance of Uyghurs is varied enough to include types one might associate with a significant number of different peoples throughout Eurasia. This diverse genetic history makes it difficult for most Uyghurs to pass as Han Chinese, hampering any efforts to fully assimilate them into the Han population. The fact that Uyghurs are the largest ethnic group in China that is obviously differentiated physically from the Han has imbued the relationship between Uyghurs and Han with a clear racial dimension, which has undoubtedly impacted the Uyghurs' place in modern China and marked them as 'others' in a society that has generally associated homogeneity with stability.

While the concept of a unified Uyghur nation did not develop until the twentieth century, the gradual Islamization and Turkification of their homeland that took place between the tenth and thirteenth centuries did much to develop a unified culture in this region and to lay the foundations for the modern Uyghur identity. By the time that the Qing Empire conquered this region in the mid-eighteenth century, this unified culture was apparent in the local population. While they had yet to adopt the Uyghur ethnonym, this population was united by a shared sense of space, customs, language, religion, and the oral transmission of texts.[23] In this sense, Uyghurs today

should be considered as the Indigenous People of the region they view as their homeland. According to the UN, Indigenous Peoples are those inhabiting a region prior to the conquest, occupation, and/ or settlement of that land by those of different ethnic or cultural origins who come to dominate that territory.[24] However, the PRC is adamant that Uyghurs are not indigenous to their homeland and that this region has always been part of a larger China, an assertion that fuels tension between Uyghurs and the Chinese state.[25]

This tension has generally been over one critical question related to the Uyghur homeland: to whom does this region belong and, thus, to whom should be given authority over the governance and development of its population and territory? Perhaps the most vivid indicator of the opposing attitudes of modern Chinese states and Uyghurs towards this question is the divergence between the names each gives to this territory. Modern Chinese states assert that the region's rightful name is Xinjiang (or 'New Frontier'), a name given to the region by the Qing Empire after its conquest and the official name given to it since the 1880s when the area was first incorporated into a modern polity based in China. Most Uyghurs consciously don't utilize this name in their everyday discourse given its obvious colonial overtones. Some Uyghurs prefer the name *Shärqi Turkistan* (or 'Eastern Turkistan'), which stresses the indigenous nature of its Turkic population and evokes the history of two short-lived independent states of the same name that were established in parts of the region in the 1930s and 1940s respectively. Other Uyghurs inside China prefer the use of *Uyghur Diyari* (or 'Uyghur Region') as a means of avoiding the use of Xinjiang, a preference that is more pronounced today as authorities now view the use of 'Eastern Turkistan' as 'extremist' behavior.[26]

I have chosen to generally avoid calling this region either 'Xinjiang' or 'Eastern Turkistan' in an effort to avoid being perceived as taking a stance on political questions of sovereignty. Instead, I employ the terms 'Uyghur region' or 'Uyghur homeland' to describe this territory, except when referring to state or Uyghur nationalist characterizations of the region. While acknowledging this area as the 'Uyghur homeland' may appear to be a political stance in the eyes of the

Chinese government, I believe this is an objective description of the historical relationship between Uyghurs and this territory. As such, it is not meant to reflect a position on the political question of whether this region should be an independent state or a part of the PRC.

The debate about this territory's rightful name is symbolic of the tenuous relationship between Uyghurs and modern China and the long simmering conflict that characterizes this relationship. This conflict has varied in intensity historically, sometimes being manifested in low-level resistance and at other times fostering outright violent conflict, but it has been consistently present on some level since the Qing conquest of the Uyghur homeland. A central argument of this book is that the PRC's decision shortly after 11 September 2001 (9/11) to characterize the ongoing resistance of Uyghurs to Chinese rule as an international 'terrorist threat' fundamentally altered the relationship between modern China and Uyghurs, perhaps rendering their long-simmering conflict ultimately unresolvable for the foreseeable future.

One of the reasons that the PRC was able to so readily implicate Uyghurs in GWOT was that the war was declared against an ambiguous enemy. 'Terrorism' itself has no universally accepted definition and is primarily a political label used to discredit non-state actors engaged in armed resistance against a state or society. But since my analysis relies in part on a determination of whether Uyghurs have represented an *actual* 'terrorist threat' to the PRC and the world, it is critical that the book adopts a working definition of 'terrorism' to clarify its perspective on what should and should not be considered a 'terrorist threat.' In doing so, the book also takes a stance on what should be considered as legitimate and illegitimate political violence perpetrated by non-state actors by holding non-state actors to the same standards as states in terms of the international regulation of armed conflict.

WHAT IS TERRORISM?

Famously, in his historical examination of 'terrorism,' Walter Laqueur suggested that the phenomenon defied definition because any attempt to achieve international consensus on the subject

'would lead to endless controversies.'[27] Implied in Laqueur's state-ment is both that 'terrorism' has long been characterized as an ille-gitimate form of armed struggle, and that many international actors seek to maintain a vague definition of the phenomenon because such imprecision allows them more latitude to use the label selectively, omitting it to shield those non-state militant movements they sup-port and employing it to condemn those they oppose. This political manipulation of the 'terrorist' designation is frequently evoked via a quote from a 1975 novel about the 'troubles' in Northern Ireland: 'one's man's terrorist is another man's freedom fighter.'[28]

However, GWOT fundamentally changed the calculus involved in the political arbitrariness of being branded a 'terrorist' historically. Prior to GWOT, it was assumed that those deemed to be 'terrorists' by one global power could usually rely on another global power to recognize them as 'freedom fighters.' While I would argue that the politically motivated arbitrariness of branding a group as 'terrorists' did not disappear with the advent of GWOT, after September 2001 there was a concerted, albeit overtly political, effort to establish an international consensus about who should be considered 'terrorists' and, thus, enemies in this new global war. Through political 'horse trading,' numerous states sought to get non-state Muslim actors with whom they were in conflict on this new list of global enemies. China was one state that succeeded in this endeavor in 2002 when it received international recognition that it faced a 'terrorist threat' from a small group of Uyghurs who had settled in Afghanistan. This book argues that this recognition was unwarranted and politically motivated, but to make such a claim, it must do something first that the international community has failed to do. It must define 'terror-ism' or at least provide a working definition of this term as it is used in this book.

The book's critical analysis of GWOT is not meant to be dis-missive of 'terrorism' as a real concern to the world. The events of 9/11 were horrific and should be considered crimes against human-ity, as should the 2004 Beslan School Massacre in Russia; the 2008 attacks in Mumbai, India; the 2011 mass attacks on Utoya, Norway; the 2014 attacks in Gamboru and Ngala in Nigeria; the 2014 knife

murders in Kunming; the 2015 mass killings in Paris, France; the 2019 attack in Christchurch, New Zealand; and hundreds of other similar attacks, including the politically motivated mass shootings that have plagued the US in recent years.

What is universally contemptible about all of these acts of violence is neither the ideology and political aims that are behind them (although these are frequently reprehensible) nor the identity of those who carried them out and the groups to which they belonged. Rather, the characteristics of these acts of violence that make them all worthy of condemnation is that they deliberately targeted innocent civilians who had no direct connection to the political grievances of those who carried out the attacks. In my opinion, any objective definition of 'terrorism' and subsequent condemnation of 'terrorist acts' should address this core point as a means of protecting innocent people from the violence of political conflict, regardless of the nature of that conflict.

In essence, this position is an attempt to hold non-state actors accountable to the same standards as states in political armed conflict. Whether or not one agrees with either side of an armed conflict is a purely political question that is dependent upon one's values and interests in that conflict. However, the international system has recognized that violent political conflict is part of global reality and has often been a necessity for given populations to realize their rights and defend themselves from repression or conquest. This is why the international community has created rules of engagement for war and has established institutions to enforce these rules. Among those rules is the stipulation that, during war time, parties to the conflict should not deliberately target civilians. State actors that do so are considered war criminals, and non-state actors who do so should be as well, thus rightfully earning the stigmatized label of 'terrorists.'

This is not a radical position. In fact, it was proposed in 2002 by an eminent Israeli expert on 'terrorism,' Boaz Ganor, as a means for making GWOT a more rationalized and winnable war and for truly protecting innocent civilians from the violence of political conflict. As Ganor writes:

A correct and objective definition of terrorism can be based upon accepted international laws and principles regarding what behaviors are permitted in conventional wars between nations. These laws are set out in the Geneva and Hague Conventions, which in turn are based upon the basic principle that the deliberate harming of soldiers during wartime is a necessary evil, and thus permissible, whereas the deliberate targeting of civilians is absolutely forbidden. These Conventions thus differentiate between soldiers who attack a military adversary, and war criminals who deliberately attack civilians.[29]

As Ganor suggests, this same principle which is applied to states during wars should be extended to non-state actors engaged in political conflict. Non-state actors who deliberately target civilians for politically motivated violence should be considered 'terrorists,' and those who attack military, police, and state institutions for such purposes should be understood as engaged in guerilla warfare. It is certainly reasonable that a state would respond to such guerilla warfare with the use of force against its perpetrators under internationally recognized rules of engagement for war, but that does not mean that those they are attacking should be considered 'terrorists' and universally condemned.

By Ganor's logic, such a distinction both protects innocent civilians and recognizes the right of non-state actors to partake in armed resistance. After all, if all non-state actors were denied such rights, neither our modern world system nor democracy as a form of modern governance would exist. There would have been no anti-colonial liberation movements resulting in independent post-colonial states, and there would have been no revolutions replacing the age of monarchies with the forms of modern statehood that exist today. For Ganor, this objective and action-based distinction also resolves the 'terrorist-freedom fighter' divide that is so obviously plagued with political subjectivism.

According to Ganor's proposed definition of 'terrorism,' which this book adopts as its working definition, the criteria marking a 'terrorist act' are that the act is violent, politically motivated, and deliberately targets civilians.[30] For the purposes of the book's working definition, I would add that this suggests implicitly that the act is premeditated and usually (but not necessarily) undertaken as a means of striking fear in the larger population. It should go without saying that anybody carrying out such a 'terrorist act' should be held accountable as a 'terrorist' and forced to face punishments that, like those for war criminals, are both severe and founded on objective analysis and concrete evidence.

This working definition relies on a strict interpretation of what constitutes a civilian. For example, it differs from the definition provided by the US State Department. In the US government definition, 'the term "terrorism" means premeditated, politically motivated violence perpetrated against noncombatant targets by subnational groups or clandestine agents.'[31] As Ganor points out, the US definition protects military personnel, security organs, and state institutions in ways that they are not protected in a war between states, since it would be considered 'terrorism' for a non-state actor to conduct a surprise attack on them while they are not actively engaged in combat, whereas such tactics are acceptable and expected in conventional warfare.

According to this working definition, very few acts of violence perpetrated by Uyghurs can be clearly determined to be acts of 'terrorism,' going back as far as the early 1990s and especially up until 2013. Furthermore, the lack of confirmed details about those violent acts allegedly perpetrated by Uyghurs that might be considered 'terrorism' prevents one from conclusively determining whether or not they should be characterized as such. This brings into question the PRC's insistence on, and the international community's recognition of, an allegedly viable 'terrorist threat' within the Uyghur population in the early 2000s.

While the book provides this working definition as a means to salvage the concept of 'terrorism' from meaningless subjectivity, it still employs 'scare quotes' when using the term in the text to signal that it is being employed subjectively, usually by the Chinese state as a means of discrediting Uyghur resistance and even dehumanizing the Uyghur people as a whole. When the book refers to its own working definition of this term in order to objectively determine whether, in my opinion, an act should be universally condemned as 'terrorism,' it explicitly notes this. Likewise, the book uses scare quotes when it refers to the related terms of 'extremism' and 'separatism,' which the Chinese state frequently employs interchangeably with 'terrorism' as interrelated threats embodied in what it refers to as the 'three evils.' However, it is important to note that, in my opinion, the subjective and politically charged nature of the terms 'extremism' and 'separatism' renders them virtually useless as objective descriptors and unworthy of more objective working definitions.

While this explicit recognition of the subjectivity of these terms may appear to be a minute academic point to some readers, it is critical to de-construct these terms' subjectivity precisely because they have become so ubiquitous and powerful. As a result, much of the world has been de-sensitized to the ways that states have suspended human rights and committed acts of brutal violence in the name of combating an undefined enemy that we all assume we know. This is because the label of 'terrorist' serves to ultimately dehumanize those whom it designates. In the context of this book, this term's power to dehumanize is particularly evident in the ways that the PRC has justified its cultural genocide against the Uyghur people in the name of 'counterterrorism.'

THE DEHUMANIZATION OF BEING BRANDED A 'TERRORIST'

Given the horrific events of 9/11, it is not surprising that GWOT quickly succeeded in dehumanizing 'terrorists' in a manner that was unprecedented in modern warfare. This dehumanization was not as much a product of the rhetoric of the war as it was of the manner in which this conflict has been waged and against whom. This has not been a war against another state with vested interests, but a conflict with a category of people, which is considered to be irrational and amorphous. This enemy has no boundaries, but can recruit its ranks from anywhere. Thus, the US assumed at the war's outset that the rules governing state-to-state conflict need not apply because it was not fighting a rational enemy, but protecting society from an existential threat that could draw its ranks from society itself. As the philosopher Slavoj Zizek suggests, this was part of a new way of thinking about conflict that was already taking hold prior to 9/11.

As he states, 'we no longer have wars in the old sense of a regulated conflict between sovereign states in which certain rules apply (the treatment of prisoners, the prohibition of certain weapons, etc.).'[32] In place of such regulated wars between states, Zizek suggests that 'new' conflicts have few rules and are posited as being about the mitigation of threats from rogue populations who are considered as *unlawful combatants*, criminally resisting the forces of the universal order.'[33] According to this logic, states play a benevolent role in the conflict by bringing peace and order through the eradication, pacification, or quarantining of the populations posing the threat. GWOT, which is the epitome of these new types of conflicts, constructs its 'terrorist' enemy as unlawful and illegitimate, neither politically motivated combatants nor simple criminals. Instead, the 'terrorist' enemies of GWOT are outside the realm of civilized life and undeserving of the rights afforded those inside. They are portrayed almost as a biological threat to the civilized world, which must be either eradicated or indefinitely quarantined by any means necessary before their ideology spreads to others like a disease.

In this sense, Michel Foucault's articulation of the concept of 'biopolitics' is particularly useful in understanding the logic of GWOT. For Foucault, biopolitics represents a modern political regime in which the state frames all of its actions as ensuring the health of society, which includes protecting society from threats to that health emanating from either inside or outside its own population. He suggests that a biopolitical regime imagines society as a living organism, the health of which depends upon fostering the productive actors within it while excluding the infectious potential of those who are unproductive or, even worse, counter-productive. As such, the state must defend society from being infected by these unproductive and counter-productive elements, which must be 'banished, excluded, and repressed' in order to keep the organism of society healthy.[34] This logic is evident in Foucault's explanation of the goals of war in a system of biopolitics: 'the enemies who have to be done away with are not adversaries in the political sense of the term; they are threats, either external or internal, to the population and for the population ... in other words, killing or the imperative to kill is acceptable only if it results not in a victory over political adversaries, but in the elimination of the biological threat to ... the species or race.'[35]

Applying these concepts to GWOT, one can understand the ways in which the war has served to dehumanize its 'terrorist' enemies. By framing them as a threat as opposed to a foe, it strips them of any political aims or history of oppression. Rather, like a cancer, they are imagined as merely irrational purveyors of death and destruction. As such, they also do not warrant the rights provided to those within 'healthy' society. For this reason, Zizek argues that the 'terrorist' enemies of GWOT have become the modern equivalent of the ancient Roman concept of *homo sacer* ('sacred' or 'accursed' man), those who were banished from the religious and political community and not afforded the protection of Rome's laws.[36]

This construction of GWOT's 'terrorist' enemies as *homo sacer* was perhaps first most apparent in the decision of the US government to extra-legally intern suspected terrorists in Guantanamo Bay Detention Center, quarantined indefinitely without the status of either 'prisoner of war' or 'criminal,' outside the protection of the law.[37] But it is also a truly global phenomenon, where states around the world have used the narrative of 'terrorism' to construct a transnational geography of uncontrolled spaces inhabited by dangerous populations, which need not be afforded legal protections, but must be quarantined or eradicated to prevent them from becoming a security (or infectious biological) threat to others.[38] This is obviously also the logic of China's mass internment camps in the Uyghur homeland and its attempts to eradicate Uyghur culture in the way that one would seek to cure a disease.

In addition to being characterized as an existential threat to society, the enemies of GWOT are also culturally profiled. They are all Muslims. The threat they pose is seen as emanating from a certain 'extremist' strain in Islam that could hypothetically infect any Muslim. Thus, at the war's outset, the US and other western states sought to counter this threat by making a distinction between 'good' or 'moderate' Muslims and 'bad' or 'extremist' Muslims. However, with time this led to profiling any Muslim as a potential carrier of the 'extremist' strain of Islam, leading to Islamophobic calls for the exclusion of all Muslims from society as a means of protecting society from this 'extremist' strain. This logic is apparent in Donald Trump's 'Muslim travel ban' in the US as well as in the rise of hate crimes against Muslims with no affiliation to 'terrorist organizations' in both Europe and the US.[39] Similarly, in many minority Muslim countries around the world, including China and India, Islamophobic calls for the exclusion of Muslims have become apparent both in state policies and in popular discourse. I would argue that GWOT's biopolitical logic of eradication or quarantining a threat that is culturally profiled as an 'extremist' strain within Islam fosters an aggressive Islamophobia that is ultimately pregnant with genocidal tendencies. This has been apparent in Myanmar's exclusion of the Rohingya and, more importantly to this book, in China's mass internment of Uyghurs and its more general war on Uyghur culture and identity.

In this context, one can understand the potential traumatic effects of being labeled as a 'terrorist' in the age of GWOT. It immediately brands a population as a virtual biological threat to the entirety of the global system and as deserving not just of marginalization, but of complete obliteration or intensive quarantining. For this reason, the international recognition of an alleged 'terrorist threat' within the Uyghur population in 2002 is a critical juncture in the story of how a cultural genocide has unfolded in the Uyghur homeland since 2017. While the biopolitical logic of GWOT is not the primary reason that China began its all-out assault on the Uyghur people and their identity, it certainly informs and justifies the inhumane manner in which this assault is being administered.

STRUCTURE OF THE BOOK

This book's analysis sits at the nexus of local and global phenomena. On the one hand, it examines how the Uyghurs' present situation has been in part facilitated by a global narrative about the perceived threat of Islamic 'terrorism' since 9/11. On the other hand, it analyzes how this narrative has been employed by the Chinese state as a means of engaging with a much longer and localized history of colonial relations between modern China and the Uyghurs. While this intersection between localized and globalized analysis is present throughout the book, the first two chapters respectively set up the local and global contexts of the Uyghurs' present dire situation inside China.

The first chapter frames the local context of the book's analysis through a *longue duree* history of Uyghur relations with modern China up to 2001, emphasizing the colonial nature of this relationship. Chapter 2 shifts the book's narrative to the global phenomenon of GWOT and its impact on the Uyghurs and their relationship to the Chinese state. Chapter 3 proceeds to develop an alternative narrative about the alleged 'terrorist threat' posed by Uyghurs up to 2013, which is based on my own research, arguing that the alleged 'terrorist threat' to Chinese society from Uyghur jihadist groups was virtually non-existent up to 2013 and has remained minimal ever since.

The last three chapters of the book chart developments on the ground inside the Uyghur homeland since 2001, examining how the intersection of Chinese settler colonialism and the narrative of the presence of a 'terrorist threat' within the Uyghur population contributed to an increasingly tense relationship between Uyghurs and the state. Gradually, this led to an increased targeting of Uyghurs as a dangerous and ultimately existential threat to Chinese society, a logic that has eventually resulted in the state-led strategy of cultural genocide we are witnessing today.

Chapter 4 explains that, despite the narrative of a 'terrorist threat' from Uyghurs established internationally in 2002, very few, if any, Uyghur-led premeditated acts of political violence took place inside the Uyghur homeland during the first decade of GWOT. As a result, PRC policies towards the Uyghurs in the early 2000s initially differed little from those implemented by the Chinese state in the 1990s, albeit applied more aggressively and with more impunity given their framing as a 'counterterrorism' effort. Chapter 5, which covers the period 2013–2016, demonstrates how the first decade of the PRC's disingenuous claims of a significant Uyghur 'terrorist threat' as a justification for the suppression of Uyghur dissent eventually led to a self-fulfilling prophecy of Uyghur militancy both in China and abroad. This process was largely initiated by the PRC's increased scrutiny of Uyghurs as a 'dangerous' population following the 2009 Urumqi riots, but it was also reinforced by several acts of Uyghur-led violence in 2013–2014, which increasingly looked like actual 'terrorist' attacks, in Beijing, Kunming, and Urumqi. Chapter 6 explains how the events of 2013–2016 laid the foundations for the campaign of cultural genocide that began in earnest from 2017. The chapter provides details of the intensity and invasiveness of this campaign, demonstrating that it is systematic, violent, and ultimately aimed at eliminating Uyghur identity as we know it. In particular, the chapter focuses on the complex of policies that have driven the campaign, including the mass internment system, the pervasive surveillance network, and attempts to transform both the landscape of the Uyghur homeland and the lives and culture of Uyghur people.

The concluding chapter examines the likely future outcomes of the cultural genocide presently taking place in the Uyghur homeland by seeking to answer three critical questions. How will the present crisis end? What are its ramifications for the future development of GWOT? And what can be done to stem the present processes of cultural genocide in the Uyghur homeland? This is followed by some final words about what the Uyghur cultural genocide tells us about the ominous direction in which the world is headed in the twenty-first century.

1

COLONIALISM, 1759–2001

One of the reasons it is so devastating to be labeled a 'terrorist' in the context of the Global War on Terror (GWOT) is that the war has successfully characterized its enemy as lacking in legitimate grievances – motivated instead by an irrational ideology based on an extreme and intolerant interpretation of Islam. In the case of the Uyghurs, this effectively strips them of their historical grievances with modern Chinese states, which are more important to understanding the present conflict between the PRC and Uyghurs than is a narrative of Islamic 'extremism' or 'terrorism.' Thus, in an effort to elucidate these historical grievances behind the tense relations between Uyghurs and the PRC today – which are often obscured by a narrative focusing on 'terrorism' – this chapter provides a historical overview of this relationship, beginning with the Qing conquest of the Uyghur homeland in the eighteenth century and concluding on the eve of GWOT in 2001. In doing so, it makes the case that this relationship has always been, and continues to be, colonial in nature.

In academic circles, it is somewhat controversial to describe the relationship between modern China and the Uyghurs in terms of colonialism. James Millward, one of the most prominent historians of Qing rule in the region, has until recently shied away from the colonial label, noting that the phenomenon of colonialism is too difficult to detach from the dominant role of European powers globally at this time and that the Han themselves viewed European powers as seeking to control them in a colonial manner.[1] Likewise, Justin

1 Man with rooster walking past the statue of Mao in Kashgar, January 1990.

Jacobs, who studies the rule of Republican China in the region, has argued that using the discourse of colonialism to discuss the relationship between modern China and Uyghurs has been problematized by the broad and incendiary political associations that this term evokes.[2] Nonetheless, both Millward and Jacobs acknowledge that modern China's control over this region is a legacy of imperial conquest and rule, whether it is termed colonialism or not.

Some of the new generation of international scholars studying the Uyghurs and their homeland have been less reticent to embrace the terminology of colonialism in describing modern Chinese rule of this region and its people.[3] While some of these scholars suggest that modern China's rule of the Uyghurs and their homeland may not be colonialism in a 'classic sense' or a 'direct replication' of European colonial domination, they also assert that one cannot ignore the similarities between European colonialism and China's conquest and subsequent rule over Uyghurs and their homeland. This is also apparent in more recent literature on the Qing Empire, such as that produced by Max Oidtmann, which freely refers to this empire as colonial in character.[4]

A recent article by Dibyesh Anand goes even further in asserting this argument, suggesting unequivocally that contemporary China has become a 'colonizing nation-state' in its rule of the Uyghurs.[5] For Anand, China's rule over both the Tibetans and Uyghurs are clear cases of colonial domination over both territory and populations, and he suggests that glossing over this fact in scholarly writing only contributes to the continued existence of these forms of domination.[6] Furthermore, Anand suggests that colonialism is not merely a part of modern China's past relationship to Uyghurs and their homeland; it is a process of domination that continues and, in many ways, is intensifying in the present.

This chapter adopts Anand's perspective that modern China's relationship with the Uyghurs and their homeland has always been, and continues to be, one best characterized as colonial. Framing this relationship as a colonial one explains the prominence in it of what Partha Chatterjee has called a 'rule of colonial difference' and what Anand calls 'paternalistic control.'[7] In other words, modern Chinese states have clearly distinguished the Uyghurs and other local Turkic people as fundamentally different from and inferior to the dominant Han population and, thus, incapable of either becoming equals to the Han or of even knowing how best to care for themselves. As a result, modern Chinese states' attempts to assimilate Uyghurs have suffered from the classic dilemma of colonial powers trying to 'civilize' the colonized and make them more like themselves while simultaneously never accepting them as equals. I would argue that this attitude towards Uyghurs has been a defining characteristic of all modern Chinese states' rule over this population.

If this chapter frames modern China's relationship with Uyghurs and their homeland as fundamentally colonial in nature, it also recognizes that this particular colonial relationship is relatively unique in several ways. First and most notably, this is a case where colonialism still persists in the twenty-first century. In most instances of colonial conquest around the world, the colonizing powers eventually accommodated the peoples they colonized by relinquishing at least partial control of their homeland, allowing for either independent statehood or enhanced rights and recognition as the region's indigenous population. In the case of modern China's colonial relationship to the Uyghurs and their homeland, neither of these processes of de-colonization have taken place. There have been several moments in the history of modern Chinese history where the state tentatively began processes of accommodation that could have resulted in de-colonization, but it has always stopped short of recognizing the Uyghurs as being indigenous to their homeland and deserving of either sovereignty over the region or of special rights to self-governance within it. Ultimately, this inability of modern Chinese states to de-colonize their relationship with the Uyghurs and their homeland is marked by the fact that it has neither acknowledged its conquest and subjugation of this region nor recognized the Uyghurs as the indigenous population of their homeland.

Second, the Uyghur homeland is a colony that is geographically contiguous to China. Such situations generally foster one of two different colonial relationships – a frontier colony that is held at arms-length from the colonial metropole and a settler colony that is absorbed into the colonial power's polity and settled by the dominant colonizing population. In the history of modern China, the Uyghur homeland has largely been constructed as a frontier colony where the local population was able to remain demographically dominant, at least in the Uyghur heartland of the southern Tarim Basin, and the Chinese state retained control of governance and resource extraction while seeking to establish and maintain Han dominance in the region's north, including its capital of Urumqi. Arguably, with the creation of the PRC, the state sought to absorb the entirety of the Uyghur region and its indigenous population into a larger 'socialist nation-state,' but it was largely ineffective in this goal for the first thirty years of communist rule, especially in the southern Tarim Basin.

While the PRC had already succeeded in drastically altering the demography of the region by the 1960s and substantially so by 1980 through the massive re-settlement of Han citizens from outside the region, most of the Han who had come to the region remained in the north or in the military colonies of the Bingtuan. Most of the southern Tarim Basin remained overwhelmingly Uyghur in population, and few Uyghurs welcomed either assimilation into a Han dominated state culture or education in the Chinese language. This inability to fully integrate the region and its people into the PRC was due to a variety of reasons including the political and economic chaos of the PRC's first thirty years, but it was also facilitated by the state's view of this region as a buffer-zone and frontier, particularly vis-à-vis the Soviet Union.

This situation only began to change in the 1980s during the reform period when the region's economic potential beyond resource extraction was first recognized. Much of the history of PRC rule since then has been characterized by the state's efforts to fully incorporate this region and its population into the larger political and economic system of a changing communist China. Following an initial period of accommodation in the 1980s, which could have paved a path for integration through partial decolonization, the decades that followed have involved a steadily escalating attempt to forcibly integrate this region and assimilate its people into a unified PRC, representing a gradual shift from viewing the region as a frontier colony to viewing it as a settler colony. Unsurprisingly, much of these efforts have been concentrated on the Uyghur heartland in the southern oases of the Tarim Basin, which had previously remained largely uninfluenced by Han culture.

Lorenzo Veracini, who is one of the pioneers in the study of settler colonialism, suggests that while other forms of colonialism generally exploit the colonized population in addition to their territory as a virus lives off other living cells, settler colonialism only needs the land to thrive like bacteria living on surfaces without the need for a living host.[8] Thus, Veracini notes that settler colonists tend to favor colonies with less density of indigenous populations and tend 'to execute the transfer/removal of the Indigenous Peoples they encounter.'[9] Given the density of the Uyghur population, particularly in the southern oases of their homeland, the PRC's shift towards a more robust settler colonialism in the Uyghur region has not been easily accomplished, perhaps belying the reason why this process has been both slow and conflictual.

In many ways, the academic debate about whether or not one should refer to modern China's relationship with the Uyghurs and their homeland as colonialism is less relevant than whether Uyghurs themselves view this relationship as such. The development of the Uyghur nation, particularly in the twentieth century, was shaped by a recognition of their colonial situation within modern China. As a result, Uyghur nationalist historiography inevitably frames its nation's resistance to Chinese rule as part of an anti-colonial national liberation struggle.

This conflict between modern Chinese states and the Uyghurs over the territory known respectively as Xinjiang and Eastern Turkistan has often been viewed by both parties as a zero-sum proposition of either Chinese or Uyghur sovereignty, but these are not its only possible outcomes. As in many post-colonial states, one can imagine a situation where the PRC's recognition of the Uyghurs' status as the Indigenous People of their homeland, with special rights within that territory, could lead to a relatively harmonious incorporation of the Uyghurs and their homeland into the PRC's polity and society. This chapter points to several moments in history where modern Chinese states appeared to be moving towards such accommodating policies in their governance of the Uyghurs and their homeland, but in each case, these efforts have been temporary and rolled back in favor of policies that were more reflective of a paternalistic rule of colonial difference. Unfortunately, the extreme nature of the PRC's present approach to governing its Uyghur population may have finally closed the door to such an approach to decolonizing the relationship between Uyghurs and modern China.

QING CONQUEST AND RULE: HOW THE UYGHURS AND THEIR HOMELAND BECAME PART OF MODERN CHINA

While the PRC goes to painstaking lengths to suggest that the Uyghur homeland has always been a constituent part of China since ancient times, such arguments are completely disingenuous.[10] Indeed, the area that is today officially called the XUAR has a long history of interactions with empires emanating from China, but it has also had a similarly long history of interactions with a variety of empires from Central Asia and has served as the center of its own empires at times. A proper reading of history suggests that this region only really started becoming a constituent part of a larger China when the Qing Dynasty conquered it in the 1750s, and only became integrated into a larger Chinese territorial polity in the late nineteenth century when the Qing made it a province of its domain.

In part, this is because the late Qing, like many empires of its time, was the first imperial power to conquer the Uyghur homeland that would gradually adopt the modern trappings of statehood which could eventually serve as the basis of a Chinese nation-state. However, initially the Qing control of this region differed little from past empires that had conquered this region, and it specifically adopted many of the practices of its direct predecessor, the Zunghars. The Qing would establish its imperial outpost in the northern region that had been the heart of the Zunghar Empire and which, to this day, is known as Zungharia.[11] Additionally, when the Qing conquered the southern oases of the Uyghur homeland known as the Tarim Basin, it would also initially rule this region indirectly through elites from the local population as the Zunghars had done.[12]

Qing conquest and early rule: continuity with the past

The Qing conquest of the Uyghur homeland almost destroyed the entire population of the region's previous rulers, the Zunghars, and required a protracted military campaign to defeat Muslim resistance from the region's southern Tarim Basin. By 1759, the Qing had replaced the Zunghars as the masters of the entire region, and in doing so it adopted many of the Zunghars' means of rule. As the Qing created its imperial outpost in roughly the same location as the Zunghars' capital near the present city of Ghulja, it borrowed a practice from its predecessor by resettling significant numbers of Muslims from their homes in the southern Tarim Basin to help build and feed this outpost.[13] Similarly, with regards to its rule of the Tarim Basin, where most of the ancestors of the present-day Uyghurs lived, the Qing adopted essentially the same indirect system of rule as the Zunghars, relying on the Muslims' own *Bäg* system, which consisted of local leaders essentially administrating issues of daily importance.

While, unlike the Zunghars, the Qing's administration in the region during its first century of rule would benefit from a bureaucracy that had a penchant for documenting its subjects in the same manner of European colonial powers at the time, this did not really translate into the region becoming a physical colony of the empire. The Qing only really maintained outposts in the region, populated with military divisions and administrators mostly led by Manchus and Mongols, and the number of representatives from the conquering power in the region remained small. For this reason, historian Rian Thum has referred to the Uyghur homeland's status at this time as a 'dependency governed by a Manchu-dominated military' rather than an integral part of the empire.[14]

This ambiguity of the region's position in the Qing Empire became more obvious in the early nineteenth century. In response to the financial strains that controlling this region demanded, the imperial court began debates in the 1820s regarding whether the empire should continue to invest in controlling the Tarim Basin at all.[15] As a result, when a series of substantial Muslim rebellions broke out in the 1860s, first in Gansu and later in the Tarim Basin and Zungharia, the Qing did not expend undue energy to re-establish control of the region, and they eventually withdrew entirely.

While most Uyghur nationalists tend to view these revolts as part of their history of national liberation struggles, it is difficult to justify such an interpretation given the rebellions' multi-national character. Furthermore, the largest state to develop out of the revolts was led by Yakub Beg, who had come from the Ferghana Valley in present-day Uzbekistan and had no real connection to the Tarim Basin.[16] Finally, no unified concept of a modern Uyghur nation even existed at this time, with the local populations identifying with multiple allegiances – Muslim, settled or nomadic, and Turkic.

After the Qing withdrawal, Yakub Beg sought to establish a unified state of sorts throughout most of the region, but there was also a separate independent para-state in the north known as the Ili Sultanate, which controlled the area around the former Qing military complex near Ghulja. Sensing a power vacuum and worried about the growing power of Yakub Beg, who was seeking British support for his state, the Russian Empire responded by conquering the Ili Sultanate and occupying its territory in the Ili valley. While the Russians ruled this region for only about a decade and publicly proclaimed that they were only maintaining control of the region until the Qing returned, their actions, which were arguably much more akin to colonialism than Qing rule had been, suggested a concerted effort to leave their mark in the region if not to remain there indefinitely.

Given the Qing Empire's weakness at this time, there were fierce debates within the imperial court regarding whether or not to re-enter the region and seek to conquer it again.[17] In the end, those arguing for re-conquest won the day, and the Qing began a military campaign in the north of the region in 1876. By 1880, the Qing had reconquered the region, with the exception of that part in the Ili valley controlled by Russia, and in 1881, Russia returned most of this territory to the Qing in accordance with the Treaty of St Petersburg.[18]

However, Russia's impact on the Uyghur homeland and its population through its decade-long occupation of the Ghulja area was to have long-lasting ramifications. A substantial majority of the local Muslims in this northern area took the opportunity afforded them on the return of the region to the Qing to re-settle across the border in the Russian controlled portion of the Ili valley, which is now part of Kazakhstan.[19] This created a substantial Uyghur population on the border of Chinese-controlled territory that would be influential throughout the modern period.

Late Qing colonialism and the creation of Xinjiang

Once the Qing had officially retaken the entirety of the region in 1881, the imperial court was quick to reform the region's administration to integrate it more closely with the governance of the empire's overall territory, declaring it in 1884 an official province entitled Xinjiang, or the 'New territory,' a name that had already been used less formally by the Qing for the region.[20] This occurred at a time when the Qing itself was changing. It was both adopting the hallmarks of modern statehood and becoming more dominated by the Han ethnic group that increasingly made up the bulk of its bureaucracy. As such, it was evolving into the basis for a nascent Han-dominated Chinese nation-state that would seek to absorb the new Xinjiang province and its people into its domain. As part of this process, the *Bäg* system was eradicated in all but a few locations and replaced with a bureaucratic network of territorial entities led by mostly Han administrators. To create a bridge with the local population, local Muslims, many the descendants of former *Bägs*, were hired as 'clerks,' a significant demotion from their former positions.[21]

Along with this marginalization of the local Muslim population in governance, the Qing also initiated policies aimed at assimilating this population, or at least its elite. The most critical aspect of these policies involved establishing an educational network in the Mandarin language, which had become the *lingua franca* of the Manchu-led Qing Empire. As Zuo Zongtang, the architect of the re-conquest, noted, 'if we wish to change their peculiar customs and assimilate them to our Chinese ways (huafeng), we must found free schools (yishu) and make the Muslim children read (Chinese) books, recognize characters, and understand spoken language.'[22] In addition to reading and writing, the schools promoted Confucian thought as the de facto ideology of the empire. In the last years of the Qing Dynasty, this Confucian-based educational system was replaced in Xinjiang, as was the case in China proper, with a modernized scholastic system based on western concepts of science. However, neither the Confucian nor the new modern educational system succeeded in transforming the local population or even in attracting many Muslim students.[23]

Thus, by the last years of the Qing Empire, which itself was becoming more Chinese than Manchu, its administration of Xinjiang appeared much more like colonialism. Indirect rule had been replaced by more invasive administrators from the colonial metropole, and conscious attempts were being made to assimilate the local population into Han culture. However, the region still remained a frontier colony that was only tenuously connected to the empire rather than a settler colony that could readily be absorbed into a future Chinese nation-state. The local population generally continued to live their lives as they had previously before the region had become a province. They mostly practiced their religion unfettered, spoke their native languages, had their own informal means of self-governance, practiced agriculture, and traded. They also maintained relations with other Muslims speaking closely related Turkic languages in the Russian Empire, and they frequently traveled to Russian territory to trade, and beyond for religious education and pilgrimage. In addition, they continued to develop and utilize their own educational systems, which co-existed alongside those created by the Qing. These systems included both the traditional religious education network associated with Islamic clergy and the more modernized Muslim schools based on the usul-i-jadid method that combined religious education with modern studies of literature, history, math, and science.[24]

REPUBLICAN CHINA IN XINJIANG AND THE RISE OF MODERN UYGHUR NATIONALISM

The fall of the Qing Empire involved little of the revolutionary zeal that fueled the demise of other empires around the world during the late nineteenth and early twentieth centuries. The revolution was neither really anti-colonial, being driven by the dominant Han ethnic group, nor inspired by a disenfranchised class of citizens as in Russia. Furthermore, Republican China essentially inherited the territory of the Qing Empire, including its tenuous colonial appendages like Xinjiang and Tibet. In this sense, the fall of the Qing did not entirely mark a transition from 'empire to nation-state,' but a transition to a new concept of 'national empire,'[25] While this was similar to the transition from the Tsarist Empire to the Soviet Union, unlike the USSR, Republican China did not acknowledge the excesses of its imperial predecessor or the rights to self-determination of those it had colonized.

Given that the 'imperial form' had not been jettisoned by the new state that replaced the Qing Empire, it is not surprising that the revolution of 1911 had little initial impact on the lives of the Muslims in the Uyghur homeland. This would change over time as the different Han administrators in charge of the region for Republican China would seek to control the lives of the local population with more zeal. Nonetheless, throughout the Republican period, the region would remain mostly a frontier appendage to the nascent Chinese nation-state, run by a series of Han governors with ambiguous relationships to central power, whose primary goal was maintaining control of the region, not integrating it into a larger modern China. At the same time, this period would witness the birth of Uyghur national consciousness, mostly established around the modern concept of anti-colonial self-determination and the desire among the region's Muslims to differentiate themselves from the ruling Han people. Over the next several decades, this national awakening among the local Muslim population would lead to the establishment of two short-term para-states, which sought independence from China during the 1930s and 1940s respectively.

Early Republican rule's continuity with Qing rule and the birth of modern Uyghur nationalism

The first Han administrator to run Xinjiang after the fall of the Qing was Yang Zengxin, who would rule the region until 1928. Most historians view Yang as an authoritarian ruler, who commanded loyalty and made the region into his own personal fiefdom.[26] However, he also modeled his mode of governance after early Qing rule in the region by deliberately limiting the state's involvement in the lives of local Muslims. Yang sought to fulfill his duty of maintaining control over a frontier region, but he made little effort to integrate this region or its population into a new Republican China. As Yang is cited as writing, 'if I am able to maintain one portion (of the country), and the (central) government is able to maintain another, is this not for the best?'[27] Part of his maintenance of this region included being particularly cognizant of the potential for revolt and foreign intervention. He especially worried that the USSR could have designs on Xinjiang, as it had demonstrated its ability to do so in Mongolia, and he was well aware that the local Muslim population could be mobilized for such ends. Yang's fears were also fueled by an awakening at the time of modern Uyghur nationalism, which was substantially influenced by the USSR's Leninist ideals of anti-colonial national liberation.

The formation of a modern Uyghur nationalism was a gradual process, which involved numerous influences from abroad, some of which appealed more to some Uyghurs than to others.[28] While this process had arguably already begun in the late Qing period, when it was highly influenced by Muslim reformist ideas from around the world, it gained significant momentum after the Bolshevik revolution and the establishment of a movement of Muslims who had left the Ghulja region for Russia in the 1880s and were now concerned with achieving the recognized status of 'nationality' within the Soviet Union during the 1920s.

Prior to the 1920s, there was a sense of collective identity among the settled Turkic Muslims in and from the Uyghur homeland, which was based on a shared sense of space, history, customs, language, and the oral transmission of texts, not to mention shaped by their obvious difference from Han and Manchu administrators.[29] However, this had yet to be expressed in the form of modern nation-hood, with its related concept of the nation-state, and the ethnonym 'Uyghur,' which referred to an ancient Turkic empire in the region, was not in use at this time. The national designation of 'Uyghur' was established by Uyghur Bolshevik sympathizers, in what is today Kazakhstan, during the first years of Soviet rule and recognized by the USSR in the 1920s.[30] Of particular concern to Yang was that this nascent nation's ideology was based in Leninist anti-imperialist rev-olution and celebrated the history of Uyghur resistance to Chinese rule as the centerpiece of its historiography.[31] These developments apparently worried Yang enough for him to establish a consulate in Soviet Central Asia in order to track these developments and their influence on the many seasonal workers from southern Xinjiang who worked there intermittently.[32]

Despite his concerns, Yang never had to contend with a seri-ous revolt from the Muslims of Xinjiang. In fact, the one Muslim revolt he actively suppressed was not against his rule or against Chinese rule more generally, but against the abuses of power of a local Muslim prince in Kumul, who was infamous for the abusive treatment of his subjects.[33] In general, Yang had mostly maintained the status quo in the region during an extremely turbulent period. However, he had made many enemies among other Han administra-tors in the process, and he was eventually removed from office by assassination in dramatic fashion carried out by waiters at his own dinner party.[34]

Paternalistic control in Republican rule and local resistance

Yang was succeeded by his disciple, Jin Suren, as governor of Xinjiang in 1928. While Jin adopted many of Yang's policies, he seemed less attuned than his predecessor to the potential ramifications of dis-content among the local Muslims. Like Yang, he fostered a group of loyal Han administrators, who together benefited from a system of graft, but he was greedier than Yang and failed to spread the wealth sufficiently among the local Muslim elite.[35] Furthermore, he instituted an even stauncher security apparatus than did Yang, and established a system of internal passports that kept watch on the movements of the local population.[36] Additionally, he levied large taxes on agricultural production as well as on the butchering of animals, encouraged state-led land reclamation projects, and forbade local residents to make the *Hajj* pilgrimage to Mecca.[37] Such encroachments on the daily lives of the local Muslim population would inevitably prove fatal for Jin, who experienced significant resistance from local Muslims throughout his brief rule.

The first substantial signs of resistance by the local Muslim population to Jin's rule occurred in the Kumul Khanate in 1931. The Khanate was a holdover administrative unit from Qing times where Kumul's Muslim population enjoyed nominal self-rule implemented by a hereditary monarchy, which Yang had maintained. While Kumul's Muslims had revolted against their own Khan in 1912, they still preferred their situation compared to that elsewhere in the region since, among other things, they were able to institute limits on Han land ownership.[38] When the Khan who had served under Yang died in 1930, Jin made moves to abolish the Khanate and establish more control over its territory. However, the dead Khan's son and successor, with the assistance of several key figures in his royal court, resisted this decision and led a substantial revolt in the region.

While Jin sought to quickly and violently suppress this revolt, the rebels were able to solicit support from a variety of quarters, and the rebellion spread beyond Kumul until, 'by the end of 1932, every corner of Xinjiang was aflame.'[39] To deal with this situation, Jin had received military reinforcements from decommissioned soldiers who had fought in Manchuria and came to the region via the Soviet Union. At the head of this new army supporting Jin was Sheng Shicai, a ruthless fighter with grand political ambitions. Sheng would lead the effort against the Muslim rebels, but he also simultaneously orchestrated a coup against Jin that led to Sheng's de facto leadership of the province and to his eventual assumption of the position of regional governor.

35

In taking over de facto power, Sheng inherited a region that was in open revolt on all fronts from the local Muslim population. As a result, he allegedly signed an agreement with Khoja Niyaz Haji, one of the original organizers of the revolt in Kumul, that divided Xinjiang between a southern Muslim-led government and a northern one retained by the provincial administration.[40] This paved the way for the founding of the first Eastern Turkistan Republic (ETR) in southern Xinjiang in 1933.

While Uyghur nationalists often portray the First ETR as the original manifestation of a modern Uyghur nation-state, historian David Brophy has rightfully challenged this characterization.[41] While some of the founders of the First ETR were influenced by the Soviet-born Uyghur nationalist ideology, the resultant para-state was built more on its population's common identity as Muslim Turks. However, it would be equally erroneous to characterize this state as exclusively religious in nature as other studies have suggested.[42] Rather, the political movement that formed this para-state brought together a broad array of indigenous intellectuals inspired by a variety of ideologies of self-determination that were popular at this time, including modernist Muslim nationalists inspired by the *Jadid* movement, Leninist anti-imperialist liberationists, and Islamic traditionalists. What united them was a desire to remove Chinese rule of their homeland and to establish an indigenously ruled state. This motivation was especially evident in the more religiously oriented rebels from Khotan, who called for the removal of Han residents, the abolishment of the use of the Chinese language, and the renaming of Chinese place-names in the local Turkic vernacular.[43]

The First ETR was to be very short-lived, never attracting significant external support. In the end, the Soviet Union assisted Sheng's military to repel Dungan (Hui) attempts to take the provincial capital of Urumqi, an act which sent the Dungan armies south to sack the still fragile ETR based in Kashgar, which essentially fell by March 1934.[44] However, the legacy of the First ETR would be incredibly important to subsequent developments in this region, including to this day. In addition to its importance for the subsequent evolution of politics in Republican Xinjiang, this para-state has served in recent years as the centerpiece for the historiography of Uyghur religious nationalists. In this role, the Republic is presented as not only an effort to liberate the region from Chinese rule, but also to liberate it from the rule of infidels.

Sheng Shicai's Sovietization of Xinjiang

When the dust had settled on the wreckage of the First ETR, Sheng Shicai had emerged as the governor of Xinjiang, and the Soviet Union as his patron. Although Sheng remained a representative of the Nationalist government in Nanjing in name, in spirit it has often been said that he was more loyal to Moscow and the Soviet Communist Party, of which he became a member.[45] While much of the Tarim Basin initially remained under the control of the Dungan armies that toppled the ETR and were loyal to Nanjing, Sheng was able to employ his Soviet patronage to establish a powerful state in the north and eventually regain control of the Tarim Basin by 1937.

Initially, Sheng dealt with the discontent of local Muslims in the region by instituting the first instance of a Chinese administration adopting accommodationist policies towards the Uyghurs that were based in Leninist ideals of anti-imperialism.[46] The new policies sought to engage the local Muslim people on their own terms but also promoted a culture of socialist modernism as had been the case in Soviet Central Asia following the Bolshevik revolution. To accomplish this, the Soviets provided Sheng with much guidance through Soviet advisors, many of whom were ethnic Uyghurs, and promoted the inclusion of local Uyghurs with Soviet sympathies in Sheng's administration.[47] Additionally, the Soviets invited nearly 30,000 Uyghurs from Xinjiang to study at Soviet universities where they were completely indoctrinated in the full range of Marxist-Leninist ideology, especially as it related to Soviet nationalities policy.[48]

With this assistance, Sheng created something akin to a Soviet-inspired multi-ethnic state in Xinjiang. He co-opted much of the leadership of the First ETR, including its president Khoja Niyaz

Haji, into the government, and he greatly increased the number of Muslims in his administration of the Uyghur homeland, based on the experience of the Soviet *korenizatsiia* (or nativization) policy.[49] The Soviet Uyghur advisors in the region also pushed for the adoption of the Uyghur ethnonym by Sheng's administration and succeeded in having it officially recognized in 1935 as a descriptor for the region's largest Turkic-speaking population.[50] This official recognition of the Uyghur nation was accompanied by a variety of efforts, supported by Soviet Uyghur advisors, to establish a narrative of this nation's history and literary development as well as by campaigns to raise the profile of the Uyghur language.

If these accommodationist policies were likely welcomed by many of the local Muslims, and especially by those with pro-Soviet sympathies, other policies that Sheng borrowed from the Soviet Union, such as the bolstering of his secret police, would be less welcome. In general, Sheng's administration was even more dedicated to suppressing dissent than those of his predecessors, employing security organs with direct links to Stalin's infamous NKVD, whose aggressive tactics it generally adopted.

Sensing a resurgence of Uyghur religious nationalism in the Kashgar region, which Sheng worried might lead to renewed revolt, the provincial administration sought to suppress it, purging some of the local Uyghur leaders, taking control of the local newspaper, and seeking to bring teachers from the Soviet Union into local schools.[51] These restrictive policies and purges of local elites resulted in yet another revolt in 1937 in Kashgar and Khotan, which was orchestrated by some of the remnants of the leadership from the First ETR.[52] With Soviet assistance, including troops and air support, Sheng quickly suppressed the revolt, setting in motion a massive purge of Uyghurs from Sheng's administration and the targeting of other Uyghur nationalists throughout the province. This campaign coincided with, and adopted the language of, Stalin's own purges as Sheng began mass executions of Uyghurs throughout the region, justified by accusations of Trotskyism and associations with foreign imperialists just as was happening across the border in the USSR.[53] Subsequently, Sheng virtually obliterated the Uyghur elite and intelligentsia and sought to recruit an entirely new and more loyal group of native intellectuals and officials.[54]

Soviet influence on Sheng continued to increase after the purges of 1937 and 1938, and Sheng allegedly even suggested to Stalin in 1941 that the USSR incorporate the Uyghur region into the Soviet Union.[55] However, a year later Sheng began a drastic change in his policy towards the USSR as he sought to cut ties with his patron. In 1942, Sheng ordered the arrest of some one hundred of the most prominent communists and Soviet sympathizers in the region, accusing them of plotting a conspiracy to take over the region and incorporate it into the USSR.[56] Simultaneously, Soviet cultural societies and institutions in the Uyghur region were closed, and thousands of local residents who had worked with Soviet advisors and workers or who had studied in the USSR were arrested for their links to the alleged conspiracy.[57]

Thus, having just undergone a purge of alleged anti-Soviet elements, the Uyghur population was now subjected to a purge of its pro-Soviet elements. As a result, the attitudes of the local Muslim population had turned against Sheng. Feeling betrayed by Sheng, the Soviet Union saw an opportunity to utilize this dissatisfaction among the local Muslims as a means to topple Sheng himself. According to Russian scholar Valery Barmin, the Soviet Politburo had already discussed the option of creating a cross-border Uyghur resistance movement for this purpose in 1943.[58] However, with his Soviet patrons gone, Sheng had already lost much of his power and was not destined to stay in the province long enough to experience Soviet retribution. In 1944, he was removed from power and given a national-level position in China proper.

Even though Sheng was now gone, the Soviets continued their planning to undermine Republican China's control of the Uyghur homeland. During 1943 and 1944, the USSR would disseminate propaganda among the Uyghur population to highlight the Han's colonial rule over them and their homeland in an effort to incite revolt.[59] In the meantime, the Soviet Union was in discussions with local Uyghurs about supplying them with weapons and advice for a planned revolt in the northern region of Ghulja just across the Soviet border.

*The Second ETR and the apex of Uyghur self-determination in
modern China*

In October 1944, the Soviets would help these rebels carry out a
revolt that broke out in the three districts surrounding the northern
city of Ghulja, a region once briefly controlled by the Russian Empire
in the 1870s. Armed with Soviet weapons and assisted by Soviet
advisors, this rebellion entered the city of Ghulja on 7 November
where it declared the establishment of a second independent ETR
on 12 November 1944.[60] Appearing to have aspirations of extending
this new independent state to the entirety of the Uyghur homeland,
it continued to fight Chinese troops throughout 1945, threatening to take the provincial capital of Urumqi by September of that
year.[61] It was at that point that the rebels' Soviet patrons apparently
intervened to stop their advance and proposed to broker peace talks
between the rebels and the Guomindang (GMD). As a result of the
peace talks, the GMD agreed to the establishment of a coalition
government in the Uyghur region, which substantively involved the
leaders of the ETR and gave them de facto control over the Ghulja
region.

The Second ETR would exist in its de facto autonomous form
throughout the rest of the 1940s, and it succeeded even more than
its predecessor from the 1930s in establishing the symbols of modern
nationhood. With Soviet assistance, it published journals, news-
papers, and textbooks. It also made its own currency, had its own
uniformed army, its own school system, and, of course, its own
flag and national anthem.[62] While, like the First ETR, this semi-
autonomous state was formed explicitly as a multi-national polity,
many Uyghurs have since viewed it as the prototype for a secular-
based Uyghur nation-state, and its ethnic Uyghur leadership has
entered the pantheon of Uyghur nationalist heroes.

Although the Soviet Union continued to sponsor and sought to
control the actions and ideology of the Second ETR, it would be
inaccurate to view it merely as a Soviet puppet state. Many of the
local Uyghur supporters of the Second ETR saw the state as the first
step towards an anti-colonial national liberation movement, and the

state's leadership often acted autonomously more in the interests of the local population than in those of their Soviet patrons. The content of media produced in the autonomous state frequently focused on topics related to Soviet socialism, but it also addressed issues related to the development of Uyghur nationalism and the role of Islam in social life, subjects that were no longer tolerated in the Soviet Union after the 1920s.[63]

Perhaps in recognition of the power of the ETR to mobilize local Muslims, the GMD also empowered local Muslims in its administration of the region's new coalition government. In particular, this included giving critical positions in the coalition government to three prominent Uyghur intellectuals who were sympathetic to the GMD: Isa Yüsüp Alptekin, Muhämmäd Imin Bughra, and Mäsud Sabri.[64] In addition, the GMD's first governor of the new coalition government, Zhang Zhizhong, established locally elected councils in the region and mandated that the Uyghur language be used side-by-side with Chinese in government at all levels.[65]

In many ways, the Xinjiang coalition government that existed from 1945 to 1949 represented the most accommodating administration to the region's local Muslim population in modern history, including to this day. In this sense, it held great promise for a decolonized future of the relationship between modern China and the Uyghurs. Uyghurs had become intimately involved in the governance of their homeland and recognized as essentially equal citizens of China with the dominant Han, and a public debate among Uyghur politicians discussed the relative merits of independence and autonomy for the Uyghur homeland.[66] Emblematic of these accommodating policies, in 1947 Zhang resigned his post as governor and was succeeded by one of the three primary local Muslim GMD officials, Mäsud Sabri.

Mäsud's brief leadership greatly empowered other Uyghur nationalists in the coalition government, leading to the increasing use of 'Turkistan' in place of 'Xinjiang' in official communications, the expansion of Uyghur language education, including new curricula that discussed the history of the Turkic people, and the further strengthening of the role of the Uyghur language in governance.[67]

41

However, just like the brief period of accommodation experienced under Sheng Shicai, this new empowerment of indigenous Muslims was destined to be short-lived and reversed.

Once the Chinese Communist Party (CCP) had seized control of Beijing in January 1949, the GMD leadership in the region knew that their days were numbered. As a result, Isa Yüsüp Alptekin and Muhämmäd Imin Bughra fled the country via Kashmir and finally found refuge in Turkey where they would lead a Uyghur nationalist movement in exile.[68] In August 1949, Moscow helped to broker a meeting between a CCP delegation and the core leadership of the ETR. It was agreed at this meeting that the ETR would help facilitate the entry of the People's Liberation Army (PLA) into the region and that the core leadership of the Republic would be invited to participate in the First Plenary Session of the Chinese People's Political Consultative Conference in Beijing.[69] The five leaders who left for Beijing via Kazakhstan allegedly all died in an airplane crash in Siberia en route to the conference on 27 August 1949.[70] Subsequently the ETR was dissolved, as was the provincial coalition government, as the People's Liberation Army (PLA) established PRC rule in the region. The remaining local Muslim leadership of both the GMD and the ETR were left with the choices of declaring allegiance to the Chinese communists, fleeing the country, or being liquidated. Mäsud Sabri, who remained in the region in opposition to the communists, would be executed in 1951.

CHINESE COMMUNIST RULE AND THE BROKEN PROMISES OF ETHNIC AUTONOMY, 1949–1980

When the GMD authorities in the Uyghur region surrendered to the CCP in September 1949, the First Field Army of the PLA easily entered the region and took a leading role in setting up communist power in it by the end of the year. During the first years of communist rule, the PLA would play the role of occupying force in the region, which largely remained a frontier colonial appendage to the PRC as it had to Republican China. However, the transition from Republican rule to the PRC did translate into a fundamentally different approach to China's polity and society, which would have vast ramifications for the Uyghur region's status as a frontier colony. Maoist ideology advocated for a flattening of difference in society, which was also assumed to be anti-imperialist. As a result, initially the PRC sought to adopt the Soviet version of decolonization that had become known as 'Soviet nationalities policy' and integrate the Uyghur homeland as an integral part of a Chinese communist state. This would partially extend the accommodationist policies in the Uyghur region that had characterized the coalition government between the ETR and GMD and raise expectations for a new post-colonial reality in the region. However, these expectations would not be met as the PRC took a more assimilationist approach to the region in the late 1950s that would escalate throughout the 1960s and 1970s.

Initial accommodation and the role of the Soviet Union

The Soviet Union played an important role in encouraging these early accommodating policies, especially after the signing of the Sino-Soviet Treaty of Friendship, Alliance, and Mutual Assistance in 1950. This treaty allowed for a return of Soviet advisors and industries to the Uyghur region, as well as for the continued education of Uyghurs and other local populations from the region in the USSR. Soviet involvement in the region during this time likely also contributed to the decision to invite many Uyghurs and other local non-Han people, primarily former ETR officials, to take prominent roles in the CCP's initial governance of the region. This also made demographic sense given that Uyghurs in 1949 still made up 75% of the region's population in contrast to only 6% consisting of Han.[71] With many Uyghurs and other Turkic Muslims playing a prominent role in governance in the region, state schools and universities with Uyghur-language instruction were created, and Uyghur language publishing expanded.

Soviet advice to the CCP also likely played a critical role in the creation of regions of ethnic autonomy inside China that appeared similar in structure to the Soviet Socialist Republics of the USSR. In the Uyghur region, this led to the creation of the Xinjiang Uyghur

43

Autonomous Region (XUAR) in 1955.[72] While the establishment of the XUAR marked a recognition of the Uyghurs' attachment to, and historical role in, this region, it stopped short of the independence theoretically allotted to the Soviet Republics, which had the constitutional right to secede from the USSR if they chose. The XUAR and other autonomous regions in the PRC were never given such a right and instead were only allotted 'theoretical autonomy.' Furthermore, not only was secession not provided as a constitutional right, but was condemned as a serious danger to the state's success. This condemnation was achieved through a feat of 'double-speak,' which labeled all anti-colonial liberation movements inside China as 'pro-imperialist.' As an editorial in a state paper declared in 1951, 'at this point, any nationality movement that seeks to separate from the Chinese People's Republic (CPR) to become independent is reactionary since, objectively considered, it would undermine the interests of the various nationalities, and hence would work to the advantage of imperialism.'[73]

While Soviet involvement in the establishment of socialist rule in the region helped to extend some of the accommodationist policies from the coalition government of the late 1940s, it also likely played a role in early attempts to transform the social life of Uyghurs. Rian Thum has suggested that the PRC, likely with Soviet guidance, quickly moved to dismantle the religious institutions of the region, outlawing traditional Muslim courts, subsuming clergy into a state managed system, and redistributing land from the *Waqf* system that had used land trusts to support mosques, madrassas, and shrines throughout the region.[74] However, given that these radical measures were taken simultaneously with land reform that provided Uyghur agriculturalists, who had previously worked rented lands, with their own property, the mass of the local population appears not to have resisted the changes.

The end of accommodation and the Sino-Soviet split

Ironically, the period of CCP accommodation in the XUAR began to end shortly after autonomy was declared in 1955. Already by this

44

time, Soviet influence in the region was on the wane as tensions increased between Mao and Khrushchev. As a result, the PRC quickly began reducing Soviet influence in the XUAR, and by 1957, it had stopped the importation of books and journals from the Soviet Union entirely, including those in the Uyghur language.[75] Additionally, the reform of the Uyghur alphabet into Cyrillic to match the Uyghur language in the USSR and allow for shared textbooks across the border, which began in early 1956, was halted, and a new plan was adopted to create a Latin alphabet for the Uyghur language in China to be introduced by 1960.[76]

As the PRC was gradually purging the Uyghur region of Soviet influences, it also began implementing the 'Hundred Flowers Campaign' in 1956. Encouraging people, and especially Party members, to openly criticize Party policies with which they disagreed, the campaign suggested the desire to involve citizens in governance, but it would ultimately be used to attack those who spoke out. In 1957, this campaign was quickly followed by an 'Anti-Rightist Rectification Campaign,' which punished those people who had criticized the state in ways the CCP deemed ideologically inappropriate. In the Uyghur region, this 'Anti-Rightist' campaign translated into a purge of nationalists among the local Muslim population, including many former ETR officials, and those purged were publicly criticized and sentenced to forced labor. According to one Chinese Party historian, during this campaign, 1,612 cadres among the local Muslims of the Uyghur region were labeled 'local nationalists,' the majority of them being forcibly sent to labor camps for re-education.[77] As a result, it was becoming clear that the Soviet-inspired partially accommodationist policies of the early 1950s were coming to an end.

During this time, the PRC was also settling more Han in the region, helping to alter its demographics. Borrowing loosely from the history of Qing military-run farms in the region, the PRC established the Xinjiang Production and Construction Corps (XPCC), or Bingtuan, in 1954.[78] This institution allowed the PRC to quickly move de-mobilized soldiers from the PLA and surrendered ones from the GMD to the XUAR, employing them both as production corps in the service of agriculture, making them de facto settlers, and as a militia ensuring security. This institution has remained critical to PRC policies in the XUAR to this day.[79] In many ways, the XPCC has long served as the symbol of the CCP's colonial approach to the region, creating a segregated system for settlement and economic exploitation while simultaneously providing an occupying military force.

In addition to the Han being sent to work on the XPCC, as many as two million Han came to the region fleeing famine caused by the Great Leap Forward (GLF) during the late 1950s and early 1960s.[80] However, the GLF's impact on the Uyghurs and their homeland went beyond this influx of Han settlers to the region. Instituting the collectivization of agriculture, the GLF likely represented the most concerted effort to disrupt the daily life of the mass of Uyghurs in the region up until that time. As Rian Thum has suggested, the GLF 'not only brought economic disaster and, in many cases, starvation, but also tore apart Uyghur social structures' as it transformed village life.[81] While the formal institutions of religion had already been dismantled during the early 1950s, the GLF also initiated the first state policies to discourage Uyghurs as individuals from practicing religion.[82] Furthermore, the creation of collective farms offered opportunities for more general attempts to assimilate Uyghurs into a Han-dominated PRC culture, as state slogans increasingly discussed the necessity of the 'blending of nationalities' for the success of socialism.[83]

In response to these increasingly repressive policies, many Uyghurs sought ways to flee their homeland during the later 1950s and early 1960s. The largest group fled to the Soviet Union, which had accepted Uyghur immigrants since the early 1950s as part of a larger campaign to repopulate the USSR in the aftermath of World War II.[84] By the late 1950s, the number of Uyghurs leaving their homeland for the Soviet Union increased significantly, and by 1961, it had reached a fever pitch as it became clear that Sino-Soviet relations were headed towards a conflict. In the spring of 1962, Soviet authorities had virtually opened their border with the XUAR in the Republic of Kazakhstan to any local Muslims who were willing to leave, and local CCP authorities appeared to be complicit in this as they provided buses leaving Ghulja for the Soviet border.[85] When it was announced on 29 May 1962 that the buses would no longer leave for the border, many Uyghurs who held tickets for the bus panicked, assuming that the border had already closed. A protest ensued that was allegedly suppressed with gunfire, resulting in scores of Uyghur deaths.[86] In the wake of this disturbance, some 67,000 Uyghurs and many ethnic Kazakhs fled towards the border and were allowed to leave over the course of the next several days.[87] Shortly after this incident, the Sino-Soviet border was officially closed to all travel and trade in 1963.

At the same time as these Uyghurs were arriving in the USSR, the Uyghur region of China was closing off from the rest of the world. Along the Soviet border in the Ili Valley, which had long served as the entry point of Russian and Soviet influence to the region, military-run XPCC farms were set up as a buffer zone, and the residents of the region were denied the ability to leave the country.[88] As China isolated itself from the Soviet Union, a power struggle ensued at the upper echelons of the CCP as a result of the debacle of the GLF. In this struggle, the regional Party Secretary of the Uyghur region, Wang Enmao, pulled back from the mass collectivization effort and followed the new economic policies of Mao Zedong's rivals. However, this was soon to end as Mao unleashed the chaotic Great Proletarian Cultural Revolution (GPCR) throughout the country in 1966 as a last-ditch effort to maintain his control of the CCP.

The chaos of the Cultural Revolution and its assimilationist policies

Most of the scholarship on the GPCR in the Uyghur homeland has focused on the political struggles between Red Guard youth who had come to the region to challenge the power of long-standing Party leader Wang Enmao.[89] These political struggles certainly impacted those Uyghur officials and intellectuals who had remained within the CCP in 1966, but the impact was somewhat unevenly distributed on the majority of Uyghurs due to the chaos that surrounded this period in PRC history. Nonetheless, the GPCR did involve an unprecedented effort to assimilate Uyghurs into a Han-dominated

socialist culture and resulted in an exponential increase of Han settlers in the region.

Given that a major thrust of this youth-propelled Cultural
Revolution was attacking the three 'olds' (old ideas, old customs, and
old habits), it was inevitable that the many zealous Han youth who
came to the region during this time to promote revolution would
also attack Islam and Uyghur culture. There were reports in 1966
that Red Guards had targeted Islam extensively in the region, closing
mosques, burning religious books, and arresting suspected Muslim
clergy.[90] Additionally, there is anecdotal evidence that efforts were
made to ban indigenous forms of dress and force all Uyghurs to
wear clothing modeled after the PLA uniform, to turn mosques into
pig farms as a means of deliberately desecrating Islam, and to force
Uyghur women to wear Chinese hairstyles.[91] Finally, most of the
secular Uyghur elite who still remained in the country, including
academics and artists, were sent to labor camps for 're-education.'

However, the extent and impact of these assimilationist actions
are less clear given the chaotic ways in which power was wielded at
this time. For example, the fact that schools virtually ceased operating during the GPCR meant that many Uyghurs emerged from the
period illiterate and unable to speak the Chinese language. As one
Uyghur recounted, whom I interviewed in the 1990s and who had
been a teenager in Ghulja at this time, he mostly sought to stay
at home with his family and avoid the ongoing political struggles
and street fights that he interpreted as a Han matter. While this
may have characterized the experience of many Uyghurs, a recent
dissertation on the impact of the GPCR on Uyghurs clearly demonstrates that the Red Guards were also successful in recruiting
Uyghur youth, especially from the educated urban populations in
the Uyghur region.[92]

Regardless of the extent or impact of the GPCR's assimilationist aims vis-à-vis the Uyghurs, it is clear that this chaotic political
campaign left an impression on all Uyghurs who lived through the
period. The XPCC settlements had evolved into bases for Red Guard
youth from China proper who had dedicated themselves to transforming the rural population of the region into modern socialists.[93]

While authorities in Urumqi allegedly sought to limit the impact of such groups of radical youth in the countryside so as not to incite another Uyghur rebellion, it is likely that these Red Guards did succeed in subjecting many rural Uyghurs to humiliating persecution for their traditions and religious beliefs.

In this context, it is not surprising that violent Uyghur resistance to Chinese rule once again emerged during this period. Drawing from the experience of the Second ETR and at least tacitly supported by the USSR, an insurgency allegedly calling itself the Eastern Turkistan People's Revolutionary Party (ETPRP) reportedly emerged at this time to fight for an independent Eastern Turkistan state in the Uyghur region based on Soviet styled socialism.[94] Allegedly having existed between 1968 and 1970, the ETPRP reportedly carried out numerous attacks during the GPCR before being defeated in a battle with PLA troops in the foothills of the mountains near Kashgar.[95] According to recent PRC sources, the organization was liquidated in 1970 when local authorities arrested close to 6,000 Uyghurs accused of being involved in it.[96]

The Cultural Revolution likely altered the lives of Uyghurs more than any periods of modern Chinese rule that predate it. It successfully destroyed many Uyghur cultural and religious institutions, temporarily curtailed the use of the Uyghur language in official documents, broke up communities and social capital, and fostered an uneducated generation of Uyghurs who had no sustained access to standard education. It also facilitated a major demographic shift in the region. Between 1953 and 1967, the population of Han had already increased almost six-fold from 300,000 to 1,791,000, but, by 1982, the Han population had exploded to 5,287,000, almost equaling that of the Uyghurs in the region but mostly concentrated in the north of the region or on segregated XPCC bases.[97] However, even this period's extreme policies, demographic shift, and interventions in the daily lives of Uyghurs had failed in truly integrating this region into China proper. The distance of the region from the rest of China and the legacy of colonial difference seemed to limit the Cultural Revolution's impact on Uyghurs in important ways, including shielding some Uyghur populations from the movement's most

49

radical intentions. This was particularly true for the rural Uyghur population in the southern oases of the Tarim Basin.

UYGHURS AND THE XUAR IN THE REFORM PERIOD, 1980–2001: ACCOMMODATION, DEVELOPMENT, AND THE INTENSIFICATION OF SETTLER COLONIALISM

When Deng Xiaoping emerged as leader of China after the end of the Cultural Revolution, there was yet another opportunity to decolonize the relationship between the PRC and the Uyghurs. Deng's reform agenda had substantially changed the state's attitude towards this region and its role in the state's development. The PRC had shifted from isolating itself from outside influences to engaging the outside world, especially economically. In this context, the Uyghur homeland became a potentially important region geo-strategically, which could serve as a bridge to engage countries to the west and south-west for which the region had long served as a buffer zone. As a result, the PRC was to initiate a gradual project of integrating the Uyghur homeland and its population as a bridge to, rather than a buffer from, states bordering on China.[98] It was probably during this period that the region became more integrated into a larger China than during any time prior in modern Chinese history. For the first time in the history of modern China, the state would have the capacity and resources to focus on integrating the Uyghur homeland into a larger Chinese polity and society, and it would likewise have more motivation to do so given the region's emerging geostrategic significance. The PRC had a variety of options at its disposal to do so, including engagement with Uyghurs as the indigenous population of the region as well as forcibly seeking to assimilate them and colonizing their homeland. After briefly flirting with the former, it would decide to adopt the latter.

The 1980s and the last attempts at accommodation

During the early reform period, the PRC ostensibly initiated its first policies of accommodation vis-à-vis the Uyghurs since the

1950s, raising hopes in the region that the PRC's relationship to the Uyghurs and their homeland might be decolonized and result in real ethnic autonomy. Apparently at the urging of Hu Yaobang, the youngest of the reformist officials in the CCP Central Committee at the time, the PRC adopted a resolution in 1980 calling for cultural and economic reforms in the XUAR and allowing for a substantial number of the Han officials and XPCC members stationed in the region to return home to China proper.[99] The results were quickly felt in the region as the Uyghur alphabet was returned to a modified form of Arabic writing, Uyghur schools and university sections were re-opened, mosques were re-established, and there was an explosion in Uyghur language publishing. Hu Yaobang would subsequently rise to the positions of Party Chairman and General Secretary of the CCP in 1981 and 1982 respectively, ushering in a period of increased freedom in the Uyghur homeland and elsewhere in the PRC for the next six years.

This period of accommodation had already started narrowing in its scope by 1987 with the purging of Hu Yaobang, and it narrowed even more with the Tiananmen Square protests of 1989. Ultimately, reforms were halted prior to granting any increased ethnic autonomy or facilitating a regional demographic shift in Uyghurs' favor. Still, the 1980s allowed for a Uyghur cultural renaissance and for a re-emergence of Islam in the region, which would raise Uyghur expectations for the future and reverse most of the cultural erasure that had transpired during the Cultural Revolution. When I first visited the XUAR in January 1990, the impact of the previous decade of accommodating policies was clearly visible. Although many rural Uyghurs continued to wear the coats and hats styled after the PLA's uniform that were popularized during the Cultural Revolution, small mosques had popped up everywhere, and public displays of religiosity were common, especially in the south of the region. The revived Arabic script for the Uyghur language was now also visible everywhere, and the Latin alphabet that had been propagated during the Cultural Revolution was virtually non-existent.

Furthermore, many of the Uyghur intellectuals and religious scholars who had spent time in labor camps and prisons during the

Cultural Revolution had been released and were allowed to teach and publish again. While few of these intellectuals dared to write standard history books, many did write historical novels, some of which discussed the periods of the First and Second ETRs and others that asserted the Uyghurs' indigeneity to the region.[100] Additionally, religious scholars who had been released from prison opened informal schools and began once again propagating Islam on their own terms without scrutiny from the state.

Many Uyghurs who lived through the 1980s to this day call this time the 'Golden Period' in recent Uyghur life, remembering it for the hope it provided for a different future and a different China. In retrospect, if these accommodating policies had been sustained, it is likely that Uyghurs would have more readily integrated with Chinese society during the 1990s, especially if the PRC had recognized the XUAR as the Uyghurs' homeland and had instituted substantive ethnic autonomy there. While the accommodations of the 1980s once again stopped short of such policies that could have decolonized the relationship between the PRC and Uyghurs, the cultural liberties and religious freedom they did afford to the local population would be difficult to reverse.

The 1990s: between settler colonialism and integration

If, during the 1980s, the PRC sought to integrate the Uyghur region and its population into a reforming PRC through accommodation, in the 1990s, this integration would mostly be promoted through economic opportunity. Indeed, the economic growth of the PRC under Deng's reforms brought Uyghurs new opportunities, and many took advantage of being able to open businesses or even travel abroad to do trading. However, political space was simultaneously tightening as Uyghur publishing and music came under more scrutiny from censors, and religious freedoms were severely curtailed. These reversals of civil liberties would combine with the hope created by the fall of the Soviet Union and the creation of independent states in Central Asia to increase Uyghur calls for self-determination over the course of the decade, at times being articulated violently. As a result, the PRC would institute a series of campaigns to attack signs of Uyghur resistance in the region that, in many ways, overshadowed the PRC campaign to develop the region and integrate it more into Deng's vision for a new China. This interplay between Uyghur resistance and corresponding state repression would begin almost immediately at the outset of the decade.

In April 1990, a major disturbance broke out in a rural area of the XUAR called Baren township near the southern city of Kashgar. Although the details of the 'Baren incident' remain unclear, the event ended in the occupation of local government buildings for nearly three days until Chinese military and security forces were able to take back the buildings and either kill or arrest the Uyghurs who had occupied them. Some reports suggest that the violence that broke out in Baren was spontaneous, occurring after the Chinese military clashed with some 200 Uyghur demonstrators protesting against recently applied limits on the number of births allotted to minority families.[101] Other reports, including official Chinese sources, maintain that the incident was a premeditated attempt to overthrow state control of this small rural area by a religiously oriented pro-independence group calling itself the East Turkistan Islamic Party (ETIP).[102]

The actual truth may lie somewhere in between. There are credible accounts that the disturbance was initiated when a group of young religious Uyghurs began a protest regarding a variety of PRC policies targeting Muslim beliefs. However, there is also credible evidence that the leader of this protest, Zäydin Yüsüp, had indeed created an organization by the name of ETIP that intended to wage an armed struggle to liberate Uyghurs from Chinese rule and had been stockpiling stolen weapons for this purpose. When the protest was attacked by security forces, the members of ETIP who organized it were ready to respond with armed resistance.

The combination of an ideology of self-determination with Islamic religiosity apparent in the Baren incident raised fears in the government that Uyghurs may be organizing a religiously inspired violent resistance movement to Chinese rule. These concerns of the government were amplified two years later when two buses were blown up in the city of Urumqi.[103] While there are few details available about these bombings, there was evidence that they were organized by Uyghurs who had studied with the same informal religious teacher as had those involved in the Baren incident.

These worries about Uyghur resistance to Chinese rule were exacerbated by the dissolution of the Soviet Union in December 1991. This event sparked fear throughout the CCP that the PRC could face a similar fate to the now defunct USSR, but it sparked particular fear amongst those CCP officials responsible for governing the Uyghur homeland. Already in the late 1980s, the opening of the Sino-Soviet border had allowed Uyghurs to reunite with family members who had fled to the USSR in the 1950s and early 1960s. Thus, many Uyghurs from China had witnessed the twilight of Soviet power, the fall of communism, and the emergence of Central Asian nation-states, and they had done so in the company of Uyghur nationalists who had once fought against Chinese armies to achieve similar goals in their homeland during the 1940s. For many Uyghurs, these events renewed hope of attaining independent statehood. As one Uyghur I met in the XUAR in 1994 noted plainly, 'now there is a Kazakhstan, a Kyrgyzstan, and an Uzbekistan, where is Uyghurstan?' While there is no evidence that such sentiments had led to a substantial organized Uyghur resistance, the PRC was concerned that it might.

As a result, the PRC security campaign in the XUAR, which had been initiated after the Baren incident, intensified in 1991 with the fall of the USSR. This campaign targeted Uyghur expressions of nationalism as well as Uyghurs' religious revival under the guise of combating 'separatism' and 'unsanctioned religious activity.' Through this campaign, between 1990 and 1995, security forces arrested some 1,831 Uyghurs under suspicion of nationalist and religious sentiments, claiming they were members of 'separatist counter-revolutionary organizations, illegal organizations, and reactionary gangs.'[104] Additionally, the state created a strict process of vetting for Muslim clergy that required regular political exams testing their loyalty to the PRC, and closed many of the smaller community mosques that had been built during the 1980s.[105]

While this crackdown on Uyghur dissent and religion appeared to be reactive to Baren and the fall of the USSR, it was not until 1996 and the leaking of 'Document No. 7' that it would become clear that the PRC's strategy for suppressing Uyghur religiosity and calls for self-determination was systematic. This document, the contents of which were allegedly resolutions from a high-level Party meeting, laid out a strategy that simultaneously sought to integrate Uyghurs and their homeland more solidly into the PRC while eliminating what the state considered to be 'separatism' and 'unsanctioned religious activity.' On one hand, the document instructed officials to 'speed up economic development and improve the life of people,' referring to economic construction, reform, and China's 'open-door policy' as the 'bases of maintaining stability in Xinjiang.'[106] On the other hand, it mandated aggressive security measures targeting Uyghur dissent, which it alleged was supported by 'international counter-revolutionary forces led by the United States of America.'[107]

In addition to requiring a stronger and more active presence of military and security organs in the Uyghur region, this document also advocated limiting the spread of 'separatist ideas,' which the PRC viewed as being at least partially related to independent religious activity. Thus, the document mandated a strict regulation of religious observation in the region, including the curbing of construction for new mosques and the closing of informal religious schools and 'Qur'an studies meetings.'[108] It also called for enhanced surveillance of Uyghurs and the media they consumed, especially in the south of the region where it suggested there was a need to 'establish individual files' on Uyghurs suspected of 'unsanctioned religious activities' or of harboring self-determination aspirations.[109]

Despite, or perhaps in part due to, the extensive control measures called for by 'Document No. 7,' another major disturbance broke out in the region in February 1997 in the northern town of Ghulja near the Kazakhstan border. Although accounts of this event are contradictory, it appears to have begun with a protest by Uyghurs against limits on religious observation, and it spiraled out of control after security forces clashed with protestors, leading to multiple casualties.[110] The PRC reaction was again very heavy-handed, and the town was put under curfew and its transport connections to the rest of the region cut off for two weeks.[111]

Less than three weeks after the 'Ghulja incident,' three bombs exploded on public buses in the capital city of Urumqi, which killed nine and seriously injured twenty-eight people.[112] While no specific organization took credit for the bombings, and little details about the incident are available, it occurred on the day of memorial services for the recently deceased Deng Xiaoping, suggesting political motivation. These violent events in Ghulja and Urumqi led to a renewed region-wide crackdown on Uyghurs that was much more intense than others during the early 1990s.[113] The crackdown resulted in countless arrests and further restrictions on Uyghur religious behavior, which was now limited to men over eighteen at state-sanctioned mosques. At the same time, the PRC also began to cut off the cross-border ties between China's Uyghurs and those in Central Asia and used the newly established Shanghai Cooperation Organization (SCO) to ensure that Central Asian security organs would silence the political activity of the Uyghurs living in their countries.[114]

This extreme crackdown on dissent and closure of access to Uyghurs outside the PRC provided a new impetus among young Uyghurs in northern urban areas to follow state-prescribed paths towards integration into the PRC's Han-dominant culture.[115] Seeing few other available options, many such youth made the decision to study in Chinese-language schools and to pursue careers that might break the ethnic segregation between Han and Uyghurs, while others immersed themselves in Islam as a means of resisting assimilation into Han culture.[116] However, few of the clear majority of Uyghurs who lived in rural regions, especially in the south, were even provided opportunities for integration, finding themselves in constant conflict with local security organs.

As the crackdown in the wake of the Ghulja events and the Urumqi bombings expanded over the following three years, violence in the region also increased. Gardner Bovingdon documents approximately 38 incidents of violence that took place in the Uyghur region between February 1997 and the beginning of 2001, but it is striking that most of these incidents of violence can be explained as attacks on the police and security organs, which were spearheading the crackdown and the frenzied search for 'separatists' in the region.[117] The few instances that did not involve violence against police were mostly assassinations of local religious clergy who had become the face of religious regulation in the region and a few bombings utilizing home-made explosives, about which virtually no details are available. Even more noticeable is that reports of violent incidents in the region virtually disappear in 2000 and 2001.

In retrospect, the 1990s represented a period when the PRC sought to integrate Uyghurs and their homeland more solidly into the state, but without undertaking the accommodations to the local population required to incentivize such integration. Having found the power of market economics, the government presumed that economic liberalization would erase the over two centuries of colonial relations that had fueled tension in the region. The Chinese state seemed to hope that Uyghurs would be satisfied to integrate into a new China where 'to get rich is glorious' and assimilate into a Han dominant culture without any recognition of their unique relationship to their homeland and cultural roots. Indeed, during this time, a portion of urban Uyghurs in the north did get rich, and some of them, especially in Urumqi, sought to integrate into a newly reformed PRC by assimilating to a Han-dominant culture. However, others, especially in the south where economic opportunities were minimal, viewed economic liberalization as a new means of facilitating the region's colonization and one that was more explicitly articulated as Han settler colonialism.

There were clear reasons for such an interpretation of Chinese policies at the time. By 2000, the Han who had left after the Cultural Revolution had been replaced by a new generation of migrants, maintaining the Han portion of the region's population almost on par with that of the Uyghurs, representing 40.6% and 45.2% respectively.[118] Unlike those Han who had been sent to the region during the Cultural Revolution, however, these new migrants were coming to the region voluntarily to take advantage of economic opportunities generated by development, increased resource extraction, and commerce with the neighboring former Soviet republics, suggesting that they were there to stay and would likely be followed by more. While these new migrants mostly settled in the north of the region, state policies, especially the establishment of a rail link from Urumqi to Kashgar in 1999, were already seeking ways to bring more Han migrants to the southern oases, which had remained mostly Uyghur in population.

If the region had long looked like a frontier colony of modern China, these new developments suggested the initial stages of an intensified settler colonialism where Uyghurs could eventually be overwhelmed. At the same time, the state was viciously attacking the Islamic faith among Uyghur believers, forcibly removing a portion of their identity and culture.[119] Finally, it was clear that the PRC had completely stepped back from its promises in the 1980s to provide Uyghurs with more autonomy over their homeland, and the space for Uyghur political discourse had been mostly erased as any questioning of state policies became grounds for accusations of 'separatism.' With the declaration of a broad state development campaign to 'Open Up the West' at the end of the decade, these characteristics of settler colonization would only increase, especially in the southern oases of the Tarim Basin, where they would meet with increased resistance from the local Uyghur majority.

FROM FRONTIER COLONY TO SETTLER COLONY?

The Uyghurs have long had a contentious relationship with modern Chinese states that originates from a history of conquest and colonialism. In itself, these colonial origins do not set this relationship apart from majority-minority ethnic relations in a host of post-colonial states which began as colonies around the world. However, what does make the relationship between modern China and Uyghurs unique is that these colonial origins have never been fully acknowledged by Chinese states as a precursor to initiating a process of decolonization or post-colonialism as has been the case in most other former colonies. As a result, the region is, in many ways, still a colony of the PRC today, an observation that will not come as a surprise to most Uyghurs reading this book.

During its more than two centuries of history, this colonial relationship has involved a variance in state strategies for controlling the region and its peoples, but these policies have never served to truly integrate the region and its people into modern China. Arguably, modern Chinese states, and especially the PRC, have long desired a more blatant absorption of this region and its population into their polities, but their efforts to do so have been consistently thwarted by a lack of state capacity as well as by distance and their own paternalistic attitudes of colonial difference towards the local population. As a result, the region, and especially its mostly Uyghur populated south, remained on the margins of modern Chinese society into the 1990s, akin to a frontier colony.

This tenuous position of the region in modern China allowed Uyghurs to maintain cultural distinctiveness and largely avoid assimilation. Thus, when the 1990s began, the Uyghur language was still far more prominent as a mode of communication amongst Uyghurs than was Chinese, Uyghur children were still afforded an education where Uyghur was the primary language of instruction, and Uyghurs were largely free to pursue their own cultural rituals and even to practice Islam. This relative cultural freedom had likely tempered Uyghur resistance to what had essentially been a long-term colonial occupation of the Uyghur homeland. However, events during the 1990s presented new challenges to this state of relative equilibrium. Suddenly, the PRC was more directly involved in the region than ever before, and state-led development was transforming the landscape, especially in the north, to look more like the rest of China. Simultaneously, the state was also rolling back the political, cultural, and religious freedom of Uyghurs in the name of fighting 'separatism.' In many ways, the Uyghur homeland was becoming more integrated into China than ever in the 250 years reviewed in this chapter, but, for many Uyghurs, this felt as if their homeland was under siege from a new stage of settler colonization, which was intended to marginalize, if not entirely displace, them.

It is worth stating that at the end of the 1990s, there still existed a policy option for the PRC that could have allowed for the peaceful integration of the Uyghur homeland into modern China. However, that policy option would have required the PRC doing something unprecedented; it would need to acknowledge the region's past colonization and the Uyghurs' indigenous status, followed by accommodations that would have given Uyghurs a lead role in the region's future development. This chapter highlights numerous moments in the history of modern China's relationship with Uyghurs and their homeland when the beginnings of such processes appeared to have been set in motion, but they were all eventually curtailed and reversed.

Instead of pursuing such accommodationist policies towards the Uyghurs and their homeland in the early 2000s, the PRC would adopt a strategy that would ultimately marginalize and dehumanize the Uyghur people as a whole. It would suggest that Uyghur dissent in the region was actually the product of a 'terrorist threat' linked to Al-Qaeda in the context of the US-led GWOT. This decision came as a surprise to those who had followed developments in the region over the last decade because there were few signs that such a 'terrorist threat' existed among Uyghurs. While there were significant incidents of Uyghur resistance to Chinese rule in the 1990s, some of which had turned violent, there was no evidence that any of this resistance was led by a specific organization, let alone one linked to Al-Qaeda. Furthermore, with the exception of the 1992 and 1997 Urumqi bus bombings, which both remain shrouded in mystery, there was no violence allegedly perpetrated by Uyghurs in the 1990s that could be described as 'terrorism' under the working definition of that term provided in this book's introduction.

Nonetheless, the PRC did decide in October 2001, on the heels of the 11 September attacks on the US, to link Uyghur dissent in China to the global 'terrorist threat' that was the focus of the emerging US-led GWOT, and it would be successful in getting at least partial international recognition of this threat. These events would ultimately facilitate the PRC's further settler colonization of the Uyghur homeland by justifying the increased marginalization and repression of its indigenous population as an existential threat to Chinese state and society. As such, they did not only initiate another stage in the long contentious and colonial relationship; they also fundamentally altered this relationship, ultimately making any attempts to peacefully decolonize it unimaginable in the foreseeable future.

2 Häsän Mäkhsum giving a religious lecture in Afghanistan, circa 1998–2001.

HOW THE UYGHURS BECAME A 'TERRORIST THREAT'

Uyghurs were classified as a 'terrorist threat' in the early 2000s, not because of anything Uyghurs did; they were classified as such through a politically motivated process initiated by the PRC and, after intensive lobbying, reified by the US. While this classification only branded one small and little-known Uyghur exile group in Afghanistan as a 'terrorist organization,' it has subsequently had major ramifications for all Uyghurs everywhere and especially in China. This classification was unquestionably pursued by the PRC opportunistically, but it was also the ambiguous nature of the US-led GWOT's enemies that made it possible.

HOW GWOT IDENTIFIES ITS AMBIGUOUS ENEMIES

It is important to note that the 'terrorist' enemies of GWOT have been ambiguous since the very beginning, and this was likely a deliberate decision of those who declared the war. When, on 20 September 2001 President George W. Bush addressed Congress and the American people, laying out his proposed response to the attacks on the US that had occurred nine days earlier, he famously declared a broad war on 'terror' that would begin with Al-Qaeda, which had been identified as the perpetrators of the attacks, but 'not end until every terrorist group of global reach has been found, stopped and defeated.'[1] In characterizing this vague enemy, Bush confidently noted that 'the terrorists practice a fringe form of Islamic extremism that has been rejected by Muslim scholars; ... [their] directive commands them to kill Christians and Jews, to kill all Americans, and make no distinction among military and civilians, including women and children.'[2] While Bush's characterization of these 'terrorists' suggested a formidable and evil foe, their actual identity remained mostly undefined and open-ended, likely deliberately so. As of this book's publication, this war is still with us, and its enemy remains as ambiguous and demonized as ever. This ambiguous framing of the war's enemy ensured that GWOT would be an open-ended war that could be articulated in different ways by different actors around the world. In many ways, it is not a war at all, but a narrative that can serve as a political tool in the hands of states to advance a variety of different agendas.

Indeed, the US would set the precedent for the use of this war as a political tool as it quickly pivoted to make its version of GWOT more about fighting 'rogue states' in the international system than about fighting the vaguely defined 'terrorists' that Bush had described. The US invasion of Afghanistan, whether justified or not, at least had a direct connection to the 11 September attacks as the base of operations for Al-Qaeda, which had ordered the attacks. However, by January 2002, when George W. Bush gave his infamous 'Axis of Evil' speech, it had become clear that the US was intending to fight not only states who were allegedly providing support and sanctuary to 'terrorists,' like Afghanistan, but also those states which *might do so* in the future due to their unsanctioned manufacture of 'weapons of mass destruction.' In particular, Bush noted that Iraq, Iran, and North Korea were all allegedly in the process of creating such weapons, which they *could* provide to alleged 'terrorists.' As he ominously declared, 'states like these, and their terrorist allies, constitute an axis of evil, arming to threaten the peace of the world.'[3] From that time on, the Bush administration's version of GWOT became more about regime change in Afghanistan and Iraq than about destroying alleged 'terrorist organizations.'

In the context of this book, the US manipulation of GWOT's ambiguous enemy to target unrelated enemies is primarily important for the precedent it set for other states. Elsewhere, such manipulation has generally not been used to justify targeting international enemies as the US had done, but instead as justification for attacking domestic opponents, especially if they are Muslims. The amorphous nature of GWOT's enemies and their wide geographic dispersal has invited such a response, especially from authoritarian regimes seeking excuses to discredit domestic dissent of all kinds. Furthermore, since the war is inherently global, it has its own international architecture, which can be manipulated by states to brand domestic opponents as internationally recognized 'terrorists.'

GWOT's 'terrorist lists'

Within this global anti-terrorism architecture, one of the most important tools for states wishing to implicate domestic opponents as enemies in GWOT is the system of international 'terrorism lists' that serve to recognize groups as global 'terrorists.' In essence, being put on such a list in the context of GWOT serves the purpose of a 'scarlet letter,' justifying the violent targeting of the groups and individuals in question wherever they might be located and whatever may be their actual goals and actions. While numerous countries keep such lists, only one list portends to demonstrate the general international consensus on whom should be categorized as a 'terrorist,' especially in the context of GWOT. This is the so-called United Nations Security Council (UNSC) 'Consolidated List.'

This list was originally created by the UNSC in 1999 under Resolution 1267 as a means of sanctioning Al-Qaeda and the Taliban for their involvement in the 1988 bombing of the US Embassy in Tanzania.[4] However, it became substantially more powerful following the declaration of GWOT when it began including any organization or individual alleged to be associated with Al-Qaeda and the Taliban. While this list quickly became the primary means of identifying the 'terrorist' enemies in this new war, criteria for inclusion had nothing to do with the acts carried out by a given group and was instead determined through 'guilt by association.' Other lists that would prove to be powerful in the post-2001 environment include those of the US and the EU, given that these lists represent the 'terrorists' targeted by the leading militaries mobilized in GWOT.

As Lee Jarvis and Tim Legrand have argued, these lists are the basis for 'vast aspects of the Western world's counter-terrorism frameworks.'[5] Initially, they were meant to provide a legal means for targeting alleged 'terrorists' for a variety of international sanctions, but in the context of GWOT, they have also justified state-initiated violence against those represented on them. As such, states have used them to deflect political criticism of controversial extra-legal actions taken against those listed, including non-sanctioned assassinations, extra-judicial detentions, and surveillance not allowed by domestic law. As Jarvis and Legrand point out, the designation of groups as 'terrorists' on these lists has become 'a fulcrum of states' counterterrorism capabilities and ambitions.'[6]

In this context, it was not surprising that the PRC would aspire almost immediately after GWOT's declaration to get Uyghur groups recognized on these international lists. The Chinese state had long dealt violently with dissent from Uyghurs, particularly when it was suggestive of aspirations for self-determination, and the PRC's violent suppression of Uyghur dissent had increased throughout the 1990s, drawing sustained international criticism. While the international community is generally critical of the violent suppression of self-determination movements, in the context of GWOT, dealing with 'terrorists' violently is not only tolerated by the international community, but encouraged. Thus, the PRC had strong motivation after 9/11 to portray all Uyghur dissent as 'terrorism' and aligned with GWOT's ambiguous enemies.

BRANDING UYGHURS AS A 'TERRORIST THREAT'

During the early days of GWOT, the PRC had yet to directly link Uyghurs to the 'terrorists' against which the war was being waged, but this would change by October 2001 when the Chinese state began a concerted effort to re-brand its concerns about Uyghur calls for independence as an international 'terrorist threat' linked to Al-Qaeda. While the PRC's sudden characterization of Uyghurs as being part of international 'terrorist' networks in the context of GWOT seemed out of place at the time, in retrospect it made perfect sense given China's experiences during the 1990s in former Soviet Eurasia where the labels of 'terrorist' and 'extremist' were in common usage as a means of discrediting domestic opposition. The PRC's initial interaction with this discourse would emerge from its involvement in the 'Shanghai Five' group, which later became the Shanghai Cooperation Organization (SCO).

The 'Shanghai Five' and the origins of China's narrative of the Uyghur 'terrorist threat'

The 'Shanghai Five' group, representing China, Russia, Kazakhstan, Kyrgyzstan, and Tajikistan, was formed in 1996 as a means of resolving issues of border demarcation and diplomatic relations between China and the four states of the former Soviet Union which it bordered. At its initial meeting in Shanghai, it agreed to establish annual meetings, which were held in Russia (1997), Kazakhstan (1998), Kyrgyzstan (1999), and Tajikistan (2000) respectively. The agenda at these meetings would quickly expand beyond border demarcation and diplomatic relations to focus increasingly on security concerns.[7] In these subsequent Shanghai Five meetings, the PRC's concern about Uyghur nationalist aspirations would become an increasingly important part of the concessions it sought from its neighbors, especially following the Ghulja incident and Urumqi bus bombings of 1997. The Chinese government was well aware of the activities of the Uyghur nationalist communities in Kazakhstan and Kyrgyzstan, and it worried that these exiles in Central Asia were fueling calls for independence among China's own Uyghurs.

Given the PRC's preoccupation with the Uyghur issue at the time, it was not surprising that security concerns were dominant in the discussions of the Shanghai Five group in Almaty in 1998 where the group added a new dimension to their collaboration – 'combating separatism, religious extremism and international terrorism,' a trinity of threats that would eventually become known as the 'three evils.'[8] In 2001, when the group returned to Shanghai for its annual meeting, it announced the founding of a new regional security cooperation organization that became known as the SCO. One of the first orders of business of the new SCO was to draft and ratify the 'Shanghai Convention on Combating Terrorism, Separatism and Extremism' that was adopted in June 2001, roughly three months before the 11 September attacks on the US.[9]

The power of the 'three evils' was that it blurred the lines between three different perceived threats, equating them as a unitary threat in the policies of the states concerned. For the PRC, it was critical that 'separatism' was included in this trinity of security threats to allow coordination on combating Uyghur calls for self-determination. As Jiang Zemin would note at the Almaty meeting, the five countries represented 'should strengthen mutual support in safeguarding the national unity and sovereignty of our nations,' a thinly veiled call for international collaboration in the PRC's fight against Uyghur calls for self-determination.[10] By contrast, the inclusion of 'terrorism' and 'extremism' in this list was more likely the initiative of the former Soviet states, all of which had experience in using the flexible discourse of 'terrorism' and 'extremism' to discredit domestic opponents in the eyes of the international community, particularly given the region's proximity to Afghanistan. However, most importantly, this trinity of threats allowed all six SCO members (Uzbekistan had been added to the group in 2001) to link their own domestic opponents, whether they were independence movements or merely political competitors, to the quickly escalating international security concern of 'Islamic terrorism.'

While its engagement with Russian and Central Asian discourses on 'terrorism' and 'extremism' through the Shanghai Five and the SCO did not result in an immediate transformation of the Chinese state's framing of its alleged Uyghur 'separatist' threat domestically, it did lead the PRC to begin interchangeably using the 'terrorist' and 'separatist' labels in its reports of Uyghur dissent to the outside world. In a January 2001 report about the destruction of an alleged Uyghur independence organization, the PRC claimed that the group had been involved in multiple 'terrorist acts.'[11] Similarly, in March 2001, the highest-ranking ethnic Uyghur Party official in the XUAR at the time, Abulahät Abdurishit, suggested to journalists that Uyghur 'separatists' in the region were receiving assistance from 'international terrorists.'[12] While the appearance of this narrative about Uyghur 'terrorism' in Chinese state discourse was still fairly rare at the time, it had already become a nominal part of that discourse prior to the 11 September attacks, albeit on the margins of broader accusations of Uyghur 'separatism.' As such, when George W. Bush declared a worldwide war on international terrorism in late 2001, the PRC already had a good idea of how to implicate the Uyghurs in that war.

China's campaign for international recognition of a Uyghur 'terrorist threat'

Signs of the PRC's intent to brand what it had previously framed as Uyghur 'separatism' as a 'terrorist threat' already appeared about five weeks after the 9/11 attacks. In being asked about a conference held at the European Parliament by the East Turkistan National Congress, a Europe-based Uyghur advocacy group, a spokesperson for the Chinese Foreign Ministry on 19 October went on a tirade about the group being a 'terrorist organization.' Going much further than previous PRC uses of the narrative of 'terrorism' to describe Uyghur dissent, he noted:

> The force for East Turkistan is a terrorist force with the objective of splitting China. It has closely colluded with the international terrorist organizations to undertake numerous horrible violent terrorist acts in China and its neighboring countries, leading to great casualties. Under the backdrop of increased international cooperation against terrorism, the force for East Turkistan is trying to disguise itself under the pretext of human rights, democracy and safeguarding the minority's rights to carry on its splittist activities. However, these tactical changes cannot change its nature as a terrorist organization.[13]

This explanation of the 'Eastern Turkistan terrorist threat' lacked details, but it outlined a general argument that would be refined by Chinese state officials in the coming weeks and months as it became clear that the PRC was explicitly seeking to implicate the Uyghurs in GWOT.

In an impassioned speech before the UN General Assembly on 11

November 2001, the PRC Minister of Foreign Affairs, Tang Jiaxuan, pledged China's support for the fight against the international 'terrorist threat' and signaled the PRC's emergent framing of Uyghur dissent as a part of that threat. He noted, 'China is also threatened by terrorism; the "Eastern Turkistan" terrorist forces are trained, equipped and financed by international terrorist organizations; the fight against the "Eastern Turkistan" group is an important aspect of the international fight against terrorism.'[14] While the PRC had made vague suggestions earlier in 2001 that Uyghur independence activists were receiving assistance from international terrorists, this accusation by the Foreign Minister was being made more forcefully at a high-profile international event. However, the vague phrasing of this statement, just like that of the foreign ministry spokesperson weeks before, left much to the imagination. Who exactly were the 'Eastern Turkistan terrorist forces' to which they were referring, and from which 'international terrorist organizations' were they receiving financing?

Likely in response to such questions, the PRC Permanent Mission to the UN appears to have released a brief explainer two weeks later that sought to clarify these earlier statements.[15] This document, entitled 'Terrorist Activities Perpetrated by "Eastern Turkistan" Organizations and Their Links with Osama bin Laden and the Taliban,' claimed unequivocally that China faced its own 'terrorist threat' that was directly connected to Osama bin Laden, enemy number one in GWOT. In the document, the PRC suggested that this terrorist threat came from a vague group called the 'Eastern Turkistan' forces, which included over 40 organizations located around the world.[16] It also highlighted eight of these organizations dispersed around the world in Turkey, Central Asia, Pakistan, Afghanistan, and Switzerland as explicitly advocating violence in their political platforms.[17] In addition to these groups, the document also mentions a variety of other organizations that had allegedly carried out acts of violence inside and outside of China during the 1990s.[18]

To most outside observers with knowledge of Uyghur political groups at the time, these claims sounded absurd. Most international scholars studying Uyghurs or their homeland had never heard of the majority of these organizations and did not perceive those named with which they were familiar as a 'terrorist threat.' Having studied Uyghurs in Kazakhstan since the early 1990s and being familiar with Uyghur nationalist organizations in the region, I personally had only heard of a few of the organizations claimed by the document to be active in former Soviet Central Asia. I was aware of the United Committee of Uyghurs' Organizations, known as *Ittipaq* in Central Asia, which was an attempt to create an umbrella organization for a variety of Uyghur secular nationalist groups in the region, but I also knew this group had few resources, was rife with divisions, and possessed no capacity to carry out acts of violence, let alone inside China. While I was also aware of the Eastern Turkistan Liberation Organization (ETLO) as a more religious nationalist group with ties to Turkey and made up mostly of more recent Uyghur arrivals from China, I knew that this group was small in number and had been virtually destroyed by Kazakhstan's security apparatus in 1999–2000 thanks to agreements made with China through the Shanghai Five. It was difficult to believe that either of these groups were connected with Osama bin Laden and Al-Qaeda. Such connections sounded even more absurd for the Eastern Turkistan Youth League based in Switzerland, which was overtly secular and focused on supplying information about the plight of Uyghurs to the international community.

The one organization named in the document that reasonably raised some speculation about a potential Uyghur connection to Al-Qaeda and the Taliban was the Eastern Turkistan Islamic Movement (ETIM), which allegedly was operational in Afghanistan. No international scholars studying Uyghurs at the time had ever heard of this group, but they also knew little about Uyghurs in Afghanistan. It was plausible that a militant Uyghur group could have established itself there given its proximity to the Uyghur homeland, its relative openness to offering safe haven to different Muslim rebel groups from around the world, and the widespread negative attitudes of Uyghurs to Chinese rule. Furthermore, if such a group did exist, it also seemed plausible that it might have become associated with

Al-Qaeda, as was allegedly the case with the Islamic Movement of Uzbekistan (IMU), a group of religiously oriented Uzbeks, which was in opposition to the government of Uzbekistan and had fled to Afghanistan in the second half of the 1990s.

Furthermore, the PRC document presented more detailed information about ETIM than about any other Uyghur group it was accusing of being part of the 'Eastern Turkistan terrorist forces.' The document claimed that ETIM was led by a Uyghur named Häsän Mäkhsum and had received $300,000 in support from Osama bin Laden and the Taliban.[19] It also asserted that the organization commanded a 'China Battalion,' and its fighters, after being trained in Afghanistan, fought in combat 'in Afghanistan, Chechnya and Uzbekistan, or returned to Xinjiang for terrorist and violent activities.'[20]

While the plausibility of these assertions raised speculation that some Uyghurs could in fact be establishing ties with Al-Qaeda, it attracted little international attention because none of this information could be easily corroborated. There was scant evidence of this group's existence aside from the PRC's claims, and the US military apparently found very few Uyghurs among the militants in Afghanistan after it had invaded the country in late September 2001. Therefore, even if there was any truth to the PRC's claims about Uyghurs seeking to carry out violence inside China from bases in Afghanistan, it did not seem that these alleged Uyghur militants had substantial enough connections to Al-Qaeda to qualify them as a serious concern in the context of GWOT.

However, the PRC remained persistent about its claims of a Uyghur-Al-Qaeda connection and continued to lobby the international community to recognize this connection's relevance to GWOT.[21] In January of 2002, the PRC's State Council Office of Information would release a far more detailed report on Uyghur ties to 'terrorism', which also called for international action against the nebulous 'Eastern Turkistan Terrorist Forces' named in the first report. This second document, entitled '"East Turkistan" Terrorist Forces Cannot Get Away with Impunity,' started with a confident statement on the 'terrorist threat' posed by Uyghurs to China as well as to neighboring regions:

Over a long period of time – especially since the 1990s – the 'East Turkistan' forces inside and outside Chinese territory have planned and organized a series of violent incidents in the Xinjiang Uygur [sic] Autonomous Region of China and some other countries, including explosions, assassinations, arsons, poisonings, and assaults, with the objective of founding a so-called state of 'East Turkistan.'[22]

This opening statement in the document is followed by a brief historical description of the origins of Uyghur self-determination movements, both seeking to refute Uyghur claims that the XUAR is their homeland and linking the Uyghur history of self-determination movements to a narrative of 'international terrorism' and 'Islamic extremism.' This section includes assertions that the Uyghur homeland had been a constituent part of China since 60 BC and that Uyghurs are not ethnic 'Turks' at all, arguing that Uyghur calls for self-determination under the banner of 'Eastern Turkistan' were part of an international conspiracy to split and weaken China that had been subsequently radicalized by 'extremist Islam' and 'international terrorist networks.'[23] While this fantastical account of the history of the Uyghurs and their homeland is easily refuted by historians, it provides insight into the logic of the PRC's application of a 'terrorism' narrative to Uyghur calls for self-determination as well as of China's melding of the 'three evils' as an intertwined unitary threat of 'separatism,' 'extremism,' and 'terrorism.'

While this historical section of the document would not garner much international attention, the following section of the document, which provided alleged evidence of 'terrorist acts' purportedly perpetrated by Uyghurs, would eventually play a critical role in the international recognition of one Uyghur group as a 'terrorist threat.' This section confidently declares that 'from 1990 to 2001, the "East Turkistan" terrorist forces inside and outside Chinese territory were responsible for over 200 terrorist incidents in Xinjiang, resulting in the deaths of 162 people of all ethnic groups, including grassroots officials and religious personnel, and injuries to more than 440 people.'[24] Then, it provides an illustrative list of violent events, mostly from the 1990s, that it classifies as 'terrorist acts,' categorized by 'explosions,' 'assassinations,' 'attacks on police and government institutions,' 'poisonings and arsons,' and 'instigating disturbances and riots.'[25] Given the lack of detailed information available about these incidents from other sources, it is difficult to know the actual circumstances of any of the described events, whether they occurred as described, and whether they should legitimately be characterized as 'terrorism.'

However, even taken at face value, very few of them qualify as 'terrorism' using this book's working definition of the term because the overwhelming majority either did not target civilians or did not even constitute premeditated political violence. The 'assassinations' allegedly targeted government officials or religious clergy working for state-run religious bodies active in the region's religious regulation. Even if these were premeditated and politically motivated, they should be viewed more as acts of guerilla warfare than as 'terrorism.' The alleged 'attacks on police and government institutions' obviously did not target civilians. The claims of 'instigating disturbances and riots,' including the Baren events of 1990 and the Ghulja events of 1997, do not fit any acceptable definition of 'terrorism' as they began as peaceful protests, and the claims of 'poisoning and arson' include too little information to allow one to easily establish a narrative of 'terrorism' about them. The only violent incidents that, if taken at face value, may involve 'terrorist' tactics, per this book's definition, are the five different series of explosions discussed in the report. Unfortunately, little is known about these events, and most of them were never reported until the release of this particular document. The two incidents which appeared to involve 'terrorist' tactics about which reports do exist are the bus bombings in Urumqi in 1992 and 1997 respectively. However, neither of these bombings were ever claimed by an organization, and little is known about the details of those arrested for them.[26]

This list of violent acts allegedly perpetrated by Uyghurs during the 1990s, if even partially accurate, certainly offers a snap-shot of the resentment that was building among Uyghurs at this time regarding Chinese rule of their homeland, but it provides no evidence of a 'terrorist threat' or even of an organized militant threat. Most of the acts of violence outlined in the document appear to have been spontaneous outbursts of violent rage or the settling of personal vendetta rather than premeditated acts of political violence against Chinese rule. Even if some may have been perpetrated by self-styled militants seeking the liberation of the Uyghur homeland, only two appear conclusively to target civilians.

Following these descriptions of past violence, the document, like the previous communique from November 2001, asserts that the vaguely defined 'Eastern Turkistan Terrorist Forces,' who had allegedly carried out all of this violence, are supported by Al-Qaeda and the Taliban in Afghanistan. However, unlike in the previous document from months earlier, the PRC did not mention a litany of diaspora nationalist groups involved in this nebulous organization, but focused on its branch in 'South Asia' and particularly on ETIM, which was alleged to operate in Afghanistan.[27] In particular, the document sought to outline further details of this group's allegedly close relations with Al-Qaeda and Osama bin Laden. Given that the US had apparently detained several Uyghurs who had fled Afghanistan for Pakistan in late 2001, there was at least some reason for the US to view the PRC's claims about ETIM and its Al-Qaeda links as plausible, but there also remained much suspicion in the US that China was opportunistically exploiting GWOT to further repress Uyghurs.[28]

Despite the many holes in the document's argument, this report would be critical to the fate of the Uyghurs in subsequent years. It would become the foundational document in a flawed narrative about the role of Uyghurs in the international 'terrorist threat' that would spread throughout the world and that continues to be reproduced by 'terrorism' experts to this day. However, the document's influence in this regard would not be fully realized until its arguments were adopted by the US and the UN in designating ETIM as an international 'terrorist organization' later in 2002.

The international recognition of ETIM as a 'terrorist threat'

On the day that the State Council Information Office of the PRC released this detailed document requesting assistance from the international community in combating its alleged 'terrorist threat' from Uyghurs, PRC representatives attended a donor conference in Tokyo where it pledged $1 million in assistance to Afghanistan's reconstruction and an additional $3.6 million worth of humanitarian goods, essentially in support of the US-led rebuilding of Afghanistan.[29] While few details are known about the contents of US-China bilateral talks at this time, it appeared that Beijing was trying to leverage its support for GWOT to get the US to recognize the alleged 'terrorist threat' from Uyghurs and its purported connections to Al-Qaeda. In the public statements made by US officials throughout late 2001 and most of 2002, it was obvious that they were feeling pressure from China on this issue, but initially the US government was also resistant to this pressure.

George W. Bush and China's Jiang Zemin had met on the sidelines of the Asia-Pacific Economic Cooperation forum (APEC) in October 2001 where they 'reached an agreement on the formation of a medium and long-term bilateral mechanism for exchanges and cooperation in the fight against terrorism.'[30] However, while at APEC, Bush also stated that the PRC should not attempt to use GWOT as an 'excuse to persecute minorities,' a comment that appeared particularly targeted at China's treatment of its Uyghur population.[31] Subsequently, the US State Department's Coordinator for Counter-Terrorism, Ambassador Francis Taylor, visited Beijing in early December 2001 to participate in talks on counterterrorism collaboration with China.[32] While these talks were generally fruitful, one of the areas of disagreement was regarding the branding of Uyghur dissent as a 'terrorist threat.'

Taylor acknowledged in his Beijing press conference that US troops had found some 'Chinese citizens from western China' in Afghanistan, but he was also adamant that 'the US has not designated or considers the East Turkestan organization as a terrorist organization,' further suggesting that 'the legitimate economic and social issues that confront people in Northwestern China are not necessarily counter-terrorist issues and should be resolved politically rather than using counter-terrorism methods.'[33] The Assistant Secretary of State for Democracy, Rights, and Labor, Lorne Craner, reiterated this point in March 2002 while introducing the US State Department's Human Rights Report on China, noting that the PRC had 'chosen to label all of those who advocate greater freedom in [Xinjiang], near as I can tell, as terrorists; and we don't think that's correct.'[34]

However, in August 2002, something appeared to have changed in the US government's public proclamations about the alleged 'terrorist threat' involving Uyghurs. On 19 August 2002, Deputy Secretary of State, Richard Armitage, drafted a document recognizing ETIM as an international 'terrorist organization' and a threat to the US. As the document read in the Federal Register, 'I hereby determine that the Eastern Turkistan Islamic Movement (ETIM) has committed, or poses a significant risk of committing, acts of terrorism that threaten the security of US nationals or the national security, foreign policy, or economy of the United States.'[35] Presenting this policy change in a press conference on 26 August while in Beijing, Armitage noted that ETIM had 'committed acts of violence against unarmed civilians without any regard for who was hurt.'[36]

Two days later, this news was followed by shocking statements from a spokesperson for the US Embassy in Beijing claiming that ETIM had been planning attacks on US interests in collaboration with Osama bin Laden and Al-Qaeda, including a planned attack on the US Embassy in Kyrgyzstan.[37] The spokesperson added that ETIM had carried out more than 200 terrorist attacks in China, including bombings, assassinations, and arson, resulting in at least 162 deaths and 440 injuries.[38] As the journalist from the *Washington Post* who reported on these statements noted, these were figures obviously taken directly from the January report issued by the PRC's State Council Information Office.[39] However, there was an important difference – the PRC document had attributed these numbers to the work of numerous alleged Uyghur groups all characterized as part of a nebulous 'Eastern Turkistan Terrorist Forces,' while the US Embassy blamed all of them entirely on the mostly unknown ETIM.[40] This mistake would subsequently enter into the general narrative about ETIM that was reproduced going forward as ETIM became consistently portrayed, both by the PRC and by international 'terrorism' experts, as the singular organization responsible for all alleged Uyghur-perpetrated violence in China during the 1990s.

It was unclear what had transpired between March and August 2002 to precipitate this sudden US support for the PRC's narrative about a 'terrorist threat' involving Uyghurs. The explanation given by US officials remained vague, citing undisclosed classified information about the nature of ETIM. For example, in early December 2002, then Assistant Secretary of State for East Asian and Pacific Affairs, James Kelly, would defensively state that the decision to designate ETIM as a 'terrorist organization' had been made during the summer of 2002 'not as a concession to the PRC, but based on independent evidence that ETIM is linked to al-Qaeda and has engaged in deliberate acts of violence against unarmed civilians.'[41] Seven years later, when asked about the evidence for designating ETIM as a 'terrorist organization' at a Congressional hearing, Randall Schriver, the US Deputy Secretary of State for East Asian and Pacific Affairs in 2002, would likewise claim that there was credible evidence of ETIM's terrorist activities beyond that provided by Chinese authorities, but he also added that he could not disclose this credible evidence since it was 'classified.'[42] This 'credible evidence,' if it exists, presumably remains classified to this day.

There were a number of events that had transpired over the course of 2002 which could have yielded this alleged 'credible evidence' that served to change US policy. The US had already interned 22 Uyghurs in Guantanamo Bay Detention Center earlier in 2002, and intelligence gathered from these detainees could have changed US attitudes towards ETIM's designation as a 'terrorist organization.' Furthermore, the accusations that ETIM plotted to attack the US Embassy in Kyrgyzstan could have contributed to the decision. However, it is unlikely that either of these factors inspired the about-face in US policy. The transcripts of the tribunals with Uyghurs in Guantanamo, which were later released, offer no evidence of the group's ties to either Al-Qaeda or the Taliban, eventually leading the US to release all of its Uyghur detainees.[43] There were also numerous holes in the story about the planned ETIM attack on the US Embassy in Bishkek. The US Embassy in Bishkek never made a statement on the planned attack, which was instead announced by the US Embassy in Beijing, and Kyrgyzstan authorities merely cited the Uyghurs' possession of maps for all foreign embassies in the country as evidence for the alleged planned attack on the US.[44] Given how quickly news about this alleged attack disappeared from the media at a time when an Al-Qaeda plot against the US would be perceived as an act of war, it is likely that there was very thin evidence behind it.

It is much more likely that the US decision to recognize ETIM as a 'terrorist threat' was driven by a need to court China's further support in GWOT. In particular, by August 2002, the US government was already contemplating how to gain international support for an invasion of Iraq. Having delivered his infamous 'Axis of Exil' speech in January 2002 implicating Iraq in GWOT, and setting the stage for future military action, President Bush was, according to Colin Powell, already getting military advice in early summer 2002 on how such an invasion might take place.[45] Furthermore, it would be only a few weeks after the recognition of ETIM that President Bush would make his impassioned case before the UN General Assembly to hold Iraq accountable, noting that the US would work closely with the UN Security Council, of which the PRC is a critical member, to do so. Thus, it is not surprising that articles published by both *The New York Times* and the *Washington Post* at the time were already speculating that the US designation of ETIM as a 'terrorist organization' could go a long way towards getting China on board to a Security Council resolution allowing the invasion of Iraq.[46] While there is no concrete evidence that the recognition of ETIM as a 'terrorist organization' by the US was done as a quid pro quo act to gain Chinese support or complicity for the invasion of Iraq, it is noteworthy that China never proposed a Security Council resolution to prevent the US invasion.

It is important to note that the US did not only bilaterally recognize ETIM as a 'terrorist organization,' but also actively participated multilaterally in an effort to have the UN do so. On 11 September 2002, on the first anniversary of the attacks on the US, the US jointly with Kyrgyzstan, Afghanistan, and China asked the UN to impose sanctions on ETIM as a 'terrorist organization' under UN Security Council Resolutions 1267 and 1390.[47] On the occasion of the UN's inclusion of ETIM on its 'Consolidated List,' the US Department of Treasury also issued a press release that welcomed the designation, repeating once again the assertion that ETIM was responsible for over 200 terrorist attacks, 162 deaths, and over 440 injuries, figures taken directly from Chinese documents meant to characterize the violence allegedly perpetrated by multiple Uyghur organizations.[48]

Thus, within the first year of GWOT, the PRC had successfully implicated at least one small group of Uyghurs in the war with the support of the US and the UN. Furthermore, these actions taken almost two decades prior under suspect circumstances remain in force, as ETIM is still listed on the US Terrorism Exclusion List as well as on the UNSC 'Consolidated List' of 'terrorists' to this day. This has had numerous ramifications for the Uyghur people as a whole since 2002, and continues to plague them as the PRC claims its mass internment of Uyghurs is an appropriate response to a serious 'terrorist threat.' The Uyghur ethnic group as a whole has suffered from this designation because, while the US and UN had not adopted the PRC's larger narrative that all Uyghur advocacy groups worldwide were part of a singular 'terrorist network,' the branding of ETIM as a 'terrorist organization' allowed the Chinese state to arbitrarily label virtually any Uyghur group or individual as a member or associate of ETIM, ultimately placing all Uyghurs under suspicion of potentially being its members or sympathizers.

When the PRC announced its first official 'terrorist' list in December 2003, for example, it included two Uyghur advocacy groups in Germany and their leadership, suggesting that these groups were aligned with ETIM.[49] As a result, Dolkun Isa, who is now the leader of the World Uyghur Congress (WUC) but at the time was one of the German Uyghur activists on the list, was issued an Interpol 'Red Notice' that greatly hindered his international travel, including to the US, until it was finally removed in 2018.[50] Likewise, the

22 Uyghurs in Guantanamo Bay, while all eventually released, were held for years as suspected 'enemy combatants' as the US military sought to connect them to the phantom ETIM 'terrorist organization.' However, the most serious harm done to the larger Uyghur population by the international designation of ETIM as a 'terrorist organization' would be the plausible narrative it provided the PRC that a persistent and dangerous 'terrorist threat' existed within the Uyghur community of China. By suggesting that ETIM was active within the Uyghur homeland's population, the Chinese state would justify almost two decades of violently repressing Uyghur dissent, and eventually Uyghur culture, in the name of 'counterterrorism.' If ETIM's listing on US and UN 'terrorism' lists helped to establish this narrative in 2002, the work of 'terrorism' analysts would serve to perpetuate it going forward through a deeply flawed body of literature that portrayed ETIM as a cohesive organization with a long history that, while based abroad, also had members in the Uyghur homeland.

JUSTIFYING AND MAINTAINING ETIM'S BRANDING AS A 'TERRORIST THREAT'

With the US and UN 'listing' of ETIM as a 'terrorist organization,' it was inevitable that this organization would become an object of analysis among 'terrorism' experts after 2002. Within a year of the 9/11 attacks, the number of such experts grew exponentially in the US and Europe. Their role in GWOT would be to provide background and up-to-date information about the many 'terrorist organizations' that had been identified since the war's beginning. These experts would come from a variety of different backgrounds, including academia, the intelligence community, the policy community, and the military. They would also inhabit a variety of institutions, including think-tanks, consulting firms, and universities.

These 'terrorism' experts would be critical to maintaining the narrative about ETIM as a 'terrorist organization' after its controversial placement on US and UN 'lists.' While not intentionally, they have constructed a cohesive history and characterization of ETIM that is riddled with inaccurate and speculative information about the alleged 'terrorist threat' of ETIM and, particularly, about this threat's presence inside China. There are numerous reasons for these inaccuracies, including lack of knowledge of Uyghur history, culture, and especially language, the imperative to present information about organizations to which their only access is propaganda, and their own position in a vast 'counterterrorism industrial complex,' which maintains a vested interest in the continued existence of 'terrorist organizations' and the threats they allegedly pose.[51] The work of these 'terrorism' experts would be critical to maintaining a narrative of the alleged 'terrorist threat' posed by ETIM to China and the world during the first decade of the war, a time during which this threat was virtually non-existent.

Early literature on ETIM: speculation and criticism

In the immediate aftermath of the September 2002 listing of ETIM as a 'terrorist organization' by the US and the UN, numerous analysts and academics busied themselves with evaluating this threat's validity and explaining its nature to policy-makers and the larger public. This proved to be challenging due to the paucity of reliable information about this group. There were no public references to ETIM available in either English or Chinese prior to 2001, and no international experts on the Uyghurs, to my knowledge, had even heard of the group prior to the issuance of the November 2001 PRC document discussed above.[52] Furthermore, none of these analysts knew the Uyghur language, and only a small minority of them knew Chinese and had a knowledge of Uyghur culture and history. Thus, the only information about ETIM from which such analysts could draw initially were the statements provided by the PRC in the run-up to ETIM's designation as a 'terrorist organization' on US and UN lists, a few sensationalist reports from the late 1990s about Uyghur militancy (also drawing largely on PRC official statements), and speculation regarding how Uyghurs may have come to associate themselves with Al-Qaeda in Afghanistan. Despite the unreliability of the sources on which most early literature about ETIM was based, this body of work would lay a foundation for subsequent characterizations of this group.

Initial sketches of this group following its 2002 designation as a 'terrorist organization' can be found on the archived webpages of established think-tanks in the US, such as the Council on Foreign Affairs and the Center for Defense Information.[53] The characterization of the group in these short descriptions cautiously approaches questions of ETIM's capacity and the appropriateness of its designation as a 'terrorist group,' but they do all assume that the organization has long been active inside China as one of the largest, 'most extreme,' and 'most militant' Uyghur organizations seeking independence.[54] An October 2002 Congressional Research Service report on the 'terrorism threat' to China similarly demonstrated the lack of reliable information and openly admitted about ETIM and other alleged Uyghur militant groups that 'solid information about these groups remains elusive and often confusing,' but it also suggested that the groups are indeed active and involved in violence inside China.[55]

More influential in the production of knowledge about ETIM than this report or the aforementioned think-tank websites would be the first high-profile book on Al-Qaeda after the 9/11 attacks on the US, which was written by the controversial Singapore-based 'terrorism expert' Rohan Gunaratna in 2002.[56] In this 'best-selling' book, Gunaratna dedicates about three pages to ETIM and the evolution of the alleged 'terrorist threat' from Uyghurs. While this brief section of the book does not cite the Chinese government documents discussed previously, it does adopt their discourse. Without citing any specific sources, Gunaratna notes confidently that 'today, there are several Islamist groups in Xinjiang fighting for independence, and others have developed an extensive presence in Pakistan, Kazakhstan, Kyrghyzstan [sic] and Germany, where funds are raised.'[57] He suggests that this reflects a substantive transformation of Uyghur political objectives from an ethno-nationalist movement to one that is explicitly 'Pan-Islamic' in orientation. He further notes, again without citing specific sources, that 'through a coordinated network, the influx of Chinese Muslims to Pakistan and Afghanistan for indoctrination and training has been frequent in the 1990s.'[58]

In his historical account of how this threat developed, Gunaratna suggests that the Uyghur independence movement, which I assume he equates with a 'terrorist movement,' began during the Cultural Revolution and had adopted vaious names, from the Uyghurstan People's Party to the East Turkistan Party, before settling on the Eastern Turkistan Islamic Party, a name that would presumably become the Eastern Turkistan Islamic Movement (ETIM) in Afghanistan. He also draws on an unsubstantiated story about the Chinese government training Uyghurs to join the *mujahidin* in the fight against the Soviets during the 1980s to explain how this group became based in Afghanistan and eventually linked with Al-Qaeda. While Gunaratna's account of ETIM in the book is brief and only cites two obscure and undetailed sources, it is important for its inclusion in a best-selling book on Al-Qaeda.[59] As a result, many of his assertions would subsequently show up in later works trying to make sense of ETIM, keeping alive the narrative that this organization represented a significant international security risk with a long history and deep ties to transnational jihadist networks.

A 2003 academic article published in a well-established Criminology journal provides a clear example of how Gunaratna's book helped subsequently frame the characterization of ETIM among 'terrorism' experts, especially in law enforcement. The article prominently cites Gunaratna and takes at face-value the Chinese government's documents discussed earlier, bolstering their assertions with interviews conducted in China with 'faculty members in the Anti-Terrorism Division in a criminal justice university.'[60] Much of the article seeks to explain why ETIM should be considered a 'terrorism organization' in the context of the literature on 'terrorism psychology,' but this is again based entirely on the suspect evidence provided by the PRC about this group. Furthermore, sloppy research by the author leads to many confusing points that have from time to time re-emerged in literature citing his work, including an assertion that the other groups discussed by PRC documents as part of the nebulous 'Eastern Turkistan terrorist forces' are actually sub-groups under ETIM.

It is important to note that a counter-discourse about ETIM was also established at this time among regional experts. In 2004, for example, The East-West Center, a think-tank in Washington, DC, published an important report by James Millward, which critically analyzed the violence in the Uyghur homeland during the 1990s and questioned the validity of a 'terrorist threat' to the region.[61] Similarly, other scholars with knowledge of Uyghurs and their minimal links to the outside Islamic world suggested that China's characterization of a 'terrorist threat' from Uyghurs was far over exaggerated.[62] In more popular policy-oriented media, scholars likewise questioned the Bush administration's classification of ETIM as a 'terrorist organization,' implying that it was a calculated move to win China's support for the invasion of Iraq.[63]

While this counter-narrative about ETIM moderated US foreign policy positions towards the Uyghurs at this time, many in law enforcement and the military continued to assume that Uyghurs posed a 'terrorist threat.' My mother, who worked as a probation officer in New York State at the time, for example, told me that training given to her office in the early 2000s by the FBI characterized Uyghurs as a potential 'terrorist threat' to the US and ETIM as a clear part of the Al-Qaeda network. When she told the FBI agent instructor that her son studied Uyghurs, he advised her to warn me to take caution because Uyghurs were among 'the bad guys.'

This contested nature of the narrative about ETIM was further complicated by the conflicting information emerging from the battlefields of GWOT at the time. While 22 Uyghurs remained in Guantanamo Bay as accused enemy combatants, by 2004, information was emerging that many in the US military had serious reservations about this designation for at least 12 of them.[64] Additionally, in December 2003, it was reported that the Pakistani military had killed Häsän Mäkhsum, the alleged leader of ETIM, in the northwest of the country in October of that year.[65] With Mäkhsum's death, it became unclear what remained of this organization, and there was no evidence that it had any active military operations either in

China or in Afghanistan since being designated a 'terrorist organization' by the US and the UN.

In this context, the initial narrative about the alleged 'terrorist threat' posed by Uyghurs was gradually disappearing from both policy and academic discourse in the US and Europe by 2005. While think-tanks that provided their own sketches of different 'terrorist groups' tended to still have entries on ETIM, they mostly played down the seriousness of this group's threat to both China and the world while still characterizing it as a 'terrorist organization.'[66] This trend was further visible in 2006 as the US released five Uyghurs who had been interned in Guantanamo Bay Detention Center to Albania.[67] The US had decided that these Uyghurs were not 'enemy combatants' and, thus, should be released, but not to China where they would likely suffer torture, imprisonment, and/or execution. The fate of these former detainees would revive discussions in popular media about the political nature of ETIM's designation as a 'terrorist organization,' further bringing into question the relevance of this group to GWOT.

The Turkistan Islamic Party and the re-birth of the ETIM narrative

Just as it seemed as if the labeling of Uyghurs as a 'terrorist threat' was losing its relevance in the western world, a seemingly new Uyghur militant group made itself known internationally through the internet in 2004. While Häsän Mäkhsum's ETIM neither had a website nor had posted videos or statements on the internet, this new group seemed to suddenly have the resources to do so. While the organization branded itself as the Turkistan Islamic Party (TIP) rather than as ETIM, its first video, released arouond May of 2004, was an Arabic-language biography of Häsän Mäkhsum, the alleged founder of ETIM.[68] The video also advertised TIP's presumably new website – www.tipislamawazi.com. According to the website and the biographical film about Mäkhsum, TIP was merely a new name adopted by ETIM, and this name change had been made in 2000 prior to Mäkhsum's death.[69]

While TIP's website and its lone video honoring the legacy of

Häsän Mäkhsum did not initially capture much international attention, in 2006, another Uyghur Arabic-language video emerged on the internet, which appeared to be produced by adherents of Abu Musab Al-Suri, the Syrian-born Spanish citizen and well-known jihadist, calling for jihad in Eastern Turkistan. This production did not use the TIP name, but merely had a logo with the stylized name 'Turkistan' in Latin and Arabic letters in the top right corner of the video.[70] In addition to promoting jihad, the video also visually fulfilled most observers' expectations of the communications of an Islamic 'terrorist' group. Prominently displaying a black flag with the *Shahadah* (Muslim proclamation of faith), the Uyghur speakers pictured in the video, which was dubbed over in Arabic, brandished AK-47 machine guns, wore turbans and camouflage, and covered their faces.

These developments between 2004 and 2006 renewed at least a cautious interest among international 'terrorism' experts in the analysis of the alleged 'terrorist threat' posed by Uyghurs, but the community of people interested in this alleged threat in 2006 remained quite divided over its extent. A 2006 special issue on terrorism in *The China and Eurasia Forum Quarterly* demonstrates this divide.[71] Of the four articles in the issue, two written by scholars familiar with Uyghurs are explicitly dismissive of the threat posed by ETIM, stressing the PRC's over-exaggeration of its capabilities, and two, written by a Chinese scholar and by Rohan Gunaratna with a colleague named Kenneth Pereire respectively, make the case that ETIM is closely tied to Al-Qaeda and poses one of the gravest security threats to China.[72] The article by Gunaratna and Pereire, which discusses the recent aforementioned Abu Musab Al-Suri-related video extensively, further pushes the alarmist narrative about ETIM that Gunaratna employs in his 2002 book on Al-Qaeda, suggesting that the group will likely soon employ suicide bombing techniques inside China and is likely to spearhead an 'Islamicization' of the Uyghur conflict with China.[73]

While regional experts continued to question the importance, or even existence of ETIM, alarmist opinions remained dominant in the literature about the group. Pereire, who co-authored the aforementioned article with Gunaratna, also wrote a 2006 report on

ETIM for a Singaporean think-tank, suggesting that the organization represented a serious 'terrorist threat' that was 'underestimated.'[74] Likewise, a 2007 academic article by Liza Steele and Raymond Kuo concluded that 'the Uighurs' [sic] social fragmentation and discontent have spurred an Islamist salient threat of extremism that cannot be ignored.'[75]

Perhaps the clearest academic example of this alarmist interpretation of ETIM at the time is a book by Martin Wayne, which examined China's 'counterterrorism' efforts vis-à-vis Uyghurs through the prism of the counter-insurgency theories that shaped US military strategies in Afghanistan and Iraq.[76] Wayne, who is a comparative security studies expert rather than a regional studies scholar, makes the case that Uyghur militants have unleashed an insurgency inside their homeland that justifies the PRC's 'counterterrorism' efforts. Citing Gunaratna extensively, Wayne asserts that Uyghur militants have a long history of experience in Afghanistan, referring to past claims of large numbers of Uyghurs trained by the PRC to fight the Soviets, and are seeking to establish a society-wide insurgency inside the Uyghur homeland by working with the global jihad movement in Afghanistan and Pakistan.[77] In doing so, he also praises the PRC's efforts to suppress this threat, suggesting that they 'represent one of the few successes in the global struggle against Islamist terrorism.'[78] Wayne attributes this success to 'bottom-up' 'counter-extremist' strategies that seek to incentivize Uyghur integration into the PRC.

The 2008 Beijing Olympics and TIP's 'coming-out' party

If the alleged re-emergence of ETIM in the form of TIP invited increased attention from academics and analysts in 2006–2007, it would not be until the run-up to the 2008 Beijing Olympics that this interest would become widespread. This new attention to ETIM/TIP would be fueled by both the Chinese government and TIP itself. On 1 March 2008, TIP released a video message from its alleged *Emir*, Abdul Häq, who, holding a rifle in front of a map of the Uyghur homeland, warned the international community not to take part in the Olympics because his group was prepared to attack the games.[79]

While this video's poor production quality did not make TIP look very sophisticated, the threat it posed quickly escalated in the eyes of many when, within a week of the video's release, the Chinese government claimed that it had foiled an attack on a plane where a Uyghur woman was alleged to have brought gasoline canisters on board.[80] Subsequently, the Chinese authorities would also claim to have broken up numerous alleged 'terrorist' plots by other Uyghurs inside China during the same time.[81] The combination of these claims with TIP's video had suddenly made the alleged 'terrorist threat' from Uyghurs inside China a matter of world news in the spring of 2008.

Predictably, these events also caught the attention of 'terrorism' analysts in the west. The 'terrorism' monitoring websites that had been established in the years since 2001 published several analytical pieces on the alleged 'terrorist threat' posed by Uyghurs to the Olympics. The Jamestown Foundation's Terrorism Monitor featured an article by Elizabeth Van Wie Davis outlining the validity of the threat posed by ETIM in early April 2008. The author writes that US intelligence had long known of this group's links to Al-Qaeda and that camps in Afghanistan and Pakistan had trained Uyghur militants since the 1980s.[82] She also assumes that this group is behind a number of alleged violent incidents inside China in the run-up to the Olympics, posing a real threat to the games.[83] In May, *StratFor* published a three part series on the Uyghurs and their threat to the Olympics.[84] *StratFor's* analysis of the alleged 'terrorist threat' from Uyghurs was much more skeptical than that of Davis, suggesting that it was being manipulated by Beijing and that events inside China likely had little to do with ETIM.[85] Nonetheless, it still recognized ETIM as a potentially escalating 'terrorist threat.'

This interest in ETIM/TIP was further fueled by the group's subsequent video releases around the Olympic Games. One of these videos claimed responsibility for bus bombings in Shanghai and Kunming in the run up to the Olympics, which the Chinese government later denied were carried out by Uyghurs, and the other, beginning with dramatic animation of a burning Beijing Olympics flag and a simulation of an explosion in the Olympic stadium, promised further attacks the week before the opening ceremonies.[86] Indeed, in the week surrounding the opening ceremonies, there were two violent incidents in the Uyghur homeland involving alleged Uyghur attacks on security organs, military, and police.[87] While these acts were certainly not 'terrorism' per this book's working definition and there was no evidence to connect ETIM/TIP to them, the violence raised more speculation about the alleged 'terrorist threat' of ETIM/ TIP inside China.

The events surrounding the emergence of TIP and its threats against the Olympics had very much re-fueled policy debates in the US and Europe about the nature of the alleged 'terrorist threat' from Uyghurs. While public statements from western democracies continued to raise concerns about the PRC's human rights abuses against Uyghurs and to criticize the misuse of 'counterterrorism' approaches for suppressing domestic dissent, these states also acknowledged that China might have some legitimate concerns about a 'terrorist threat' from Uyghurs. Furthermore, given that there were simultaneously debates within the US government about the fate of the Uyghurs in Guantanamo, the Uyghurs were increasingly becoming a politicized issue in domestic US politics. 'Counterterrorism' expert, Thomas Joscelyn, of the Foundation for the Defense of Democracy (FDD), for example, argued in a series of opinion pieces that the Guantanamo Uyghurs' admitted interactions with Abdul Häq, who had allegedly trained most of them at a camp in Afghanistan and who was documented now threatening the Olympics, were proof of these detainees' status as 'enemy combatants.'[88] It was also at this time that the PRC's Ministry of Public Security issued additions to its 'terrorist list' in October 2008, adding eight people, all of whom were said to be core members of ETIM, with Abdul Häq at the top of the list.[89]

The post-Olympics narrative of ETIM

In the years after the Olympics, the tracking of ETIM/TIP as an alleged 'terrorist threat' by analysts and security studies academics continued to increase. Among private intelligence companies and non-profits specializing in terrorist threats, IntelCenter created a threat wall chart of ETIM/TIP leadership structure based on information from videos and TIP's website, and the Nine Eleven Finding Answers Foundation posted translations of items from TIP's website as well as of transcripts of several TIP videos.[90] Furthermore, the Jamestown Foundation, Search for International Terrorist Entities, the FDD, and other organizations specializing in analysis of 'terrorist threats' expanded their coverage of ETIM/TIP in their regular analytical bulletins. In this way, the narrative of the alleged 'terrorist threat' from Uyghurs was sustained for the foreseeable future, and international attention to it was maintained.

These events had also caught the attention of the larger 'counterterrorism industrial complex' at this time, and the US took its first substantive acts against alleged Uyghur 'terrorists' since its 2002 'listing' of ETIM and subsequent detention of Uyghurs in Guantanamo Bay. In April 2009, the US Treasury placed Abdul Häq, the presumed leader of ETIM/TIP, and the first person on China's updated 'terrorist' list released six months earlier, on a sanctions list. In the press conference that announced this action, the US Treasury spokesperson noted that 'Abdul Häq commands a terror group that sought to sow violence and fracture international unity at the 2008 Olympic Games in China; today, we stand together with the world in condemning this brutal terrorist and isolating him from the international financial system.'[91] In February of 2010, the US would go further in its pursuit of Abdul Häq, targeting him in a drone strike that was alleged to have killed him.[92]

The western analytical literature about ETIM/TIP would expand exponentially from 2008–2012. The events surrounding the Olympics provided an impetus for this increased interest in the alleged 'terrorism threat' posed by Uyghurs inside China, but TIP would also fuel this interest through the production of many new and better produced videos as well as through the regular publication of an Arabic-language magazine from 2008.[93] As IntelCenter, which specializes in the analysis of videos produced by alleged 'terrorist organizations,' points out, after having produced its first five videos between 2004 and 2008, TIP would go on to produce 55 videos between 2009 and

2012, putting it in IntelCenter's 'top-tier' of 'Jihadi video producers.'[94]

This sudden proliferation of media from TIP did much to change the global narrative about the alleged 'terrorist threat' associated with Uyghurs. If the many new TIP videos offered more material for 'terrorism analysts' to engage, it is important to note that such videos are first and foremost produced as propaganda and must be analyzed from that perspective.[95] In TIP's case, it had numerous messages it wanted to convey to different populations. To the Chinese government, it wanted to promote an image of strength and the capacity to challenge the PRC through violent tactics. To its presumed sponsors in the Arab world, for whom it created Arab language media, it wanted to demonstrate its religiosity, its knowledge of Salafism, and its association with other jihadist groups. Finally, to Uyghurs inside China, the group sought to portray a long and cohesive history that linked it to Uyghurs' historical struggle against Chinese rule, while also encouraging Uyghurs in the homeland to join them in jihad by undertaking local attacks. While these sources do provide a window into TIP's ideology, goals, and capabilities when examined critically, most analysts have approached them at face-value as communiques of an established 'terrorist organization.' Furthermore, since these analysts lack Uyghur language skills, they rely on those few videos produced in Arabic or only the visual cues from the many produced in Uyghur.

Although the 2009 Urumqi riots were obviously not instigated by TIP or any other Uyghur militant movements, they attracted the interest of 'terrorism' analysts when the Algeria-based Al-Qaeda in the Islamic Maghreb called for revenge on China for its killing of Uyghur Muslims, the first time a mainstream Arab jihadist group had threatened China publicly or had taken up the Uyghur cause more generally.[96] In addition, the Singaporean 'terrorism' expert Gunaratna would fuel claims of a 'terrorist' connection to the riots in an interview for *Xinhua* news agency where he noted that the WUC, which the government claimed was responsible for the violence, included many sympathizers of ETIM.[97] The Chinese government would also further fuel this alleged connection between 'terrorism' and the riots by reporting that it was arresting increased numbers of alleged Uyghur 'terrorists' in the post-riot crackdown in the region. Finally, these factors were exacerbated by claims in 2010 of two alleged foiled 'terrorist plots' on Chinese interests purportedly planned by Uyghurs in Norway and Dubai respectively.[98] While the unclear circumstances surrounding these alleged planned attacks will be discussed in the next chapter, it is worth noting here that, for many analysts, this appeared to provide evidence that TIP's operations, while remaining focused on China, had become internationalized and a component of the Al-Qaeda threat.

In this context, it is not surprising that 2010 saw the publication of two of the most sensationalist books on the alleged 'terrorist threat' from Uyghurs. The first, simply entitled *The ETIM*, was written by two journalists with no Uyghur language skills who meticulously, but mostly uncritically, combined Chinese state, TIP, and 'terrorism' analysts' sources to describe this group, its activities, history, and ideology.[99] In many ways, this book serves as a monument to the cohesive, yet flawed, narrative about this group that 'terrorism' analysts built during the first decade of GWOT. The second of these books was a project of Rohan Gunaratna in collaboration with both another Singaporean and a Chinese colleague from Macau, which focuses on issues of ethnic conflict in China.[100] Gunaratna's manuscript, while suggesting that the PRC should be more humane in its 'counterterrorism' efforts, also provides a very alarmist characterization of ETIM/TIP as a serious 'extremist' and 'terrorist' threat inside China.[101]

In general, the literature produced by 'terrorism' analysts and academics in security studies about ETIM/TIP between 2009 and 2012 established a much more cohesive narrative about this group than previously, but the accuracy of this narrative must be questioned given the thin evidence upon which it was based. While regional experts continued to question the validity of TIP's threat to China, 'terrorism' analysts, who located the group within international militant Muslim networks, tended to 'hype' the threat it posed to the PRC.[102] The literature on ETIM/TIP at this time had more material to draw from for contemporary analysis given the efforts of TIP's media wing, but it relied primarily on those TIP sources that were in the Arabic or Turkish languages, as well as those few that had been translated into English. It also frequently drew background information from more speculative and flawed analysis about ETIM's evolution and historical continuity published earlier, all ultimately based on PRC state claims.[103]

Thus, a decade after ETIM's designation by the US and UN, questions of this group's origins, actual nature, and assumed threat remained unclear and contested. Yet, because analysts confidently characterized the group in their work, the 'counterterrorism industrial complex' continued to assume that ETIM/TIP posed a dangerous 'terrorist threat' that justified its place on the US and UN 'terrorism lists.' This state of affairs was partly due to the liberal assumptions and lack of detailed research that go into 'terrorism' experts' comparative analysis, but it was also an inevitable product of studying a phenomenon that has no consistent definition. For most of the western 'terrorism analysts' cited here, a 'terrorist organization' is any non-state group that employs violence in the name of Salafi-inspired political Islam and is designated by a western power as 'terrorists,' but for the PRC, 'terrorism' has a broader meaning that encompasses any articulation of the unitary threat it calls the 'three evils': any calls for self-determination ('separatism'), any expression of Islam not approved by the state ('extremism'), and any act of violence perpetrated by Uyghurs ('terrorism'). Both of these definitions are extremely problematic on their own and serve the interests of those who propagate them, but their co-existence in the narratives reproduced about ETIM/TIP is even more problematic and only further obscures the accuracy of characterizing this group as a 'terrorist organization.'

The designation of ETIM/TIP as a 'terrorism organization' is all the more concerning if one looks more closely at the reality of the Uyghur militants who, at least in the eyes of 'terrorism analysts,' were associated with ETIM during the first decade of GWOT. While ETIM's international designation as a 'terrorist organization' and the plethora of literature written about the group by 'terrorism analysts' would suggest that this was a cohesive group that has a long history of carrying out violent attacks inside China and that, at least since 1998, was an affiliate of Al-Qaeda, my own analysis of those Uyghurs who are assumed to have been members of ETIM/ TIP at this time suggests that none of these assumptions are fully accurate.

3 Prominent members of TIP since 2008. Pictured from the left top corner clockwise: *Emir Abdul Ḥāq; Deputy Emir Abdushakur* (d. 2012); Commander Säyfullah (d. 2012); religious figure Abdulāziz (d. 2012). The last three were killed by drone strikes in Pakistan during 2012, presumably ordered by the US.

3

MYTHS AND REALITIES OF THE ALLEGED 'TERRORIST THREAT' ASSOCIATED WITH UYGHURS

On a snowy February day in 2019, I found myself in a courtroom in Oslo, Norway arguing about acronyms and the alleged Uyghur-led 'terrorist organizations' to which they supposedly referred. I was an expert witness for a Uyghur refugee who had gone to Syria to fight for a paramilitary group called the Turkistan Islamic Party (TIP) believing he was being trained for a war of liberation, in his homeland. He was now facing charges of 'terrorism' in Norway as a result. Given the ways that Norwegian laws about 'terrorism' are being implemented, it was unimportant what this man had done in Syria, against whom he had fought, or whether he had ever killed an innocent civilian. All that really mattered was whether he had been associated with an organization that was on a recognized 'terrorism list.' The EU 'terrorist list' includes no Uyghur groups. The UN's 'Consolidated List' includes ETIM along with several aliases for the group, including The Eastern Turkistan Islamic Party, The Eastern Turkistan Islamic Party of Allah, Islamic Party of Turkestan, and Djamaat Turkistan.[1] While the US List of Foreign Terrorist Organizations does not include any Uyghur groups, the US Terrorist Exclusion List includes ETIM along with the alias Eastern Turkistan Islamic Party (ETIP).[2] However, none of these lists explicitly mention TIP. Thus, in many ways, the defendant's fate depended upon whether TIP could be identified as the same organization as those on the various lists mentioned above.

The prosecution and its expert witness argued that ETIM and TIP were the same organization, which had become a part of the standard narrative about the alleged 'terrorist threat' associated with Uyghurs that had developed since 2002, especially among 'terrorism' analysts without specialized regional knowledge. In fact, the prosecution's expert witness, who knew little about Uyghurs and had no Uyghur language abilities, had written a report that meticulously served as a review of the standard 'terrorism' analyst narrative about the history of ETIM, its activities, and its evolution. As an expert witness for the defense, I maintained that ETIM and TIP were actually not the same organization, even if somebody associated with the former had allegedly founded the latter. This argument, while central to the court case, was only part of a larger critique I levied against the standard narrative about both ETIM and TIP. I disputed much of this standard narrative's history of these organizations' evolution, their participation in specific attacks, and the nature of their relationships with Al-Qaeda and the Taliban.

An underlying theme in this courtroom debate was the question of what type of knowledge best informs one to make judgements about a group's or an individual's classification as 'terrorists.' The prosecution's expert witness argued that such judgements were best made from the perspective of somebody focused on comparative security studies with intimate knowledge about how international jihadist organizations operate. I countered that such decisions were much better informed by local knowledge about people's grievances, how they feel about different ideologies, and what it means for them to 'belong' to an organization. Unfortunately, neither of us could argue on the merits of the legal definition of what characterizes a 'terrorist' because no such definition exists.

In the end, I believed that my argument won the day, and the prosecution's expert witness backed down on many of the points in his report that I had criticized, admitting that the details about these organizations were unclear and more needed to be researched to conclusively determine their origins and nature. While the logic of presumed innocence would suggest that my arguments and the acquiescence of the prosecution's expert witness would have been enough to have proven a reasonable doubt about the defendant's status as a 'terrorist,' the court found him guilty and sentenced him to seven years in prison. This was because, by the logic of GWOT, purported Muslim 'terrorists' are usually presumed to be guilty until proven innocent.

This chapter critically analyzes the alleged 'terrorist threat' associated with Uyghurs during the first decade of GWOT, relying on primary sources and direct evidence over and above the accumulated body of analysis and secondary discussion within the field of 'terrorism studies.' Like my testimony at the court in Oslo, these findings challenge the conventional literature on these groups, as well as the rationale behind the placement of ETIM on US and UN 'terrorism lists'. I suggest that what has been defined as ETIM and recognized as a Uyghur-led 'terrorist organization' has, in reality, been a fragmented religiously inspired Uyghur militant movement that was limited in its activities by outside actors and presented no real threat to China or the world during the first decade of GWOT. Furthermore, I find no conclusive evidence that either ETIM or TIP has ever carried out political violence deliberately targeting civilians, an act which would qualify these groups as 'terrorists' per this book's working definition. Finally, while the movement's overall motivation has always been the dire situation in the Uyghur homeland, and its overall goal to establish an independent Uyghur state there, it has had very little if any impact inside the Uyghur homeland. This critical point brings into question the PRC assertions that it faces a serious 'terrorist threat' from ETIM within its Uyghur population, a claim that has justified almost two decades of repressive PRC policies towards this population.

While my discussion of this movement's evolution, goals, factions, and allegiances draws extensively from the conventional literature written about them, as well as from the sources on which those writings are based, it is also informed by interviews with people who have participated in this history in different ways, a more in-depth analysis of Uyghur language TIP documents and videos, and a knowledge of Uyghur history, culture, and language. While this account of the history of ETIM and TIP through 2012 still suffers from a paucity of reliable information and a reliance on speculation, I believe its grounding in local histories and culture, as well as its use of Uyghur language sources, makes it a more reliable narrative about these groups than that which has dominated existing literature.

ETIM: THE PHANTOM 'TERRORIST' GROUP

As far as I can tell, no group has ever called itself the Eastern Turkistan Islamic Movement or ETIM. However, the group of Uyghurs that is usually associated with the ETIM label did exist and did establish a community in Afghanistan between 1998 and 2001 with the intent of initiating an insurgency inside China, a goal it never came close to attaining. Rather than calling this community of Uyghurs ETIM, its leader allegedly named it the Eastern Turkistan Islamic Party (ETIP) in honor of those who had battled with PRC security forces in Baren in 1990 and had called their loosely organized group by the same name. The use of this name, both in Baren by Zäydin Yüsüp and in Afghanistan by Häsän Mäkhsum, has led many in the 'terrorism' analysis world to assume that Mäkhsum's group was the same group that fought with security forces in Baren. Furthermore, since both Yüsüp and Mäkhsum were protégées of the same teacher in Karghilik, Abdulhäkim-Haji Mäkhsum, many sources suggest that this teacher was the actual founder of ETIP (aka ETIM) and that the organization goes back to the 1940s or 1950s.

Häsän Mäkhsum himself contributed to this confusion by publicly linking his group of would-be militants in Afghanistan with a long history of Uyghur religious nationalism that draws its modern origins from the first Eastern Turkistan Republic in the 1930s and sometimes even from far earlier periods in Uyghur history. As Mäkhsum stated in a 2002 Radio Free Asia (RFA) interview when asked about the origins of his group, 'the Eastern Turkistan Party has a long history; from the time that Islam was established in Eastern Turkistan to today, Islamic movements in Eastern Turkistan have never ceased; sometimes they have fought for the right to practice Islam, other times they have fought for freedom and independence, sometimes working together, other times in separate groups.'[3] It is noteworthy that shortly afterwards in the same interview he would clarify this point, suggesting that the spirit of his particular group was born in 1990 in Baren, but the group had been established in 1998 in Afghanistan. By making these statements, Häsän Mäkhsum was being neither contradictory nor misleading. Rather, he was referring to a sentiment that is shared by most Uyghur nationalists, whether religiously inspired or secular: a belief that their struggle with modern China is timeless and continuous. Uyghur nationalist historiography tends to blur the lines between the many self-determination movements that have existed throughout the history of modern China's colonial rule over their homeland, usually not distinguishing between different ideologies that have existed in these movements over time. In this sense, when Mäkhsum spoke about the long history of ETIP, he was referring to the long history of religiously inspired Uyghur self-determination movements, suggesting that these movements have had continuity in their struggle to liberate the Uyghur homeland.

In reality, Mäkhsum established his group in Afghanistan only in early 1998, and he never succeeded in making it a cohesive organization. Rather, it remained, throughout its history, a mostly informal community that sought to train an army which could one day fight the Chinese state inside the Uyghur homeland, and, even in this goal, it was thwarted by forces beyond its control. While Mäkhsum would frequently call this group ETIP in public statements, he would refer to it more often as merely the 'community' in the video footage that survived him. In essence, this community was a project initiated and implemented by Häsän Mäkhsum. As a result, the best way to understand its underlying ideology and goals is to begin with Mäkhsum's own vision of Uyghur political Islam that served to inspire this community, or at least its leadership.

The origins of Häsän Mäkhsum's Uyghur Islamic nationalism and of his community in Afghanistan

Häsän Mäkhsum's ideas about political Islam were formed during the 1980s and early 1990s. Much of the international literature on ETIM assumes that Mäkhsum and his organization were influenced by foreign radical Islamic ideologies imported from Saudi Arabia,

Pakistan, and Afghanistan, but this makes little sense in the context of Mäkhsum's biography. There were many Uyghurs who studied in Pakistani madrassas in the 1980s and 1990s, but Mäkhsum was not among them. Similarly, while Pakistani traders likewise frequented the Uyghur homeland during this time, these travelers did not seem to have had any particular influence on Mäkhsum's religious thoughts. Finally, while some high-profile international sources on ETIM suggest that its ideology was influenced by Uyghurs who had been trained by the PRC to fight alongside the *mujahidin* against the Soviets during the 1980s, there is no evidence that the PRC ever trained Uyghurs for this purpose.[4] Even if there were a limited number of Uyghurs somehow trained by the PRC to fight in Afghanistan in the 1980s, I have never met a Uyghur with knowledge of this operation, and nobody with this profile is documented as having anything to do with Häsän Mäkhsum.

Instead of being influenced by Islamic teachings that had come to China from outside, Häsän Mäkhsum's vision for his community in Afghanistan appears to be the product of indigenous ideas about political Islam. Born in the Yengisar region of Kashgar, Mäkhsum was sent by his family at the age of 13 to study Islam under the tutelage of a Sheikh named Abdul Qadir, with whom he lived and studied informally for seven years. In 1984, Abdul Qadir brought Häsän to Karghilik to study under Sheikh Abdulhäkim-Haji Mäkhsum, the same religious teacher who would teach Zäydin Yüsüp, the Uyghur leader in the 1990 clashes with government security forces in Baren.[5] Although Abdulhäkim-Haji Mäkhsum apparently made the *Haj* to Saudi Arabia in 1984, his education took place in the Uyghur homeland during the 1930s and 1940s when his ideas about political Islam were more likely influenced by the Uyghur religious nationalism of the First ETR than by Salafist traditions emanating from Saudi Arabia.

Unfortunately, all that remains of Abdulhäkim-Haji Mäkhsum's teachings from the 1980s are the memories of his students, but one of these students whom I have interviewed reaffirms that his perspective on the nexus of politics and religion was solidly grounded in indigenous issues related to resisting modern China's colonial control of the Uyghurs' homeland. My interviewee, who was part of informal study groups organized by Abdulhäkim-Haji while they were both in prison in the late 1970s and continued to study under him in Karghilik throughout the 1980s, suggests that the Sheikh promoted a broad educational program for his students, which involved the study of the Qur'an and other religious texts, but also local literary classics and the history of both Eastern Turkistan and the world. Through this broad educational program, he allegedly advocated taking inspiration from Islam to wage a struggle for Uyghur independence from China. In this sense, Abdulhäkim-Haji Mäkhsum was likely more inspired by early twentieth-century anti-colonial *Jadid* traditions in the Uyghurs' homeland than by Saudi Arabia's Salafist traditions.[6] Rather than relying exclusively on Arabic religious texts, he apparently placed a high value on indigenous texts in the local vernacular as well as on the 'modern' educational traditions of history and literature. In doing so, he, like the *Jadids*, promoted the ideals of anti-colonial national awakening among the Uyghurs that was also grounded in their identity as 'modernizing' Muslims.[7]

Abdulhäkim-Haji's underground school in Karghilik became well known throughout the southern regions of the Uyghur homeland, and one source suggests that he taught as many as 7,000 young Uyghur men from the time of his release from prison in 1979 until the closing of his school in 1990.[8] Many of his most devoted students would stay in Karghilik for many years, teaching younger students while remaining under his mentorship. Häsän Mäkhsum would study in Karghilik from 1984 until 1990 when authorities closed the school in connection with the Baren incident.[9] Throughout the rest of his life, Häsän Mäkhsum would refer to Abdulhäkim-Haji and his teachings as the inspiration for his own form of Uyghur Muslim nationalism, which would form the basis for his community in Afghanistan.

While Häsän Mäkhsum himself did not participate in the 'Baren incident,' being in Karghilik at the time, he was certainly both inspired and affected by these events involving his fellow student. Mäkhsum would establish his nascent movement in Afghanistan in 1998 as a continuation of the spirit of the group led by Yüsüp in

Baren in 1990, consequently adopting the name Yüsüp had given this group.[10] Additionally, Mäkhsum would be arrested in 1990 during the crackdowns following the Baren incident under suspicion of being involved, leading to a six month prison term. Upon his release from prison, he was subsequently restricted to his home region and placed under surveillance by local authorities.[11] During this time, Mäkhsum apparently also served as an informal teacher of Islam, promoting the lessons he had learned from his teacher Abdulhäkim-Haji. In 1993, he was again arrested for these activities and sentenced to three years of hard labor.[12] While the terms of his release in 1996 supposedly required him to remain in the Kashgar area, he decided to leave the country in early 1997, taking a surreptitious route through Urumqi and Beijing to Malaysia and on to Saudi Arabia.[13] He would never return to the Uyghur homeland.

Apparently, Mäkhsum would spend much of 1997 in Saudi Arabia and Turkey trying to convince Uyghur exiles of the utility of beginning a guerilla war against China based on the ideals he had learned from his teacher Abdulhäkim-Haji. According to his biography on the 2004 version of TIP's website, Mäkhsum had little success in this endeavor and found few if any supporters within these Uyghur exile communities.[14] The same source suggests that he then 'travelled to a land of Jihad in Central Asia' in early 1998 and stayed there for the remainder of his life. In this 'land of Jihad,' Mäkhsum would establish training facilities aimed at fielding an army of Uyghur men to wage jihad against the Chinese state and to liberate the Uyghur homeland. This initiative was not planned by an imagined cohesive militant organization inside China that had also been responsible for the Baren events or any militant efforts predating the 1990s as suggested by many sources. Rather it was Mäkhsum's initiative alone. That said, Mäkhsum likely saw his activities in the context of the timeless struggle of the Uyghur cause, especially as that cause has been framed in terms of Islam historically, including the legacy of Baren as well as that of the First ETR.

Mäkhsum's community in Afghanistan to 2001

According to Abudullah Qarahaji, who was allegedly the deputy to Häsän Mäkhsum in this community, Mäkhsum and a small group of his followers first went in late 1997 to Pakistan from Turkey with the intention of then moving to Afghanistan, but they were initially denied entry.[15] It was only with the approval and assistance of Jalaluddin Haqqani, a Taliban commander with close ties to Pakistan's security services, that Mäkhsum and his group were able to enter Afghanistan and establish a camp in Jalalabad at some point in early 1998.[16] After some time in Jalalabad, Mäkhsum's group was apparently given space in Khost to establish operations there.[17] While they entered Afghanistan with Haqqani's approval, Mäkhsum has denied that they ever had any 'organizational relations with the Taliban,' and there is little reason not to believe his claim.[18]

By most eyewitness accounts, the Uyghur community led by Mäkhsum in Afghanistan was largely isolated from other militant groups in the country. Abudullah Qarahaji claimed that the group was able to establish three camps prior to 2001 where they sheltered as many as 500 Uyghur families, who had managed to flee China, and trained the men from these families in the use of weapons.[19] While it is possible that this is accurate, it is unclear whether these camps were coterminous or had been formed successively, what weapons training they provided, and whether the trainees ultimately answered to Mäkhsum's orders or even viewed themselves as members of a specific organization. According to Qarahaji, he knew of no incidences where those trained in these camps ever carried out any attacks against the government or civilians inside China.[20] In fact, this did not seem to be the intent of the training. As Mäkhsum himself would frequently state in the video footage that would survive him, the trainings' purpose was to prepare Uyghurs for a coming widespread jihad against the Chinese state that apparently had no particular timeline.[21]

Mäkhsum's community evidently did not have the resources to access the internet and post communications and videos during this time, but its members did frequently take video footage of themselves, and this footage turns up in many of the post-2008 videos produced by TIP. Since much of this footage is used in the TIP videos to demonstrate these would-be militants' capacities and dedication, they often feature Uyghurs training and shooting weapons, but such videos also bely the organization's general inactivity and lack of resources. It is noteworthy that the footage from this period never depicts Uyghurs in actual combat, and that the shots of training groups never include more than about a dozen men, almost always armed only with AK-47 rifles.[22] As these videos were likely taken only of significant events in the groups' activities, it can be assumed that they represent the full extent of the group's actual capacity for training, its access to weapons, and its associated membership base at its apex. It is likely that the daily access of community members to weapons and training was far rarer than these videos suggest.

While 'terrorism' experts have generally assumed that Mäkhsum's group was underwritten by Al-Qaeda and had close ties to the Islamic Movement of Uzbekistan (IMU) when the US invasion of Afghanistan began in late 2001, the available evidence does not support these assumptions. In fact, I would argue that the available information about Mäkhsum's group suggests that it was not an organization at all, but a failed attempt to create a militant movement. My research identifies a group of only about five men who were dedicated to the establishment of this community in Afghanistan. This includes Mäkhsum and his deputy Abdullah Qarahaji as well as an Islamic scholar by the name of Sheikh Bilal (aka Yüsüp Qadirkhan), and possibly Abdul Häq who apparently was in charge of training newcomers. Additionally, detainees in Guantanamo Bay, who were in a camp allegedly run by Abdul Häq in 2001, mention a person in Pakistan who appears to have arranged recruitment of newcomers and support for their travel to Afghanistan. Qarahaji suggested that the group had a leadership council consisting of eight people, which corresponds to the organizational structure posted on TIP's short-lived website in 2004, but this is still suggestive of a rather small core group of organizers.[23] Most of the others associated with this community probably did not view themselves as followers of Mäkhsum or as members of the ETIP at all. While Mäkhsum likely hoped to create a militant movement that could challenge Chinese rule of his homeland, at most he was only able to start an initiative to train individual Uyghurs in small weapons. It is particularly notable that there is no evidence whatsoever that this group ever ordered its trainees to undertake any specific militant operations or violent acts of resistance inside or outside of China.

One of the primary reasons for the failure of Mäkhsum's effort to mount a militant insurgency against the PRC from Afghanistan was his lack of external support and perhaps even his external restraints. According to Mäkhsum's deputy, Qarahaji, the group had fairly strained relations with both the Taliban and the 'Arabs,' which refers to Al-Qaeda and other Arab foreign fighters in the country at the time. In his 2004 interview with *The Wall Street Journal*, Qarahaji noted that he had accompanied Mäkhsum to a large meeting of militant Muslim groups in Kandahar in 1999 at which Osama bin Laden was in attendance.[24] At the meeting, bin Laden spoke about the importance of waging jihad in the historical lands of the Arab Muslims, Palestine in particular, suggesting that this was the first priority of global jihad. Apparently, one of the Uyghurs with Mäkhsum and Qarahaji responded by suggesting that the global jihad should focus on the most oppressed Muslims in the world where the practice of religion was under attack, especially in Eastern Turkistan, but he found little to no support for this argument.[25] According to the interview's translator, Omer Kanat, Qarahaji also remarked that the Arab groups in Afghanistan at the time looked down on Uyghurs as less orthodox Muslims, since they were not adherents to the Saudi-dominated Salafi interpretation of Islam. In this context, it is extremely unlikely that Häsän Mäkhsum received $300,000 from Osama bin Laden for the group's operations as had been suggested by the Chinese government in its original documents about ETIM, and it is more likely that, while having met him, he had no working relationship with bin Laden and Al-Qaeda at all.[26] Furthermore, while it would seem logical that Mäkhsum's group would have a working relationship with the Al-Qaeda-supported IMU given the linguistic and cultural similarities between Uzbeks and Uyghurs, my research found no evidence of such connections in Afghanistan at this time.

As for Mäkhsum's relationship with the Taliban, that appears to have been more complicated, as one might expect given the Taliban's role as the government of Afghanistan at the time. On the one hand, he allegedly had received endorsement from Haqqani for his initial entry into Afghanistan, and he likely received permission from local Taliban officials to use different lands for his training endeavors. On the other hand, there is credible evidence that the Taliban, and probably Pakistan's Inter-Service Intelligence (ISI), sought to use Mäkhsum and his group as a bargaining chip in their diplomatic negotiations with China at the time, much as Kazakhstan had used local Uyghur nationalists for similar purposes with the PRC during the same period. In Kazakhstan, security forces appeared to deliberately provide a modicum of political space to Uyghur nationalist groups, perhaps even supporting them nominally, throughout the mid-1990s so that it could subsequently crack down on these groups in the later part of the decade as a component of negotiations with China on a variety of issues from border disputes to trade issues.[27]

While most of the states in the world sought to shun the Taliban government in Afghanistan during the later 1990s, it is well known that the PRC was seeking engagement with the Afghan state. In 1999, at the encouragement of Pakistan, the PRC sent a delegation to Afghanistan to discuss cooperation and economic relations, and the Chinese officials present had allegedly made several agreements with the Emirate of Afghanistan in the process, establishing trade relations and even opening up a flight route between Kabul and Urumqi.[28] Apparently, the PRC also agreed to assist the Taliban with needed infrastructure investment, and India claimed that the Chinese company Huawei even provided the internationally sanctioned Afghan government and its military with critical telecommunications at this time.[29] In 2000, the Chinese ambassador to Pakistan became the first senior official from a non-Muslim country to meet Mullah Omar, the Taliban's leader, and they apparently solidified a series of agreements at this meeting.[30]

While the details of these agreements remain unknown, it is likely that they included stipulations for containing any Uyghur nationalist groups which might use the country as a base.[31] This was suggested by the Taliban's subsequent promises to Chinese representatives that, while it would not expel Uyghurs from Afghanistan to China, its security forces would guarantee that no Uyghur groups in Afghanistan would be a threat to China.[32] Thus, just as in Kazakhstan, it appears that the Taliban, likely with guidance from Pakistan, used the presence of Uyghur nationalists and militants on their territory to their advantage with Beijing. While the Taliban allowed Mäkhsum's group to remain, they kept close watch on its operations and ensured that it posed no threat to China.

According to Omer Kanat, who covered the US war in Afghanistan during 2001 as a foreign correspondent for RFA, the Taliban fulfilled their promises to the PRC by bringing the members of Mäkhsum's community to Kabul where they could be contained. Apparently, this transfer of Mäkhsum and his supporters to Kabul started in 1999 and would remain in place until the US invasion in 2001, as confirmed by Kanat's interview with the Taliban's then Deputy Minister of the Interior, Mullah Abdul Samad Khaksar.[33] In Kabul, Mäkhsum and his supporters were closely watched and warned not to attempt any attacks inside China. The leadership, including Mäkhsum, were apparently given housing in the city where they could be monitored, and the other community members were put on the territory of two military bases outside the city, with the men possibly being enlisted into the Taliban's army.[34] In effect, any fighting force that Häsän Mäkhsum may have gathered and trained in 1998–1999 had been completely neutralized, yet he and his community remained in Afghanistan under the watch of the Taliban in the event that they could serve as a bargaining chip with China again in the future.

If this account of events is accurate, it means that Mäkhsum not only had little to no support from the Taliban and Al-Qaeda, but the Taliban was even actively involved in limiting his activities. Generally, this account makes sense in the context of China's attempts to contain Uyghur nationalism outside its borders during this time, and it is also consistent with the few eyewitness accounts we have about Mäkhsum's community, all of which suggest that it was anything but a cohesive organization with clear plans for the future in 2000–2001. The closest thing we have to raw eyewitness accounts of Mäkhsum's community at this time are those that come from the statements of the 22 Uyghurs who found themselves in the Guantanamo Bay Detention Center after being taken prisoner in Afghanistan and Pakistan. Although all of these people had engaged with Mäkhsum's 'community,' they did not understand these interactions as representing membership in any particular group. Furthermore, their descriptions of Mäkhsum's community do not inspire confidence in this group as a capable militant organization that could pose a threat to China, let alone to the world.

Eighteen of the Uyghur Guantanamo detainees had been at a make-shift training camp near Jalalabad during their stay in Afghanistan. Two others worked for Mäkhsum's community as a food deliv-erer and a typist, one wound up among Mäkhsum's people while searching for his brother, and one may have been a friend of Häsän Mäkhsum from Kashgar in the 1990s, but had only recently arrived in Afghanistan. In reviewing their testimonies from Guantanamo, it is striking that none of them talk about Mäkhsum's community as an organization at all. Rather, they consistently portray it as a group of Uyghurs brought together by circumstances and a mutual distaste for the Chinese rule of their homeland. Finding themselves in a place where weapons were readily available, they welcomed the opportu-nity to learn how to use them in the event they ever had the chance to do so against the Chinese state, but they did not seem to have in mind any planned actions against the PRC in the near future, and most viewed their stay in Afghanistan as a temporary stop in their ongoing search for a safe place to live outside China.

Both the typist and the food deliverer characterized their relation-ship with the community as employees rather than as members, and neither knew anything about external support for the organization.[35] Those in the camp had mostly ended up there in the quest for a safe place to live outside of China, having been pushed out of Kyrgyzstan and Pakistan where they had previously lived in fear of being tar-geted for extradition to China. While some came to the camp hoping to take part in an insurgency against the Chinese state, none had sought to partake in a global jihad. In fact, none of the detainees had ever heard of Al-Qaeda until they were sent to Guantanamo.

In being asked if they had helped the Taliban and Al-Qaeda forces resisting the US invasion, all the detainees said they had no reason to fight Americans. As one detainee noted in making this point, 'a billion Chinese enemies, that is enough for me; why would I get more enemies?'[36]

The existence of the camp near Jalalabad is a bit of a mystery given that Mäkhsum's community was said to be contained inside Kabul and surrounding military camps at this time. From the testimonies of former Guantanamo detainees, it appears as if the camp had only recently been established by Mäkhsum's group. It is unclear whether this was done with the approval of his Taliban hosts, perhaps to add to the ranks of the Taliban army, or whether it was something the community was doing on its own unbeknownst to the Afghan government. Regardless, the poor conditions inside the camp as described by its inhabitants suggests that it had little if any external support. All of the former detainees noted that they had never seen non-Uyghurs on its territory with the exception of one local Afghan who worked there as a cook. Those who had been in the camp longer mentioned Häsän Mäkhsum coming to its territory twice to give talks to the trainees, and almost all of them note that the camp's primary organizer was a Uyghur named Abdul Häq.[37] All of the trainees had arrived in Afghanistan and at the camp over the course of the year prior to the US invasion of the country, and they generally agreed that this training center housed approximately 30 Uyghurs at its apex.

Perhaps most importantly, the detainees' testimony about the 'training camp' where they spent time does not fit the profile of a professional, organized, and resource-rich organization with close ties to Al-Qaeda. They describe small, old, and decrepit buildings in need of dire repair, and they note that their primary activities while at the location were to repair them and bring them back to livable conditions.[38] When asked about the training received at this camp, the detainees discuss running in the mornings and the occasional opportunity to fire a few bullets with the only Kalashnikov rifle that was available at the camp. In short, their description of this 'training camp' suggests that it provided them with very little training and that it had virtually no resources to support any kind of militant operation. In fact, most of the detainees did not recognize this location as a 'training camp' at all. As one detainee answered interrogators asking about the 'camp,' 'it was a little Uigher [sic] community where Uighers [sic] went; I do not know what you mean about the place called camp.'[39]

Most of those who lived in this desolate settlement before finding themselves in Guantanamo Bay appear to have viewed the place first and foremost as a refuge from the long arm of the Chinese state. Indeed, my 2010 interviews with Uyghur former detainees who had been released from Guantanamo to Albania in 2006 seemed to confirm as much. As I began to interview these men, who had mostly become apprentice pizza cooks in Albania's capital city of Tirana, their stories sounded very familiar. Their lives prior to being taken captive were reminiscent of the accounts of the many Uyghur traders from China I had interviewed in Kazakhstan during the mid-1990s.[40] Most of them were born in rural areas and had become involved in trading because few other career opportunities existed. Once engaged in trading, they realized that to make a living beyond subsistence, they needed to become part of the transnational trade that joins the Uyghurs' homeland to its western neighbors. As a result, they traveled westward, trying to sell Chinese manufactured goods in bordering states, particularly in Central Asia and Pakistan. Once living abroad, they no longer wanted to go back to the repressive atmosphere in their homeland, many of them fearing that a return would also result in their incarceration on political charges after having interacted with Uyghur nationalists abroad. While in the early 1990s Central Asia and Pakistan still offered a fairly safe refuge for Uyghurs leaving China, this was no longer the case by 1999.

Having experienced difficulties in Central Asia and Pakistan as those countries increasingly monitored Uyghurs on their territory for the Chinese security forces, the former detainees in Albania were forced to leave these states but did not want to return to China. Aside from one of the four interviewees who said he went to Afghanistan explicitly to seek militant training that he could bring back to China, the others reportedly went there temporarily in hope of eventually getting to Turkey. They claimed that people in Pakistan had told them that a small community of Uyghurs near Jalalabad could assist them in finding safe passageway to Turkey via Afghanistan and Iran. Although my interviewees arrived in Afghanistan at different times, they all found themselves in the same settlement near Jalalabad when the American bombing of the region began shortly after 9/11. The youngest in the group, who was 18 when taken captive, said he had arrived in the country on 12 September 2001 without any knowledge of the previous day's events. During the US invasion of Afghanistan, the camp was bombed, and there were extensive casualties. Eighteen of those who survived, including all those whom I interviewed, went to the mountains to seek safety, living in a monkey cave. After seeing a group of Arabs walking nearby, they followed them across the border into Pakistan where local people first gave them refuge and then sold them to bounty-hunters for $5,000 each.

These profiles of 'accidental jihadists' who ended up in Guantanamo likely applied to the majority of Mäkhsum's community in Afghanistan during its brief existence. Over the course of almost four years, many other Uyghurs with similar stories probably had come and left, utilizing the community as a refuge. A 2010 TIP video commemorating the life of the religious scholar Yüsüp Qadirkhan (aka Sheikh Bilal), who had allegedly joined the group in 1999 and was killed in the US bombing campaign in 2001, for example, shows him teaching around 20 Uyghur children, perhaps lending credence to Qarahaji's claim that the community once included numerous Uyghur families.[41] However, by the time of the US invasion in 2001, it appears that the Taliban's transfer of the community to Kabul and alleged forced separation of the group between the city and two different neighboring military bases had prevented Mäkhsum from creating anything like a cohesive fighting force or even a unified community.

As a result, in the chaos of the US bombing campaign in late 2001, little likely remained of the community. As Mäkhsum admits in his 2002 interview with RFA, some may have ended up fighting alongside the Taliban against invading forces, perhaps having been brought into the Taliban army while living on military bases around Kabul. Others, like the newcomers in the camp near Jalalabad, were either killed or ended up in Guantanamo Bay. Mäkhsum himself apparently would gather as much of the community as he could during the bombing and likewise lead them out of Afghanistan to Pakistan. This probably would have included Mäkhsum's small core group, some of whom might have been killed by US air strikes like Qadirkhan, and those Uyghurs who had been able to escape the military bases around Kabul.

A video released by TIP in 2017 shows Mäkhsum leading a prayer session in a snowy mountainous landscape that, by the content of the leader's sermon, appears to be during their march towards Pakistan in 2001–2002. From this video, it looks as if at most 20 followers are present.[42] While the details are unknown, this group may have at some point joined up with other non-Uyghur militants who would help them find refuge in Pakistan. It was during this time that Mäkhsum called RFA unsolicited to give an interview. In that interview, he condemned the 11 September attacks on the US and denied that his group had any organizational ties or had received any financial support from either the Taliban or Al-Qaeda.[43] As Omer Kanat, who conducted that interview with Mäkhsum, suggests, he took a significant risk in doing so because he was presumably traveling with Arab and/or Afghan militants. Kanat would request another interview with Mäkhsum some months later, but the leader replied that he could no longer communicate with him and that he had already suffered as a result of his previous interview.[44]

Not much is known about the events that subsequently transpired to the remnants of Mäkhsum's community once they had reached Pakistan. Qarahaji, Mäkhsum's deputy, later told Omer Kanat and a *Wall Street Journal* reporter that Mäkhsum had sought an option of moving the community to Qom in Iran, but the group ultimately decided to stay in Waziristan, Pakistan, where it had presumably settled with Al-Qaeda groups and the Pakistan Taliban, which controlled the area.[45] On 2 October 2003, Pakistani forces would kill Häsän Mäkhsum in South Waziristan near the border with Afghanistan under unknown circumstances, and the vision for his community and its future insurgency inside China mostly died with him.[46] Some Uyghurs have suggested to me that Mäkhsum was killed because he had refused to merge his community with allied groups of Al-Qaeda and the Taliban, which were assumed to have at least the tacit support of Pakistan's ISI for their base of operations in Waziristan, and at least one person I spoke with believes he was killed because he wanted to turn himself in to American troops and explain his objectives to them at this time. However, the truth behind his death is unlikely ever to be known.

While the story of Häsän Mäkhsum, his community, and its goals of initiating a jihad against the PRC warrants further research to form a full picture of the group's activities and allegiances, it is clear from the account above that this community was at best a nascent militant organization that had never realized its true objectives. Finding itself in a milieu of Muslim militants who sought to wage a global jihad, Mäkhsum and his followers necessarily interacted with these militants while in Afghanistan, including with the Taliban and to a certain extent with Al-Qaeda, but there is no evidence that he was linked to these groups organizationally, received funding from them, or was attracted to their ideology of global jihad. Rather, the group remained dedicated to taking inspiration from Islam to wage a war of liberation for the Uyghurs' homeland inside China, and it spent its time preparing for such a war in the hope that an opportunity would arise to put their preparations into practice. In essence, this group, which never called itself ETIM, was hardly an organization at all. It involved a small, mostly inconsequential, and loosely organized group of Uyghurs who believed they were fulfilling their debt to the Uyghur cause, but they were also captive of geopolitical machinations that kept them contained and unable to ever accomplish much towards this cause.

Given this account of Mäkhsum's community, the classification of ETIM as a 'terrorist organization' is all the more absurd. First, no organization by this name actually existed. Second, this group appears never to have had close connections to or funding from Al-Qaeda and the Taliban, who more likely sought to prevent it from realizing its objectives. Thirdly, there is no evidence that Mäkhsum's community, which was only established in 1998, had anything to do with the over 200 violent acts, 162 deaths, and over 440 injuries allegedly perpetrated by Uyghurs between 1990 and 2002 that the US State Department attributed to it. In fact, no evidence exists that it ever carried out any attacks on the PRC, or perhaps on anyone. About two years after the recognition of ETIM as a 'terrorist organization' by the US and UN, its assumed leader was now dead, and his community, which was considered to be ETIM in the eyes of the 'counterterrorism-industrial complex,' had been decimated. Yet, ETIM still remained on both of these lists and does as this book goes to print, and Uyghurs are still experiencing the consequences.

THE TURKISTAN ISLAMIC PARTY, 2004–2012: A VIDEO PRODUCTION COMPANY WITH A MILITANT WING

Little is known about the activities of the remnants of Mäkhsum's community in the years immediately after his death. It is known that his deputy Qarahaji subsequently fled Pakistan for a new safe haven, and others may have followed him. If Mäkhsum arrived in Pakistan with some 20 followers in 2002, it is possible that by 2003 only a handful remained. In fact, nothing substantial would be heard about Uyghur militants in Afghanistan or Pakistan until 2008. However, in the interim, there were a few signs that whoever did remain planned to utilize the legacy of Mäkhsum's group for the development of a new project.

The first of these signs was the appearance in 2004 of the website for a group that called itself the Turkistan Islamic Party (TIP) (www.tipislamawazi.com). On its website, which did not appear to be updated throughout its existence but notably had material in the English language as well as in Uyghur, TIP claimed that it was the same organization as the one associated with Mäkhsum and that the name change had taken place in 2000 before Mäkhsum's death.[47] However, it is noteworthy that I was unable to locate any recordings or writings reflecting this change prior to the appearance of this website in 2004. Mäkhsum, for example, uses the name

ETIP in his interview with RFA in 2002, explicitly mentioning that this name was adopted in memory of his fellow student who had organized Uyghurs in Baren in 1990.[48] Around the same time as this website's appearance, TIP also issued an hour-long film in Arabic about Häsän Mäkhsum's life, which seemed intended to draw the attention of the Arab world, and jihadists in particular, to the problems of the Uyghurs.[49] Also, as noted in the previous chapter, a video was released by alleged militant Uyghurs in 2006 calling for jihad in Eastern Turkistan, but this video neither mentions TIP nor uses its logo, which appears in their media releases from 2004.[50]

In retrospect, these media efforts may have represented different factions within the already meager remnants of Mäkhsum's group struggling to represent their deceased leader's legacy. If this was the case, it seems that only one new group would emerge from the ashes of Mäkhsum's community by 2008. This group would brand itself more deliberately than Mäkhsum's community, calling itself TIP, and promoting this brand through its famous media wing, *Islam Awazi* (or the 'Voice of Islam'). Unfortunately, there is little information about how TIP was established, and one can only speculate about the circumstances. While one questionable TIP document suggests that Abdul Häq immediately took over the leadership of the community after Mäkhsum's death, there was no information announced about this until five years later when Häq issued a video regarding the Beijing Olympics in March 2008.[51] Thus, it is more likely that this group was established gradually as Häq asserted his leadership and began cultivating a new community from whichever Uyghurs had ended up in Waziristan after 2001. Regardless of what had happened after Mäkhsum's death, it was clear that the TIP which existed in 2008 was primarily a project of Abdul Häq, who had adopted the title of *Emir*, and its allegiances and approach were quite different from those of Mäkhsum's community.

Abdul Häq's history is mostly shrouded in mystery. His given name is Mämtimin Mämät, and, unlike Mäkhsum's deputy Qarahaji, he was not among the eleven Uyghurs named by the PRC's Ministry of Public Security as wanted terrorists in 2003.[52] However, Abdul Häq is identified by most of the Uyghurs who were detained at Guantanamo as being the person in charge of their training camp, suggesting that he was either a core member of Mäkhsum's community by 2001 or a Uyghur associated with the Taliban who was exploiting those Uyghurs who had come to join Mäkhsum's community after it had already been quarantined. The first issues of TIP's Arabic-language magazine, *Islamic Turkistan*, offer some details of his early life in the Uyghur homeland and his eventual appearance in Afghanistan, at least in the terms that Häq himself wanted to be portrayed. Like Mäkhsum, Abdul Häq had apparently been sent by his family to study with informal religious teachers when he was still young, but he also states that he attended a state school from 1975 until 1980, at which time he claims to have left school to study under Abdulhäkim-Haji Mäkhsum in Kaghilik.[53] However, unlike Häsän Mäkhsum, Häq does not identify Abdulhäkim-Haji as his primary mentor. He characterizes his final and ultimate mentor as Muhämmäd Zakir Akhnad Khalifä, whom Häq claims was an adherent to Salafism, suggesting that Häq may have been more influenced by Salafi traditions than was Mäkhsum.[54] After having spent time in jail and eventually finding a surreptitious route to flee the country, which involved numerous bribes, he claims that he came to Pakistan where he met Mäkhsum's representative through a local madrassa. Subsequently, he allegedly came to Khost in Afghanistan during April 1998 and joined the community during its first year of existence.[55]

It is clear that Häq eventually did align himself and his group more closely with Al-Qaeda and the Taliban than had Häsän Mäkhsum and his community, but it is unclear when this transformation happened. This may have been a necessity of circumstances as Häq emerged as the leader for the handful of Uyghurs who, after Mäkhsum's death, remained in Waziristan, a region that was controlled almost completely by Al-Qaeda and the Pakistan Taliban at the time. However, Häq's alliance with Al-Qaeda may have also involved political calculations to garner more external support for a jihad against the PRC than Mäkhsum had succeeded in doing. When the US treasury sanctioned Häq in 2009 after the Beijing Olympics, it claimed that he had already joined an Al-Qaeda *Shura* council in Waziristan in 2005, but no sources had made such assertions prior to this.[56]

Regardless of when Häq formally established ties with Al-Qaeda, it was obvious by 2008 that he and his group were fully aligned with Al-Qaeda in northern Waziristan. This alliance also appeared to bring with it substantial resources. In 2008, TIP would launch its well-produced Arabic-language magazine published by a press usually associated with Al-Qaeda and make several ominous videos threatening the Beijing Olympics. TIP's success in garnering international attention to their video threats against the Olympics likely impressed Al-Qaeda leadership enough to provide the group with continued resources in the coming years, at least for their video productions. Additionally, it was allegedly reported by an Al-Qaeda spokesperson after the Olympics that Osama bin Laden himself had appointed Häq as both the *Emir* of TIP and the leader of a phantom group called 'Al-Qaeda in China,' which was never heard of again after this announcement.[57]

As already mentioned, TIP's video production, under the trademark of *Islam Awazi*, would grow exponentially both in quantity and quality between 2008 and 2012. In addition to being more plentiful, these videos became increasingly sophisticated, were better shot, and used more and more complicated animation. However, it is unclear that this increased and more sophisticated media presence corresponded to a significant number of Uyghur fighters in Waziristan. It is notable, for example, that the videos, at least until 2011, show few present-day images of Uyghur fighters. It would seem that *Islam Awazi* had inherited the archival footage from Mäkhsum's community in Afghanistan, and it used this footage extensively in its productions, but until 2011, there were only five Uyghurs in Waziristan who appeared in these videos – the self-proclaimed *Emir* Abdul Häq, his deputy Abdushukur, a Commander Säyfullah, the producer of *Islam Awazi* Abdullah Mansur, and a religious scholar named Abduläziz. While there may have been other Uyghurs associated with TIP at this time, it is also possible that beyond these five people there were few if any additional members until 2011.

The biographies of these five people also provide some insight to TIP's allegiances and its differences from Mäkhsum's community. Abdushukur, Häq's deputy, had been a Taliban fighter in Afghanistan during the presence of Mäkhsum's group in the country, and it is not clear whether he was ever actually a part of Mäkhsum's community. He was captured by the Northern Alliance in 2000 and spent seven years in a prison until finding his way to join TIP in Waziristan in 2007.[58] Abdullah Mansur appeared to have a similar biography, as he described coming to Afghanistan together with Abdushukur a few years prior to Mäkhsum's arrival in the country.[59] Commander Säyfullah likewise appears to have come to Afghanistan in 1997 and fought with the Taliban against the Northern Alliance prior to ever meeting Mäkhsum.[60] While Säyfullah allegedly became a member of Mäkhsum's *Shura* council, it appears that he was more involved at that time with the Taliban than Mäkhsum ever was. During the US invasion of Afghanistan in 2001, he was stuck in the north, only meeting up with Mäkhsum as he was crossing over to Pakistan in 2002. The younger Abduläziz appeared to be a relative newcomer and an aspiring religious teacher. There is no evidence that he had ever been in Afghanistan prior to 2001, and it is probable that he had initially come to Pakistan to study at a madrassa and then joined the others in Waziristan. Thus, Abdul Häq was the only core member of TIP who appeared to have been substantively involved with Mäkhsum's group, although this is itself disputable, and most of the TIP leadership had instead been more engaged as individuals with the Taliban prior to arriving in Waziristan. This likely also contributed to the group's close alliance with Al-Qaeda and the Pakistan Taliban in Waziristan.

'Terrorism' analyst Jacob Zenn, who has frequently written on this group, noted of this early period in its development that, given the prolific video production of *Islam Awazi*, TIP 'appeared to be more of a propaganda group with a militant wing than a militant group with a propaganda wing.'[61] I would suggest that it is even likely that TIP had no militant wing at all at this time. Rather, the handful of Uyghurs in Waziristan at the time probably fought in multi-national brigades associated with one of the Al-Qaeda or Pakistan Taliban factions in the north, where Abdul Häq appeared to be given a role as a military leader. However, the real heart of TIP during this period was not these fighters, but its growing media presence through *Islam Awazi*.

In terms of its propaganda agenda, *Islam Awazi* fought an information war with China on two different fronts from 2008 through 2010 – trying to get Muslims in the Uyghur homeland to wage their own jihad against the PRC and trying to get international jihadist networks to turn their attention towards China as an enemy and potential target. Numerous videos early in 2009 were obvious attempts to inspire the Uyghurs inside China to wage jihad against the state. These include a video explaining the importance of jihad as both a means of liberating the Uyghur homeland and as a fulfillment of a Muslim's obligation to God as well as an instructional video discussing the methods of waging jihad.[62] After the July 2009 riots in Urumqi, videos also explicitly used these events as inspiration to call on Uyghurs to rise up inside China.[63] These videos were bolstered by others in the Uyghur language demonstrating the strength of TIP and promising to assist in any locally initiated jihad once it began.[64] If these videos were deliberately targeting a Uyghur audience inside China, the group's Arabic-language magazine and several Arabic and Turkish language videos were more directed to potential funders and supporters from outside. One such video in Arabic that probably did have some impact on other jihadists and their supporters explained the events surrounding the 2009 Urumqi riots.[65] It was after the release of this video, that the leader of Al-Qaeda in the Islamic Maghreb made the first threats ever against China from an Arab jihadist group.[66]

While TIP videos would continue to have a similar focus on promoting jihad in the Uyghur homeland during 2010–2012, non-Uyghur themes also found their way into *Islam Awazi's* expanding video catalog at this time. This shift, interestingly, corresponds with the alleged death of Abdul Häq and the resultant leadership change in the organization. In Häq's place, Abdushukur became *Emir*, and Abdullah Mansur became his deputy. In Mansur's place as head of *Islam Awazi*, the relative newcomer, Abduläziz, took over media production. This would suggest that by 2010, TIP had very little personal connection left to Mäkhsum, but it would continue to use footage of Mäkhsum to evoke his alleged role in the group's history. However, the group was now led by two Uyghurs with a long history of service to the Taliban and one young Uyghur religious teacher who appeared to have fully adopted Salafi interpretations of Islam.

From his many appearances in videos, it would appear that Abdulaziz fashioned himself as a great Islamic scholar of jihad in the Salafi tradition who saw his role as going beyond the Uyghur cause to be a spokesperson for oppressed Muslims everywhere.[67] Starting in 2011, Abdulaziz is an almost constant feature in TIP videos, with many films being dedicated exclusively to his religious lectures, mostly focused on the obligation of jihad.[68] Additionally, Abdulaziz made many videos at this time highlighting other ethnic groups with whom Uyghurs were likely fighting in Waziristan, especially Turks, Tatars, and Muslims from the Caucasus mountains in Russia.[69]

These videos are instructive of the ties that this small group of Uyghurs had forged in the region since 2003 as they probably found themselves fighting in non-Arab multi-national forces. For example, several videos were made about a Turkish jihadist who fought with Uyghurs and had martyred himself in a suicide bombing at what looks in the video to be a Pakistani military outpost.[70] Another series of videos, both in Russian and Uyghur, made by Abdulaziz in collaboration with a Russian-speaking fighter, likely from the Caucasus, highlights their collective 'home' as *Khorasan*, a historical reference to the homeland of the non-Arab Muslims of Central and south-west Asia.[71] The use of this term may suggest the emergence of a multi-national consciousness among TIP's Uyghurs, or at least for Abdulaziz, in solidarity with other marginalized non-Arab groups as well as with the Afghan Taliban in Waziristan at this time. As such, it seemed that, by 2011, the small group of TIP fighters had become an evident part of a transnational jihad movement, albeit a minute and mostly inconsequential one representing perhaps less than a dozen Uyghurs.

Despite this increased attraction to transnational jihadism, TIP remained largely inspired by the Uyghur cause. TIP's most impassioned videos were still about the struggle for the liberation of the Uyghur homeland in Eastern Turkistan, often accompanied by haunting songs presumably written by those in the group. These videos are particularly emotional as they generally juxtapose scenes of the PRC's humiliation of Uyghurs inside the homeland with heroic and proud presumed Uyghur fighters in Pakistan and Afghanistan.[72] Additionally, it is noteworthy that the group continued to fly two flags during this time, as had been the case in Mäkhsum's community – the black flag often associated with jihadist groups and a light blue Uyghur national flag that only differed from that embraced by secular Uyghur nationalists by virtue of its inclusion of the *Shahadah* in Arabic.

The flying of these two flags was something of a metaphor for the precarious way TIP positioned itself ideologically during this period. On the one hand, it declared itself as loyal to a global jihadist network, at least in its war in Afghanistan. On the other hand, it also continued to present itself as a defender of the Uyghur nation and its struggle against Chinese occupation, a cause that the global jihadist movement was still not prepared to champion. Likely one of the primary reasons that TIP was able to straddle this contentious ideological space was that the organization remained small and almost exclusively focused on the production of propaganda. It never presented an actual militant threat to China that could have created problems for its patrons in the global jihad movement.

Another sign of TIP's continued grounding in the Uyghur cause was its credible claim to have finally directly influenced an attack inside China in the summer of 2011. Shortly after a truck of Uyghurs allegedly crashed into a crowded street in Kashgar and subsequently attacked police with knives, TIP released a video that showed one of the organizers of the violence allegedly partaking in a Uyghur celebration in Waziristan in 2006.[73] While TIP did not take credit for ordering the attack, it was the first time that any Uyghur militant group in Afghanistan or Pakistan could conclusively demonstrate that its path had crossed with Uyghurs who were returning to China to sow violence. In a more recent biography of the 'martyr' shown in the video, TIP notes that he had actually returned to China in 2008 with the intent of carrying out jihad, but he had been put in prison during the Olympics, only realizing his goals on his release through the 2011 violence in Kashgar.[74] If this connection between local violence and the group raised PRC government concerns about TIP, the arrival of more Uyghurs in Waziristan around the same time probably further amplified these concerns.

During 2011, videos suddenly emerged that show a handful of new Uyghur faces, who are portrayed as foot soldiers.[75] One such video highlights a Uyghur fighter speaking in Chinese and seeking to explain to the Chinese people why Uyghurs do not view Eastern Turkistan as a part of China.[76] This appearance of new Uyghurs in Waziristan also made sense in the context of what was happening inside China at the time. The situation in the Uyghur homeland had become increasingly oppressive in the aftermath of the 2009 Urumqi riots as the PRC established virtual martial law in the region and rounded up perhaps thousands of Uyghurs for arrests. While the riots had exploded when security forces suppressed a protest led by mostly urban secular Uyghur youth, the state targeted for arrest mostly rural religious Uyghurs. As a result, a mass exodus from China of Uyghurs, especially pious rural residents, had begun as early as 2009 and would continue for the next few years. While it has been well documented that this exodus of Uyghurs from China led to tens of thousands arriving in Turkey from 2009, it is likely that a number also made their way to join militants in Waziristan. In the context of TIP's evolution into a viable militant group, as opposed to merely a producer of propaganda, these new recruits may have presented a critical turning point for the organization.

Amidst this new influx of Uyghurs in TIP's ranks, there were also other indications at this time that the group might be evolving into a more mature militant organization, perhaps even planning international 'terrorist' attacks. First, there was a case in Dubai where authorities had allegedly foiled a planned 'terrorist' attack involving two Uyghurs assumed to be connected with ETIM/TIP. The suspects, who were arrested while trying to buy explosives presumably to carry out an attack on a Chinese mall, allegedly admitted to training with Uyghurs in Waziristan prior to coming to the United Arab Emirates. However, it is unknown under what circumstances this information was extracted from the suspects and, if they had been with TIP in Pakistan, whether the organization had actually ordered the attack.[77] Furthermore, the judge hearing the case, while finding the suspect guilty, commuted his sentence, suggesting that the arrest had been made before the suspect had truly demonstrated his intentions.

Around the same time, a Uyghur refugee was arrested in Norway for allegedly planning a terrorist attack for Al-Qaeda with two other men, an Uzbek and a Kurd. The information surrounding this alleged planned attack is also unclear in part because, as in the incident in Dubai, the plotters were arrested prematurely.[78] In February of 2019, I was able to interview the Uyghur suspect in this case, Mikael Davud, who had recently finished a seven-year prison term for this alleged planned attack. While Davud admitted to me that he intended to bomb the Chinese embassy in Oslo, he adamantly denied that he had planned the attack in conjunction with either TIP or Al-Qaeda. Rather, he claimed that he was working independently of any international jihadist group, much like the Chechens who had carried out the attack on the Boston marathon in the US. It is also noteworthy that neither Al-Qaeda nor TIP ever claimed to be involved in either of the planned attacks in Dubai or Oslo.[79] Furthermore, since 2010, there have been very few similar accusations made against TIP for organizing what appear to be 'terrorist attacks', and none that have been conclusively proven. In this context, it is reasonable to assume that these alleged planned attacks were probably not actually TIP-initiated at all.

In retrospect, 2011–2012 did represent a shift in TIP's capacities as well as perhaps in its goals, but it remained uncertain in what direction this shift was headed. The group was obviously accumulating new recruits, but it is still unclear how many of the Uyghur refugees leaving China were finding their way to Waziristan. Perhaps to take advantage of this exodus to attract more recruits, TIP's media wing, *Islam Awazi*, created numerous videos in 2012 that glorified martyrdom and the life of a jihadist, while also highlighting oppression in China.[80] Even if it is questionable whether these videos could be readily accessed inside China at this time, they could certainly be viewed by those fleeing the country in Southeast Asia and Turkey. This strategy would seemingly pay off in the coming years as TIP evolved into a viable guerilla warfare force in Syria, but not necessarily an international 'terrorist organization.'

However, the fact remains that TIP through 2012 was neither a viable guerilla warfare force nor a 'terrorist organization,' at least by this book's working definition for this term. Rather, it was first and foremost a propaganda organization that emphasized the plight of the Uyghurs inside China and the role Islam could play in inspiring Uyghurs to liberate their homeland. TIP's profile between 2008 and 2012 was quite different from that of Häsän Mäkhsum's community in Afghanistan during the late 1990s, but the capabilities of the two organizations to carry out attacks in China were not that different. TIP deliberately sought to brand itself as a jihadist group that could threaten China and seemingly entered into an alliance with Al-Qaeda and the Pakistan Taliban willingly in order to do so. It also appeared to have adopted these organizations' militant Salafist interpretations of Islam and sought to propagate these ideas among Uyghurs. However, it was mostly a shell organization, the primary activity of which was video production. Its few members, especially prior to 2011, likely contributed to Al-Qaeda's fighting force in Afghanistan as individuals rather than as a group, and their pursuit of the Uyghur cause was mostly, if not exclusively, accomplished through the propaganda efforts of *Islam Awazi*.

By the end of 2012, TIP was about to become an entirely different organization. Over the course of 2012, three of its primary leaders were killed as a small number of new Uyghurs were arriving to join the group. Abdushukur, who had taken over the group as *Emir* after Abdul Häq's alleged death by US drone in 2010, met a similar fate to his predecessor when he was killed by another US drone strike in 2012.[81] Similarly, Commander Säyfullah, who had become famous as a result of his presence in videos threatening the Beijing Olympics, and the young religious scholar Abduläziz, were both killed in 2012 by other drone strikes.[82] In effect, by the end of 2012, the only person apparently left from TIP's original core group in 2008 was Abdullah Mansur. Furthermore, the fact that the rest of the group's leadership had been killed by US drone strikes served to make the group increasingly anti-American as well as anti-Chinese.

At the same time, the group's capacity as a militant movement was changing. For most of its history, the group had demonstrated that it had a substantial capability in the production of propaganda, but it remained unclear if it had a militant wing at all or was merely made up of a handful of foreign fighters aligned with Al-Qaeda and the Pakistan Taliban in Waziristan. However, by 2011, it was clear that it was establishing a larger community in the region that rivaled the strength of Häsän Mäkhsum's community at its apex in Afghanistan. Furthermore, it had appeared to provide evidence that one of its ranks had succeeded in carrying out an attack inside China in Kashgar, albeit several years after leaving the group. As its number of fighters would continue to grow in the coming years, it was unclear whether it would develop into a militant group that would seriously challenge Chinese rule in the Uyghur homeland or, alternatively, merely into a tool of Al-Qaeda, which would exploit Uyghurs' discontent in China to recruit them for a global jihad.

WHAT MAKES A TERRORIST ORGANIZATION?

The branding of groups or individuals as 'terrorists' has been notoriously subjective and politicized in the context of GWOT. Thus, the fact that ETIM was recognized as an international 'terrorist threat' and that TIP inherited this designation tells us little about these groups' actual character. Should these groups ever have been recognized as 'terrorist organizations' and assumed to be enemies in GWOT? The answer, of course, depends upon one's definition of 'terrorism.' The UN 'Consolidated List,' which provides something of an international consensus of who qualifies as a 'terrorist,' tells one nothing about a militant group's actions, goals, or the legitimacy of their cause. Rather, whether a group is on this list is determined exclusively by their association with Al-Qaeda, the Taliban, or, more recently, Daesh. Per these criteria, Mäkhsum's group should never have been listed, since they had no formal organizational affiliation with any of these groups, but TIP would qualify, not because of its actions, intents, or actual threat to others, but because of its association with Al-Qaeda and the Taliban.

However, in terms of this book's working definition, which is based on the actions of militant groups, I would argue that neither Mäkhsum's community nor TIP qualify as 'terrorist organizations' because neither has a clear record of carrying out premeditated political violence that deliberately targets civilians. There is no evidence that Mäkhsum's group ever succeeded in carrying out any acts of political violence during its existence, let alone any which deliberately targeted civilians. In terms of TIP, these questions are more debatable. TIP claimed to have carried out bus bombings killing Chinese civilians in Shanghai and Kunming in the run-up to the Beijing Olympics, but the PRC denied these claims. Furthermore, while there were credible, but questionable, claims that TIP may have planned a 'terrorist attack' in Dubai and a bombing of the Chinese Embassy in Oslo in 2010, the organization did not claim credit for either. In reality, it is questionable whether TIP had the capacity to carry out any of these alleged acts of violence prior to 2012. Rather, evidence suggests that TIP at this time was mostly a producer of propaganda videos, which did seek to incite Uyghurs inside China to violence and strike fear in the Chinese populous. Thus, while open to debate, I would suggest that TIP was also not a 'terrorist organization' in 2012 per this book's working definition. Rather, it was a small and loosely affiliated group of Uyghurs participating in multi-national para-military groups that were fighting in Afghanistan and Pakistan. The activities that united them as a group were not this participation in Afghanistan's conflict, but their video-making exploits, which sought to impact events inside China.

Aside from not being a 'terrorist organization,' it is questionable whether TIP even posed a viable threat to the security of the PRC. Aside from the 2011 attack in Kashgar mentioned above, which involved one person who had been presumably trained by the organization years earlier, there is no clear evidence that TIP had the capacity to carry out violence inside China. Furthermore, even if the group's videos had a significant audience among Uyghurs inside China (and there is no evidence that they did), it is difficult to argue that this propaganda helped to incite Uyghurs to violence. There were very few acts of premeditated political violence reported to be perpetrated by Uyghurs inside China during GWOT's first decade and there were plenty of reasons for such violence when it did occur that had nothing to do with TIP. If the TIP videos had any real impact on events inside China through 2012, it was less to incite Uyghur violence and more to fuel the fear of a purported Uyghur 'terrorist threat' among government officials and even the Chinese public writ large. In this respect, TIP did contribute to the PRC's insecurity indirectly by inviting even harsher state repression of their fellow Uyghurs still inside China, and these repressive policies would eventually lead more Uyghurs to violent resistance in the coming years.

In short, TIP's rather voluminous video catalog as of 2012 had ensured that the topic of 'counterterrorism' remained front and center in Chinese policy discussions about Uyghurs, but I would also argue that this did not reflect an actual substantive 'terrorist threat' from Uyghurs. The atmosphere in the Uyghur homeland had become more tense during GWOT's first decade, but these tensions had little to do with 'terrorism,' real or perceived. Rather, the tensions had much more to do with development, settler colonialism, and the threat of assimilation. These pressures, not a 'terrorism threat,' would be the root causes of the Urumqi riots, and they would continue to fuel violence from both security organs and Uyghur citizens, especially in the south, in the coming years. While TIP would make videos to fan this violence, it would become more a justification for state-led violent responses to this situation than an inspiration for citizen-led violent resistance. Presumably, officials in the upper echelons of the Party knew from their access to intelligence that TIP did not pose a serious threat to the PRC, but they also likely viewed the organization as a convenient justification for more intense securitization and suppression of dissent. However, it is also likely that many lower-level officials implementing policy in the Uyghur region at this time viewed TIP as a serious threat that had infiltrated the population and needed to be mitigated by any means necessary.

4 A Uyghur man sells 'knick-knacks' in front of a newly built apartment complex, Korla 2007. © Joshua Kuchera.

4

COLONIALISM MEETS COUNTERTERRORISM, 2002–2012

During the summer of 2000, I took my last fieldwork trip to the Uyghur homeland. The region had an ominous feeling to it that seemed to foretell its future direction. I had returned to Ghulja for the first time in about three years; the city, which was one of the few Uyghur urban centers in the north, felt as if it had lost its Uyghur characteristics and become much more of a generic small Chinese urban space. Urumqi was a mass of construction, as the PRC was already aspiring to make it a commercial hub for Central Asia, and the Uyghur neighborhood of the city seemed to be gradually shrinking into a sea of Han residents. However, informal Uyghur networks were still operating there, and an academic I met in a book store quickly ensured that I had a contact in my next destination, Khotan. That evening, I took a new sleeper bus that drove directly through the center of the Taklamakan desert from Urumqi in the north to Keriya in the south and then westward towards Khotan, watching gas flares glow in the middle of the desert through the night.

Once in Khotan, it was clear that the south was still overwhelmingly Uyghur, both culturally and demographically. While the city center was surrounded by lit billboards extolling propaganda about the friendship of nationalities in China, the streets were still filled with Uyghur faces. When I visited a neighboring village that was hosting its weekly bazaar day, it seemed as if the sea of Uyghurs bustling through the narrow rural road were not in the PRC at all, with no state propaganda, Chinese language, or ethnic Han in sight. In Kashgar, I spent the day with two young students of the official state madrassa who, after meeting in a local eatery, had volunteered to talk my ears off about state restrictions on religion and the ways these regulations filtered into their religious education. As I bid goodnight to my newly befriended religious students near the Id Kah Mosque, I thought I saw some plainclothes policemen approach them as they disappeared into the night, leaving me worried that I may have caused them great harm. When I left the next morning via bus to climb the Karakorum highway into Pakistan, I saw a foreboding sign of the future: a new raised four-lane highway in a state of partial construction on the deserted outskirts of Kashgar. I couldn't help but wonder if this was an omen that Kashgar, with its monuments of Central Asian architecture and winding alleyways of traditional Uyghur homes, was on a fast-track to soon look much more like the generic second-tier Chinese city that Urumqi had become.

This was the state of the region on the eve of its introduction to GWOT. It seemed as if the Chinese government had taken control of the region more than at any point in its history and was rapidly rebuilding it to prepare it for a new role as an international commercial hub. While in the south of the region it was clear that Uyghur culture remained vibrant and resilient, it seemed that the landscape was rapidly changing and the signs of future development were already apparent. The dualist strategy laid out in the infamous 1996 'Document No. 7' of intensive development and aggressive suppression of dissent and religion had been somewhat successful in pacifying the region and its population while introducing a new stage of colonization by Han settlers. In this context, the PRC would double-down on this strategy over the next decade with a new twist. Now, instead of claiming to combat 'separatism' and 'illegal religious activities,' the PRC would be suppressing dissent in the name of 'counterterrorism' and the struggle against alleged 'extremism,' efforts that had essentially been sanctioned by the international community as justifying the suspension of human rights.

STATE PROPAGANDA'S TRANSITION FROM 'SEPARATISTS' TO 'TERRORISTS' AND THE EARLY YEARS OF CHINA'S 'WAR ON TERROR'

Initially, the international recognition of ETIM as a 'terrorist threat' had little impact on Uyghurs inside their homeland. As suggested above, the state's primary 'security concern' in the Uyghur homeland after 2001, like during the 1990s, remained indigenous calls for self-determination, which the state defined broadly as any expression of nationalism or of non-state-approved religiosity. Furthermore, its strategy for dealing with this concern had also changed little, combining development and aggressive suppression of dissent. What did change was the discourse used to justify state attempts to suppress these aspirations for self-determination. Now, instead of justifying its suppression of Uyghur political voices and religious practices as combating 'separatism,' the PRC framed such efforts as 'counterterrorism,' a security position essentially endorsed by the western democracies of the world. Furthermore, there was a noticeable increase in authorities' use of the term 'extremism,' which was also a part of the GWOT discourse, as a means of signaling the ideological support of dissent, especially when it involved religious activities not sponsored by the state. For Chinese officials, these discursive shifts did not require much of a policy recalibration because PRC ideology posited that the perceived threats of 'separatism,' 'terrorism,' and 'religious extremism' were one and the same, manifestations of the 'three evils.'

However, this discursive shift, which began almost immediately after the declaration of GWOT and even before the designation of ETIM as a 'terrorist organization,' did provide a convenient justification for the intensification of the PRC's policies in the Uyghur region. The most immediate sign of such intensification was the passing of amendments to China's criminal legal code in December of 2001, three months after 9/11 and just as the PRC was ramping up its campaign for international recognition of a 'terrorist threat' from Uyghurs. While these amendments mostly amounted to adding 'terrorism crimes' with stauncher penalties to an existing list of violations under the category of 'Endangering Public Security,' Amnesty International also noted at the time that these new crimes lacked sufficient definition to be fairly punished.[1]

In the wake of these legal and discursive changes, PRC security organs launched a substantial crackdown on dissent in the Uyghur region under the guise of combating 'terrorism' and 'extremism.' This widespread campaign, the first year of which has been thoroughly documented by Amnesty International, resulted in scores of arrests of Uyghurs suspected of harboring self-determination aspirations on charges related to 'terrorism,' many carrying death sentences.[2] At the same time, security forces also launched a massive campaign in the region to limit religious observation and access to 'unofficial' information in the name of combating 'extremism.' Through this campaign, the state would arrest dozens of clerics and civilians who practiced religious activities outside official state-sponsored institutions, and would close numerous mosques deemed to have a 'bad influence' on youth due to their proximity to schools.[3] It also limited the religiosity of daily life by prohibiting certain religious rites in the life-cycle rituals of weddings, circumcisions, and funerals, by seeking to prevent Uyghurs, especially school children and government officials, from observing the Ramadan fast, and by forcing Imams to undergo additional 'political education' on Communist Party doctrine.[4] Finally, it used the justification of combating 'terrorism in the spiritual field' to confiscate un-censored publications and recordings and to arrest numerous Uyghur artists for the writing and/or reciting of poems and stories that implicitly criticized state policy or expressed Uyghur aspirations for self-determination.[5]

While all of these efforts were similar to the crackdowns in the region during the 1990s, their new framing as 'counterterrorism,' an internationally recognized justification for the suspension of human rights, facilitated a more aggressive approach towards controlling the ways that Uyghurs behaved and thought. This was a trend that would continue with increased intensity in the years that followed, especially in the southern Tarim Basin, which accounted for about 82% of the Uyghur population at the time.[6] In fact, there is evidence that Uyghurs in the Han-dominated northern areas were largely spared the worst impacts of these campaigns, and some international scholars, whose experiences had primarily been in such Han-dominated regions, suggested that a 'Uyghur-Han rapprochement' was underway in the early 2000s due to increased Uyghur integration and a noticeable decline in alleged Uyghur-perpetrated violence.[7] However, by the end of the decade, it would be clear that such a prognosis was not even appropriate for those Uyghurs living in the Han-dominant north who, while less impacted by the state's new 'counterterrorism' campaigns, were particularly subjected to the pressures of increased development in the region.

'OPEN UP THE WEST' BEFORE THE 2009 URUMQI RIOTS: INTEGRATION OR SETTLER COLONIALISM?

While state-led development in the Uyghur homeland had increased substantially in the 1990s, its benefits were simultaneously geographically and ethnically stratified.[8] Most development had occurred in the north of the region, which was where almost 88% of the region's Han lived, while the south, which was home to over 80% of the Uyghurs, was experiencing little change.[9] The PRC was well aware of this problem, which created an obvious obstacle to the region's integration. As a result, two critical development projects were launched in the 1990s to link the north and south of the region, subsequently facilitating more cohesive regional development in the future. These were the construction of the Taklamakan Desert Highway between Urumqi and the southern region of Khotan, completed in 1995, and the new rail line from Urumqi to Kashgar, completed in 1999. While these projects set the scene for much more ambitious development efforts in the south of the region during the 2000s, this would not immediately be felt during the first decade of the new millennium. Initially most development in the region in the early 2000s was financed by a large state-led campaign primarily focused on infrastructure known as 'Open Up the West,' which was launched in 2000 to address regional economic inequality in the PRC. Despite efforts to increase development in western China during the 1990s, the west still lagged significantly behind eastern China economically, and the gap was only increasing.[10]

With regards to the Uyghur homeland and the Tibetan Autonomous Region (TAR), both of which were included in this program, 'Open Up The West' also hoped to achieve political goals by helping to halt the calls for increased self-determination voiced by these regions' residents frequently during the 1990s under the assumption that macro-economic growth would ease ethnic tensions. This faith in the power of development to resolve ethnic tensions relied on the logic of outdated theories of modernization from the 1950s.[11] These theories assumed that industrialization, the introduction of new technology, the establishment of new infrastructure, and general macro-economic growth would gradually eliminate cultural differences and historical grievances by providing new economic opportunities to all.[12] However, for development to contribute to resolving ethnic tensions in the Uyghur region, it would have required addressing the region's structural racism and ethnic stratification, which the state-led and infrastructure-focused efforts of 'Open Up The West' would not do. The campaign as it was implemented in the Uyghur homeland focused almost exclusively on mega-projects related to energy, natural resource exploitation, and transportation infrastructure, both within the region and between the region and inner China.[13] According to Nicholas Becquelin, as early as 2003, Beijing 'had reported having effectively invested more than 70 billion yuan (US$8.6 billion) in building highways, power plants, dams and telecommunications facilities in Xinjiang.'[14]

These projects would undoubtedly contribute to connecting the Uyghur region with both the national and global economy over the long-term, but they did not provide significant immediate improvement in the daily lives of most Uyghurs. In fact, in many ways, this development served to aggravate the already tense relations between Uyghurs and the state. Infrastructure construction served to further militarize the region, as the paramilitary XPCC was tasked with implementing the majority of the campaign's early construction projects, which also frequently served to displace Uyghur communities involuntarily. Uyghurs also associated this development campaign with an increase in ethnic Han civilian migration to the region, especially in the north, where the majority of economic activity remained. In this context, the campaign appeared more like encroachment on a territory that most Uyghurs consider their own, rather than an attempt to improve their lives. While a small handful of Uyghurs, especially in the capital of Urumqi, certainly became wealthy at this time through the opportunities afforded by the development campaign, the majority found themselves increasingly alienated in their own homeland. Nicholas Bequelin has suggested that this result was essentially the intent of the 'Open Up the West' campaign. He describes the campaign as a continuation of integration efforts from the 1990s, but with a more explicit assimilationist intent. Without using the term 'settler colonialism,' Becquelin notes that the goals of this campaign were in line with a colonization effort, overtly promoting 'increased Han migrations into borderland national minority areas' and the 'homogenization of the Chinese nation.'[15]

Coupled with these mega-projects, the PRC was also pushing substantial urban development in the region during the early 2000s. This process was even more controversial among Uyghurs than the aforementioned infrastructure projects, since urban renewal had more direct and tangible impact on Uyghur communities and often created displacement. Furthermore, especially in the south, where cities still had a strong Uyghur character and the division of *mähällä* neighborhoods remained a part of social structure and social capital, urban development had the potential for cultural destruction.

The most emblematic case of such displacement and cultural destruction during the first decade of the 2000s was in the city of Kashgar, viewed by Uyghurs as a historical center of their urban culture. In Kashgar, the municipal government of the city had already begun an urban renewal campaign in the first years of the 'Open Up the West' campaign. Given its geographic location along routes to the west and south-west, Kashgar was strategically positioned to become a center of the PRC's regional trade, production, and commerce that could rival Urumqi in the north. However, the heart of the city contained most of the best-preserved examples of traditional Central Asian urban residential architecture in the world, especially in the form of its old city's labyrinth of mud-brick houses connected by narrow alleyways. In order to modernize the city and turn it into an international hub of commercial activity, the local government had decided that this old city would need to be demolished. While this project would raise concerns internationally for its destruction of important historical sites, for Uyghurs in Kashgar, its impact would also include involuntary displacement and the destruction of social capital.[16] As an excellent report by the Uyghur Human Rights Project (UHRP) on the Chinese State's demolition of Uyghur communities points out, not only were the local residents of the old city not consulted with regards to the development plans, but the removal from their homes was accompanied by a large armed police presence that ensured no resistance to relocation.[17]

While the destruction of Kashgar's old city was the most publicized manifestation of the PRC's urban development in the region during the first decade of GWOT, it was not a unique case. In an effort to modernize the region's cities, traditional Uyghur communities were being displaced and symbols of Uyghur culture were being erased throughout the area's urban landscape. In Urumqi, a substantial development project during the early 2000s turned the Erdaoqiao neighborhood, the primary Uyghur community in the city, into a tourist attraction and a center of formal commerce, establishing a new expansive and sanitized bazar boasting the 'largest market of ethnic minority goods in Xinjiang,' an 'ethnic dance ballroom,' and numerous new commercial buildings.[18] In the process, many were displaced from this area of the city, further marginalizing the Uyghurs' position in this long Han-dominated city. Similarly, Ildiko Bellar-Hann provides an account of how the state in the city of Kumul razed parts of a Muslim cemetery at the same time to facilitate the development of a tourism center around a former Qing palace.[19]

ASSIMILATING UYGHURS IN THE NAME OF MODERNIZATION AND COUNTERTERRORISM

If many Uyghurs recognized these development projects as part of a creeping settler colonization of their homeland, the simultaneous projects to 'integrate' the Uyghur people that took place during the early 2000s were even more colonial in their appearance. While in the 1990s, the state had sought to entice Uyghurs in the north to 'integrate' into Han culture through economic opportunities, in the early 2000s state-sponsored programs were explicitly created for this purpose. While most of these programs remained nominally 'voluntary' and driven by incentives, the harsh crackdown on expressions of Uyghur dissent in the name of 'counterterrorism' added coercive dimensions to their implementation, especially in the rural south.

Probably the most substantial of these assimilationist policies during the early 2000s was what the PRC refers to as its 'bilingual' education program in the region. Beginning in the 1990s, the state invested significant money into promoting Chinese-language instruction throughout the Uyghur region.[20] In 2002, the state closed the Uyghur language track at the premiere higher educational institution in the region, Xinjiang University, in all subjects except Uyghur language and literature.[21] This set the stage for the decision of the regional government in March 2004 that all students at all educational levels in the province would mandatorily receive instruction in Mandarin Chinese. Officially, this was promoted as a 'bi-lingual education' policy where non-Han students could be instructed in both Chinese and their own language, but, as Adrienne Dwyer has suggested, this was actually a 'covert policy of monolingual education' because the state had consolidated most non-Han language schools into Chinese-language schools, subsequently removing the curriculum in other languages almost entirely.[22]

As Dwyer further demonstrates, these policies were accompanied by reductions in the number of publications produced in non-Chinese languages as well as by a trend to produce periodicals plus radio and television programming in these languages that were merely translated versions of Chinese-language material produced in inner China.[23] As a result, not only was the Uyghur language slowly disappearing from the region's media, but even narratives with Uyghur cultural content were being wiped out.

A more aggressive educational program that was offered to select minority students involved boarding schools in inner China, where all instruction was in Chinese. These schools, known as the 'Xinjiang Class,' were begun in 2000 with the opening of twelve institutions in different regions of China proper.[24] By 2006, they had expanded to 26 different locations where they educated 10,000 students.[25] The schools were focused particularly on political indoctrination and enforced a strict atmosphere of control that one former student compared to a prison.[26] Part of this political indoctrination included overt attempts to strip students of any religious beliefs, such as only giving one day off for major Muslim holidays, during which time students were required to partake in secular celebrations and refrain from prayer.[27]

While the state framed these education policies as a means of increasing Uyghur employability and integration in the PRC, they had substantial impact on Uyghurs' identity and social relations as well. While the policies for elementary and primary education would take time to implement, and their impact would only be fully noticeable a decade later, they were laying the groundwork for the creation of the first generation of Uyghurs who would be assumed to be completely literate in the Chinese language. Especially in southern rural areas where Uyghurs had poor if any Chinese-language skills, this would eventually drive a wedge between the youth and their parents' generation. Timothy Grose's research on the 'Xinjiang Class' schools suggests that this program's results were even more immediate if they were limited to a small number of Uyghur children. As Grose notes, these schools created particularly intense identity dilemmas for their students, who found themselves after graduation detached from Uyghur culture (sometimes not even able to speak Uyghur well) while also not quite being accepted by Han as one of their own.[28]

Another state effort to transform Uyghurs during the early 2000s involved sending workers to inner China to work and live in factory dormitories with Han. One of these programs, apparently hoping to increase inter-ethnic marriage, sent young Uyghur women from rural areas in the south of the Uyghur region to the interior of China to work in factories accompanied by language training and ideological courses.[29] Based on local news reports from the region, the UHRP was able to infer that as many as 10,000 Uyghur women between the ages of 18 and 20 from rural areas in the south participated in this program during 2006 and 2007 alone.[30] While these programs were touted as economic opportunities for Uyghurs, official accounts also noted that they would help to incorporate rural Uyghurs into the 'the "great socialist family" of the Chinese motherland' by improving their 'thinking and consciousness' as well as their manners and civility.[31] Technically, these programs were voluntary but, given the population they targeted in rural Uyghur areas in the south, it can be assumed that denying participation would bring one's family under suspicion of 'extremist' and 'terrorist' sympathies.

Thousands of Uyghurs participated in these educational and work programs during the first decade of the 2000s, but the programs still only touched a small percentage of the Uyghur population. Among those who did participate, most did not subsequently jettison their Uyghur identity or proclaim loyalty to the PRC, and many reasserted their identity through nationalism and religion.[32] In short, these programs did not really serve their intended purpose of further integrating Uyghurs into a Han-dominant culture. At most, they were able to do so for a small Uyghur elite in Urumqi and perhaps in a few other urban areas, but the majority of the population likely viewed these efforts as yet one more way that the state was seeking to destroy their culture.

Despite the ineffectiveness of such integration and assimilation measures in creating 'loyal' Uyghurs, and the pressures created by the development projects of 'Open Up the West,' there were remarkably few violent incidents reported inside the Uyghur region during the early 2000s. Justin Hastings, points out that, in contrast to the 1990s, violence during 2000 to 2008 was almost non-existent.[33] Similarly, Gardner Bovingdon's list of protest and violent incidents for this time hardly includes any that could be unequivocally categorized as acts of political violence.[34] While this paucity of violence was likely due largely to the increased security environment in the region, it also suggests that, contrary to PRC rhetoric, there was no violent 'terrorist threat' to the security of China at this time. However, it was also clear that the situation in the Uyghur region was increasingly tense. Han in-migration was expanding, Han-focused urban re-development was dislocating many Uyghurs and removing signs of Uyghur culture from the landscape, and the state was increasingly adopting assimilationist policies. For a small number of Uyghurs, this situation was offering new opportunities to enrich themselves, but for the majority, it was creating an environment of alienation. It would only be a matter of time before this alienation was to explode into violent rage.

THE TURNING POINTS: THE 2008 OLYMPICS AND THE 2009 URUMQI RIOTS

In the run-up to the Beijing Summer Olympics of 2008, the PRC increased its security in all areas of society to prevent any disruption of the games, and the Minister of Public Security announced that 'terrorism,' assumed to be specifically related to Uyghurs, represented 'the greatest threat to the Olympic Games.'[35] Given the paucity of violence involving Uyghurs since the 1990s, this seemed to be an odd concern to many international observers. Chinese authorities claimed to have raided a large Uyghur 'terrorist camp' in early 2007 in a mountainous area near Kashgar, but there was much skepticism about these claims. According to Hastings, a Spanish journalist had reported that the incident had actually been a dispute about illegal mining that turned violent and ended up in the death of a policeman, which authorities covered up as being related to 'terrorism.'[36] Furthermore, virtually nothing had been heard of the activities of ETIM for the first seven years of GWOT.

However, Beijing's rhetoric about the threat that 'terrorism' posed to the games increased significantly in the spring of 2008. This was probably, at least partially, initiated by the video released on 1 March 2008 by TIP showing Abdul Häq threatening to attack the games.[37] While the video received little initial attention from international journalists or analysts, a series of alleged foiled 'terrorist' attacks announced by authorities in March and April did. First, on 7 March 2008, Chinese authorities grounded a plane traveling from Urumqi to Beijing on which a Uyghur woman was alleged to have planned an attack with gasoline canisters.[38] Then, in April, the PRC announced that it had broken up two other alleged 'terrorist cells' in the Uyghur homeland since January and had apprehended a total of 45 Uyghurs, allegedly with bomb-making materials intended for use in attacks on the Olympics.[39] However, little information was available about these incidents, and international journalists and analysts speculated whether they had even occurred as described. Some journalists believed that these allegedly foiled plots were a creation of the government to send a message of strength as a means of deterring any attempted disruption of the games.[40] Other observers, who took the claims at face-value, noted that the explosives reported seized from the alleged 'terrorist cells' were minimal and insufficient for even constructing a car bomb, suggesting a gross over-exaggeration of the threat.[41]

Nonetheless, the hype created by the PRC about the alleged risk of 'terrorism' disrupting the games would escalate in coming months. Bus explosions in Shanghai and Kunming in May and July respectively would raise more speculation about this threat, especially given that TIP had issued an ominous video claiming responsibility for both blasts.[42] While the Chinese government officially denied that these blasts had anything to do with Uyghurs, the anxiousness about this alleged threat only grew in the country as the games approached.[43]

As a result, the PRC adopted increasingly draconian security measures towards the Uyghurs in the months leading up to the Olympics. These heightened security efforts explicitly profiled Uyghurs as a people and effectively isolated them from contact with the games' international audience. This 'quarantining' of Uyghurs in advance of the Olympics was especially visible in Beijing, where Uyghurs were reportedly refused hotel rooms, and local sources suggested that as many as 4,000 to 5,000 were either detained or expelled from the city in the months prior to the games.[44] These measures were not based on suspicions about specific Uyghur individuals, but targeted the entire ethnic group, sending a clear message to Uyghurs that they were not welcome to be part of the largest international event in China in PRC history. The Chinese state employed similar exclusionary measures against Tibetans during the Olympics, but as one report at the time suggested, 'the Uyghurs are under greater pressure ... because the government sees them not only as potential protesters but also as potential terrorists.'[45] Furthermore, these exclusionary measures in Beijing and elsewhere in inner China were accompanied by increased security efforts inside the Uyghur homeland, where virtually any Uyghur displaying open religiosity or animosity towards the state was profiled as a potential 'terrorist' and monitored closely for the duration of the games.

Two violent events did occur in the Uyghur homeland during the week of the Olympics' opening ceremonies in August 2008, but these incidents were more likely a response to the tight controls put on Uyghurs at this time than they were premeditated attempts to disrupt the games. The first incident took place in Kashgar on 4 August, a few days ahead of the opening ceremonies. According to official accounts, two Uyghurs stole a truck and allegedly rammed it into a group of soldiers during their morning march, throwing explosives and stabbing the soldiers with machetes, reportedly killing sixteen of them.[46] However, there also remained much speculation about the accuracy of these reports. In September, *The New York Times* published a lengthy article drawing on interviews with western tourists who saw the attack from their hotel room windows.[47] According to these eyewitnesses, a truck had rammed into the group of soldiers, but no explosions were heard. Furthermore, they suggested that the men seen stabbing soldiers with machetes were also wearing military uniforms.[48] Regardless of what really happened on 4 August in Kashgar, the incident served to feed the hysteria surrounding the alleged 'terrorist threat' to the games.

The second incident took place in the city of Kucha on 10 August, two days after the opening ceremonies. According to Chinese government accounts, a group of Uyghurs commandeered a taxi or taxis in the morning and allegedly proceeded to throw explosives from the car(s) at police patrols, the Public Security Bureau building, the industry and commerce administration building, and possibly several other buildings, killing police and injuring civilians.[49] When the alleged perpetrators were confronted, the government said that eight

Uyghurs assailants were killed, two were captured, two blew themselves up, and three others allegedly escaped.[50]

Little is known about the motivations for this violence. Unlike the bus explosions in Shanghai and Kunming, TIP did not claim to have anything to do with these apparently rudimentary attacks. Furthermore, it is unclear whether the acts of violence were meant to be political statements about Uyghur self-determination timed for the Olympics, acts of rage in response to the massive crackdown on Uyghurs during the games, or a reaction to something else entirely. Regardless, they were significant given the relative lack of reports of violent resistance from Uyghurs since the 2002 international recognition of ETIM as a 'terrorist organization.' Taken together with the threatening videos produced by TIP, these acts of violence would only invite more scrutiny of Uyghurs from state security organs in the coming months.

Following this violence, the Chinese Communist Party Secretary of the region, Wang Lequan, declared a 'life or death struggle' against 'terrorists.'[51] The aggressive crackdown that followed reportedly mobilized some 200,000 public security officers and armed police and included official orders to punish the families and neighbors of those suspected of being involved in the Kashgar and Kucha violence. Reportedly, an Imam in Kucha was even given a life-sentence prison term because one of the alleged attackers had attended his mosque.[52] According to official accounts, nearly 1,300 Uyghurs were arrested for 'state security crimes' in 2008, including on charges of 'terrorism,' substantially more than in previous years.[53] The oppressive environment that these measures cultivated among Uyghurs over the course of 2008 undoubtedly contributed to the tensions that exploded in Urumqi in the summer of 2009.

Less than a year after the opening ceremonies of the Beijing games, the city of Urumqi witnessed what was likely the worst incident of ethnic violence in the history of the PRC. While this incident had nothing to do with an alleged 'terrorism threat' or with any sort of premeditated violence, it would further fuel both state and Han citizen fears of Uyghurs as an inherently 'dangerous' population. As a result, it would begin a period of unprecedented repression in the Uyghur homeland that would only destabilize the region further.

This incident began in the evening of 5 July 2009 as a peaceful protest led by Uyghur youth who were demanding justice for the brutal murder of two Uyghur workers at a toy factory in Shaoguan city in China's southern Guangdong province.[54] The murders had apparently transpired during a violent clash where Han workers ambushed sleeping Uyghur workers in their dormitory after rumors had spread on the internet that Uyghur male workers had raped a Han woman.[55] This incident in Guangdong was also clearly linked to state development policies since the Uyghurs in the factory were presumably working there under one of the state-promoted work programs for Uyghurs in inner China that had been developed in the early 2000s.

The protest itself was substantial and unusual for the Uyghur region of China where, unlike in inner China, such public expressions of discontent were severely punished. However, it was also unique in that the protestors who organized it were among those Uyghurs who had chosen paths of integration into the PRC and were placing faith in the Chinese Communist Party (CCP) to apply justice for the incident in Guangdong. In fact, videos of the initial protest showed what appeared to be Uyghur university students carrying PRC flags and signs in Chinese at the front of the march, appealing to authorities on the basis of their status as citizens of China, not merely as Uyghurs.

The exact circumstances under which the protest became violent is unknown. Chinese authorities suggested that the violence was premeditated and had been orchestrated by the WUC leader Rabiya Kadeer from abroad.[56] However, most other reports suggest that the violence was a spontaneous response to security forces' aggressive attempts to stop the marchers from advancing, quickly spreading beyond the protestors to include Uyghur bystanders unleashing their anger at the state and the dominant Han ethnic group. The violence itself was raw and intense as Uyghurs throughout the city set vehicles on fire, destroyed stores, and began attacking Han civilians, leaving a reported 156 people dead.[57] The descriptions of the intense violence that took place were testament to how tense relations between

Uyghurs and Han had become in the preceding decade. The next morning, groups of Han vigilantes responded by attacking Uyghurs, allegedly while security forces looked on passively and perhaps even provided these vigilantes with weapons, and in the evening security forces swept through Uyghur neighborhoods hauling away suspected participants in the violence.[58] The violence continued for two days after the initial riot broke out; there remains no reliable account of how many were killed over the three-day period, but it is assumed that casualties were at least several hundred.

In many ways, the violent passion unleashed in Urumqi in July 2009 was a boiling over of the tensions that development, settler colonialism, and Uyghur marginalization in the region had fostered. As Rian Thum pointed out at the time, this violence marked a clear change in the shape of Uyghur resistance to Chinese rule that had now become focused on the Han as a people rather than just on the government.[59] At the same time, it also marked a clear change in the way that Han migrants to the region viewed the local Uyghur population. If the Han had long held racist stereotypes of the Uyghurs as backward and lazy, now they also considered this people to be an inherent danger. Combined with the fears of 'terrorism' allegedly associated with Uyghurs that had spread through China during the Olympics, these attitudes would facilitate among Han an increasingly exclusionary attitude towards the Uyghurs. All Uyghurs had suddenly become 'dangerous' and worthy of particular scrutiny. As Tom Cliff has suggested, for many Han in the region, the Urumqi riots, frequently referred to simply as '7/5,' unleashed an unprecedented demonization of the Uyghurs, which can be clearly compared to the Islamophobia that spread in the US after 9/11.[60] This response from the Han population within the Uyghur homeland put increased pressure on local authorities to do something about the 'dangerous' Uyghur people, and the state responded to these demands aggressively.

The official response to the 2009 riots was to further increase security measures in the region, including a virtual state of martial law for the next year. This encompassed a heavy security presence in Urumqi for months afterwards and stepped up security operations elsewhere in the region. Extensive searches for Uyghurs alleged to be involved in the violence were carried out, including door-to-door searches of Uyghur-populated apartment buildings and neighbor-hoods.[61] The number of those arrested and jailed in connection with the riots remains unknown, but the *Financial Times* reported that at least 4,000 Uyghurs had already been arrested within two weeks of the events.[62] Arrests of Uyghurs accused of involvement in the riots continued for months afterwards in both Urumqi and in other areas of the Uyghur region.[63] Among the reportedly thousands detained in connection with the riots, a substantial number remain unac-counted for, leading Human Rights Watch to categorize them as 'enforced disappearances.'[64]

Additionally, tight restrictions were placed on communications throughout the region. Immediately after the riots began, the govern-ment shut down the internet locally, only restoring it incrementally between December 2009 and May 2010. Cell phone text messag-ing was prevented until January 2010, and international phone calls were blocked until December 2009.[65] In short, state security organs put the entire region under lock-down for almost an entire year fol-lowing the riots.

While the violence in Urumqi was clearly neither a 'terrorist attack' nor related to Uyghurs' Muslim faith, the security response included more searches for alleged 'terrorists' and 'extremists' as well as a general crackdown on all religiously inclined Uyghurs, especially in the rural south of the region, whose migrants to Urumqi were blamed by many Han for the violence. During this time, the state increased its oversight of sermons given at mosques – requiring Imams to cover themes of importance to PRC policy, and making it prohibitively difficult to perform the *Haj* pilgrimage – and sought to more aggressively prevent religious teachings in private homes.[66] Unfortunately, given the almost complete information blackout to which the Uyghur homeland was subjected in the year following the Urumqi riots, the full extent of these measures remains unknown.

EXPEDIATED DEVELOPMENT, 2010–2012

Despite the apparent links between the pressures of development in the region and the 2009 riots, the state did not respond by seeking to mitigate these pressures, at least as they impacted Uyghurs. Rather, the state continued to view the riots as an indication of 'underdevelopment,' and subsequently responded by only seeking to increase its development efforts. Within a month of the riots, then CCP General Secretary Hu Jintao announced that the only solution to the 'problems' in the Uyghur region of China was to 'expedite development.'[67] The new Party Secretary appointed in the region after the violence, Zhang Chunxian, supported this assertion, noting that the state would ensure 'leapfrog development and lasting stability,' suggesting that these two concepts are inextricably linked.[68] In this sense, the government seemed to be doubling down once again on its trust in an outdated form of modernization theory, believing that more economic growth would inevitably lead to improved ethnic relations, if not the disappearance of ethnic difference entirely. However, the ways in which this was done also suggested that the PRC was looking to an even older model of development and ethnic integration for its inspiration, that of settler colonization.

In late 2009, Beijing sent three investigation teams to the region to examine ways to 'expediate development,' replaced the Party Secretary of the region, and began planning a large Xinjiang Work Forum for May of 2010.[69] This first Xinjiang Work Forum, in turn, laid out a new and more aggressive vision for the region that sought to both stimulate development and establish stability. While this strategy's goals differed little from those that the PRC had been pursuing in the region since the 1990s, its more aggressive approach was more overtly assimilationist, especially in its attempts to change the landscape and demographics of the region.

This aggressive strategy of economic and cultural integration also became more directed towards the Uyghur-dominant south after the Work Forum. While development had increased in the urban areas of the Uyghur-majority south during the first decade of the 2000s, these efforts at best maintained the development gap that had existed between north and south at the turn of the millennium. Likewise, despite attempts to implement mandatory education in the Chinese language and entice Uyghurs from the south to work at factories in inner China, the population of the southern Tarim Basin remained resistant to assimilation and the adoption of the Chinese language. Now, the PRC hoped to expedite development and assimilation efforts in the south. However, for many Uyghurs in the south, this would appear to be an intensification of the state colonization of the region, only provoking more resistance.

The approach for developing this region economically was somewhat innovative. While its logic of integration and the dissolution of dissent was still based in 1950s modernization theory, if not Marxism to which that theory was a response, its implementation was decidedly neo-liberal in a very Chinese way, and its outcomes looked more like the settler colonialism of the nineteenth century. This program was called the 'Pairing Assistance Program' (PAP) and partnered economically successful regions elsewhere in China with 'underdeveloped' locations in the Uyghur region, primarily in the south. The program initially involved 19 Chinese provinces and municipalities outside the region, all of which gained particular benefits from the region's oil and gas, pledging to contribute 0.3–0.6% of their fiscal revenue for 2011–2020 to the development of their corresponding 'sister' regions in the Uyghur region, mostly funneled through companies located in these 'partner provinces.'[70]

Thomas Cliff has asserted that this program 'epitomizes the logic of integration' since it brings the power of administrations in inner China into the development of the Uyghur region.[71] Cliff suggests that this was done as much for reassurances of stability to the Han migrants who had come to the region in the previous decades as it was for its effectiveness in driving development. With the Han population having lost confidence in local PRC administrations to protect them from the increasingly 'demonized' Uyghurs after the Urumqi riots, it was hoped that existing Han migrants would be encouraged to stay and new ones would be enticed to come to the region if the administrations of prominent Chinese cities like Shanghai and

Shenzhen were involved in planning local development. Indeed, the PAP would lead to massive urban development in the Uyghur cities of the south and appeared to be helping tip the demographic balance in these urban centers increasingly towards the Han.

The other new economic policy to come out of the Work Forum was the establishment of 'Special Economic Trading Areas' (SETAs) in Kashgar near the Kyrgyzstan border and in Khorgus on the Kazakhstan border respectively. This effort made obvious sense in the context of the PRC's use of the Uyghur region as a commercial bridge to Central and South Asia, especially given that many of the infrastructure projects connecting the region to neighboring countries during the early 2000s were already entering China at these two outward-looking geographic nodes.[72]

If the location of these two proposed SETAs made strategic sense, the context in which they were to be built were very different. Khorgus was a remote and lazy border town that could easily be built up from scratch, but Kashgar was a densely populated Uyghur-majority city that was critical to Uyghur history and identity. Thus, developing Kashgar into a SETA would necessarily involve displacement and destruction of what already existed in the city in addition to massive development of a new city. It is not surprising in this context that the PRC chose Shenzhen, China's first 'Special Economic Zone' during the 1980s, to partner with Kashgar in the PAP. Furthermore, Kashgar was slated to receive nearly half of the PAP assistance for the entire region during the program's first years.[73] As one observer at the time suggested, this effort reflected a 'frenzy to develop Kashgar in the model of Shenzhen.'[74]

In addition to the destruction of the old city and the relocation of the majority of its Uyghur inhabitants to concrete apartment buildings, the state was busily focused on developing manufacturing in the city, with plans to create an industrial park 160 square kilometers in size.[75] These developments inevitably pushed many of the native Uyghur population further into the margins of the city, if not outside it entirely. In fact, the announcement of Kashgar's future role in the region immediately fostered a housing boom, and the majority of new apartments were bought before completion by speculators from China's interior who hoped to profit on Kashgar's future role as a manufacturing and commercial center.[76]

It is important to recognize that this massive development push in the Uyghur region after 2010 benefited numerous Uyghur elites economically. As Alessandro Rippa and Rune Steenberg have pointed out in an article about Kashgar's development at this time, the money pouring into the city gave many Uyghurs opportunities to engage more in the formal economy and made some Uyghurs extremely wealthy.[77] However, the development was also very evidently marginalizing Uyghur influence on the city's overall development: large Chinese companies began to dominate the economy; the demographic balance of the city was shifting; and the Uyghur cultural characteristics of the city that had long distinguished it began to disappear. Furthermore, most of the city's inhabitants would benefit little if at all from the city's transformation, particularly given the discriminatory hiring practices of many of the Chinese companies involved in the development. Despite labor laws to the contrary, it had become increasingly prevalent after the 2009 riots for companies and even state institutions to advertise for employment with stipulations that only Han need apply.[78] Although these blatantly discriminatory hiring practices were justified by employers as linguistically driven, given the low-level of most Uyghurs' knowledge of the Chinese language, they were primarily propelled by the growing Han fear of Uyghurs as 'dangerous' as well as by the long-held stereotype among Han of Uyghurs as 'lazy' and 'unproductive.'

In addition to being shut out of major sectors of employment in the economy, many Uyghurs were also being further physically displaced by the region's development boom. As a result, many of the PAP projects involved significant efforts to build new housing stock. For example, the city of Shanghai, which had been partnered with the Kashgar Prefecture outside the city limits, pledged to 'complete resettlement projects for 80,000 households' covering four different counties in three years.[79] Additionally, regional authorities pledged to 'transform' 1.5 million houses throughout the region between 2010 and 2015, primarily in the Uyghur neighborhoods of Urumqi, Kashgar, Turpan, Hotan, Ghulja, Kumul, Aksu, and Korla.[80] While housing was usually provided to those Uyghurs who were displaced by such development, the new housing was not shaped around traditional Uyghur community structures, thus helping to break down the social capital of densely Uyghur-populated neighborhoods that had long existed in the region.

Finally, this new strategy for the region also involved continued and more intense efforts to assimilate Uyghurs into a Han-dominant culture through educational and work programs. The Work Forum, for example, had pledged to fully realize the 'bilingual education' initiative started several years earlier, with the goal of having all Uyghur children speaking fluent Chinese by 2020.[81] Likewise, enrollments in the 'Xinjiang Class' schools would steadily increase between 2010 and 2012.[82] While the work programs that brought Uyghurs to do manufacturing jobs in China's interior were suspended after the events in Guandong that sparked the Urumqi riots, the Party continued to explore ways to improve this program, which would once again be rolled out with more intensity and increased assimilationist aims after 2012.

In many ways, these post-2009 development efforts represented just another chapter in what Nicholas Becquelin has called the 'staged development' of China's Uyghur region, the logical conclusion of which is the complete integration of this region and its people into modern China.[83] However, the new stage that emerged from the Urumqi riots and that was increasingly focused on the region's Uyghur-dominant southern oases also looked even more like settler colonization than had previous development stages. As Thomas Cliff has stated, this was an attempt 'to drive the region's progression from ... a "frontier of control" (military occupation) towards a "frontier of settlement" (Han civilian occupation).'[84]

As such, these efforts also complemented a new assimilationist trend in the PRC's general relationship with non-Han people.[85] Since the early 2000s, there had been debates within the CCP policy community, especially championed by the ethnic Hui scholar Ma Rong, about the appropriateness of the ethnic autonomy model for the administration of China's territories, arguing that this model had led to the dissolution of the Soviet Union and Yugoslavia. Rong, and others aligned with him, argued that China should adopt a 'melting pot' approach to promoting a singular civic identity in place of ethnic distinctiveness and autonomy, a position that would subsequently be known as 'Second Generation Nationalities Policy.'[86] While these approaches to ethnic policy had previously been viewed as marginal to Party debates, after the Urumqi riots this was starting to change, and they were particularly apparent in the policies to come out of the Xinjiang Work Forum. In many ways, the Uyghur region would provide the perfect testing ground for many of the policies associated with the 'Second Generation Nationalities Policies,' which fit in well with the region's increasingly apparent Han settler colonization.

UYGHUR RESISTANCE AND STATE COUNTERTERRORISM, 2010–2012

In addition to these assimilationist development policies, the Work Forum also ushered in a new era of securitization in the Uyghur homeland. Following the violent and extensive crackdown on Uyghurs during the first year after the riots, the PRC would begin implementing a much-enhanced security environment in the region in 2010. This was the 'stability' portion of the state's post-riot strategy of 'leapfrog development and lasting stability,' and would be articulated increasingly in terms of 'counterterrorism.' The pressures that this increased security would place on Uyghurs, especially in the rural south, would be particularly intense, and predictably only led to a rise of Uyghur-initiated violence targeting the state.

By the first anniversary of the 2009 Urumqi riots, local officials reported that '40,000 high-definition surveillance cameras with riot-proof protective shells had been installed throughout the region.'[87] In Urumqi, there were also reports that city officials were placing permanent barriers between Uyghur and Han neighborhoods.[88] However, in the Uyghur-dominated south of the region, the environment was particularly tense. There were limits imposed on traveling outside one's home region, frequent checkpoints between cities, and ethnically profiled random searches. Furthermore, Uyghur refugees from rural areas, with whom I spoke in Turkey in 2016, repeatedly told me that they had been put under constant surveillance by local authorities for several years after the 2009 riots due to their profiling as particularly 'religious' Uyghurs. These refugees, who said their situation was akin to house arrest, reported that these measures were the primary reasons they fled the country. In addition to these efforts to monitor and control the general Uyghur population, even more substantial controls on the practice of Islam were established. Many of these controls utilized public institutions, including schools, hospitals, and mosques, to regulate Uyghurs' public behavior, beliefs, and dress, to prevent Uyghur children from embracing Islam, and to control the messages they received from their own religious leaders.[89]

In the face of this intensifying securitization, Uyghur violent resistance to police and security forces would soon become a common occurrence, especially in the Uyghur-majority south. The first report of such violent resistance since the Urumqi riots was an alleged bombing of a police station in Aksu in August 2010, but similar events would be reported over the next several years with increased frequency. While information about this violence remains limited, the majority of incidents through 2012 appear to have been clashes between Uyghurs and law enforcement officers.[90] Although Chinese officials questionably labeled all of these incidents as 'terrorist acts,' most do not fit this description per this book's working definition. Rather, they appear more like reactions to equally violent security actions in the region, and many of them obviously were provoked by the invasive security that would increasingly blanket the region.

The most publicized of these violent incidents would be a series of alleged attacks on police and security forces in Kashgar and Khotan in July of 2011. The first of these incidents occurred in the city of Khotan on 18 July. While the details are disputed, it appears that a group of Uyghur men clashed with police at a station in the city, killing several of them, taking others hostage, and setting the station on fire.[91] The *South China Morning Post* later reported that the impetus for the violent incident had been a recent ban on veiling and the wearing of black clothing among Uyghur women in the area.[92] In the end, the death toll was placed at 18, but 14 of these were from among the alleged Uyghur attackers. *The Guardian* would term the incident 'one of the deadliest encounters' the region had seen in recent years.[93] Within two weeks, a series of violent incidents also took place in the city of Kashgar. On a Saturday night around midnight, there appeared to be an unsuccessful attempt at moving explosives into the city, and a mini-van exploded. Two Uyghur men who were apparently involved fled and stole a truck that they then drove through a crowded street of food stalls, eventually jumping off to attack people in the crowd, including police.[94] Seven people were allegedly killed, including one of the purported perpetrators, and some 22 were injured. The next day, a riot broke out that appeared to begin with an attack on a restaurant where several Uyghur men allegedly threw hand-made explosives and used knives to attack people.[95] After the two days of violence had ended, some 20 people had been killed, including several of the alleged attackers.

While not claiming credit for the incidents, TIP issued a video about this series of alleged attacks in Kashgar and Khotan, calling them jihad operations. Furthermore, it was this particular video where TIP was able to document that one of the participants in the Kashgar violence had in fact been in Waziristan in 2006.[96] In the video, Abdushukur, who had taken over in Abdul Häq's place as *Emir* of TIP, read a statement that pointed to the many assimilationist policies in the region as reason for the action, including the education and work programs as well as the influx of Han migrants.[97]

The timing of these incidents within a month of each other combined with the video from TIP showing one of those involved in Waziristan five years earlier appeared to seriously concern authorities. As a result, in the wake of this violence, the PRC even uncharacteristically criticized Pakistan, one of its closest allies, for harboring Uyghur 'terrorists,' and Pakistan responded by promising to assist China in its struggle against the alleged 'terrorist threat' posed by Uyghurs in all ways possible.[98] Predictably, the local Chinese administration in the Uyghur region also responded by increasing its monitoring of Uyghurs and announcing a new campaign to police religious behavior in the name of combating 'extremism.'[99] However, it appears that not all locals were convinced of the state narrative that international 'terrorists' had carried out the violence.

As one Uyghur, interviewed by *The Wall Street Journal* in Kashgar at the time stated, 'they say the people came from Pakistan; they say they were international terrorists, but that's not true; they were local people angry with the government and with the Han Chinese.'[100] This statement, while completely anecdotal, is telling about the extent of influence from TIP in the region at the time. Indeed, TIP had been making videos promoting jihad in the Uyghur homeland throughout 2010, and it is possible that some of these videos had gotten into the hands of local Uyghurs, especially after the 2010 establishment of 3G cellular networks and the proliferation of smart phones among Uyghurs. However, it was clear that Uyghurs in the southern Tarim Basin had plenty to be angry about and did not need any provocation from TIP to engage in violent resistance.

Violence similar to that which took place in Khotan and Kashgar in the summer of 2011 would gradually become more commonplace over the next two years. Furthermore, each time violence occurred, the heavy-handed response of the state would only make matters worse. Often what was framed as a 'terrorist attack' by authorities at this time was really armed self-defense against police and security forces, which were seeking to aggressively apprehend Uyghurs they viewed as 'disloyal' to the state, often merely determined by their religiosity. This appears to have been the case in the next major violent event that would take place in December 2011 in the Guma region outside Khotan. It was reported that a group of young Uyghur men had been pursued by police as they allegedly planned to go to Pakistan, and, in the midst of a confrontation with police, the Uyghurs took hostages and eventually got into an armed conflict with the police.[101] At the end of the confrontation, seven of the Uyghurs were dead, in addition to one policeman.[102]

Even by the sparse information coming out of the region, it was apparent that such incidents only increased in frequency in 2012, involving violence initiated by both Uyghurs and police. In February, Uyghur youth in Karghilik allegedly killed 13 Han migrants to the area on the street for unknown reasons, and the police would kill all seven of the alleged attackers.[103] In March, police killed four Uyghurs during a 'raid' on what the state deemed to be an 'illegal religious gathering' in Korla but may have merely been a group of Uyghurs praying.[104] In June, six Uyghurs were apprehended for allegedly planning to hijack a plane from Khotan to Urumqi, but the details and circumstances surrounding this incident are contested. Also in June, a 'raid,' on what authorities called an 'illegal religious school' in Khotan, but which may have been just an unregistered Uyghur school, led to severe burn injuries to multiple Uyghur children.[105] In August, authorities jailed 20 Uyghurs on charges of 'separatism' for information they had posted on the internet.[106] In October, clashes between Uyghurs and Han civilians in Korla led to invasive police sweeps throughout the city's Uyghur residential neighborhoods, and a Uyghur carried out an alleged suicide attack on a border post near Karghilik on the country's 'National Day.'[107] In short, the situation in the south of the Uyghur homeland was quickly evolving into an escalating conflict between Uyghur citizens and security organs. However, the nature of this violence suggested that this conflict was not led by any organized insurgency, let alone by an international 'terrorist organization,' but was most likely an outgrowth of growing tensions between an increasingly invasive security apparatus and Uyghurs in the region, which was further aggravated by the state's assimilationist policies and increased colonization of the region.

This increase in violence facilitated an escalating cycle of repression followed by violence and more repression throughout much of the southern Tarim Basin in the following years. In the wake of every act of violence or in advance of important public events, the state increased its security presence, recruited 'volunteer' security officers to monitor public places, established numerous checkpoints, and conducted widespread security sweeps in local Uyghur communities.[108] These security measures also included explicit efforts to police public expressions of Islam.[109] In turn, after each of these intensive security lock-downs, the incidents of violence only increased.

In many ways, this emerging self-perpetuating conflict between Uyghurs and security organs in the south was a logical outcome of the first decade of GWOT in the Uyghur homeland. A dangerous combination of the Han-dominated state's settler colonialization aspirations in the region with the Islamophobic and security-obsessed narrative of GWOT had created a situation where Uyghurs and the state were pitted against each other. One of the few attempts by Uyghurs during the decade to peacefully protest PRC policies in Urumqi in 2009 was repressed by security organs and spiraled into tragic violence, clearly showing that there was no political space for Uyghurs to voice their concerns about the situation peacefully. The handful of Uyghur self-proclaimed jihadists in Waziristan that represented TIP sought to insert themselves into this situation through prolific video production, but they were really a sideshow to what was happening on the ground in the region, serving mostly to justify increased state violence against Uyghurs.

This self-perpetuating cycle of violence in the south of the Uyghur homeland would continue over the next several years and create a 'self-fulfilling prophecy' of Uyghur militancy both inside and outside China, only providing the state further justification for its suspension of Uyghur rights in the name of 'counterterrorism.' As this self-fulfilling prophecy moved out of the Uyghur homeland into inner China, it would also fuel a broader, mostly Uyghur-specific, Islamophobia that would help to build support from ethnic Han throughout the country for any measures, regardless of how extreme, that the state took against its Uyghur population, which was increasingly demonized as an existential threat to state and society.

5 'Counterterrorism' mural in village near Kuqa, 2014. The mural reads, 'The use of the internet to download and disseminate violent terrorism audio and video content will be subject to severe legal punishment.' © Zheng Yanjing.

5

THE SELF-FULFILLING PROPHECY AND THE 'PEOPLE'S WAR ON TERROR,' 2013–2016

On 29 October 2013, an SUV with a black flag bearing the *Shahadah* waving outside one of its back windows drove recklessly towards the Forbidden City in Beijing's Tiananmen Square, struck numerous people, and caught fire near the palace that has long symbolized Chinese power. It turned out that a Uyghur family had been inside the vehicle, including a man, his wife, and his mother. Five people were killed, including those in the car and two tourists, and thirty-eight were injured in the process.[1] This was the first time that the gradually escalating violence inside the Uyghur homeland had spilled into inner China, and, as such, it helped to escalate the fear of the alleged 'terrorist threat' posed by Uyghurs inside the PRC to a new level.

At the time, I was asked by *CNN.com* to write an opinion column on the incident, and in that piece, I raised skepticism about this event's connection to an organized threat with ties to international 'terrorism' networks, given the rudimentary nature of the attack.[2] The response I received from Chinese *netizens* was overwhelming and extremely violent, many sending me death threats by email. Most were incensed that an American could not recognize the equivalency between Uyghur-led violence in China and the 9/11 attacks on the US, and a few even justified policies vis-à-vis Uyghurs because 'the US had done the same thing to Native Americans.' *The Global Times* wrote a scathing editorial about my column, criticizing *CNN* for publishing it, and *CCTV*, China's state broadcaster, aired a seven-minute segment that suggested that *CNN* had 'an ulterior motive' in questioning whether this attack was terrorism.³ Chinese citizens even started a supposedly grassroots campaign to ban *CNN* from the country.⁴

While this incident garnered much attention given that it had occurred in the symbolic center of state power, it was not anywhere near the most violent incident involving Uyghurs in China in 2013. The self-perpetuating ongoing violence in the south between security organs and local Uyghurs that had begun in 2010 had been escalating throughout 2013 and had already taken far more lives than the five lost in Beijing, but it had been isolated in the Uyghur region and had mostly gone unreported by the state. It is much more likely that the incident in Tiananmen Square was an outgrowth of the tensions of this ongoing violence between security organs and Uyghurs in the south of the Uyghur homeland than being related in any way to 'international terrorism.' However, the Chinese state was adamant that the incident was an obvious 'terrorist attack' that was masterminded by TIP's adherents inside China. While TIP issued a video that congratulated the Uyghurs who had carried out what it characterized as an act of jihad, it did not take responsibility for the act or claim any specific linkage to it.⁵ Furthermore, the actual circumstances around the crash were unclear and certainly did not suggest a well-organized attack. While the black flag bearing the *Shahadah* flying outside the car window suggested at least a familiarity with the symbols of militant Islam, a husband, wife, and mother constituted a strange make-up for an alleged 'terrorist cell' aligned with international jihadist groups. Furthermore, other sources speculated that the family was possibly intentionally killing themselves rather than others, akin to Tibetan self-immolations, to protest the destruction of a mosque in their hometown in Akto a year earlier.⁶ Regardless of the actual motivations and intentions for the family's SUV crash into Tiananmen Square, it suggested that the self-perpetuating violence between disenfranchised Uyghurs and the state was not only having ramifications beyond the southern Tarim Basin, but beyond the Uyghur homeland itself.

Thus, by late 2013, it seemed that the concerns about Uyghur political violence that the PRC had over exaggerated and had labeled as a 'terrorist threat' throughout the previous decade were per-haps finally becoming a reality through a 'self-fulfilling prophecy.' Furthermore, this violence would increase over the following three years, with some of the incidents appearing to legitimately qualify as 'terrorist acts' by the working definition of this book. However, none of these developments suggested that there was any organized 'terrorist threat' within China's Uyghur population, let alone one that was connected to TIP or any other international jihadist group. Instead, almost all of the incidents appeared to have their own local peculiarities that informed their motivations and intentions. However, the fact that so many acts of violence were being carried out in isolation from each other was also indicative of how widespread the frustration and rage had become within the Uyghur population, especially in the rural south.

The PRC predictably responded to this increase in violent resistance once again with an escalation of its own state-led violence, which it justified in the name of 'counterterrorism.' While the next three years through 2016 would witness continued state-led efforts at 'expediated development' in the Uyghur homeland through the PAP, this development would be gradually overshadowed by the PRC's intense security measures in the region. Furthermore, during this period, the state would begin articulating the alleged threat it faced within the Uyghur population as emanating first and foremost from certain aspects of Uyghur cultural and religious practices that the state would identify as 'extremist.' Happening in the backdrop of continued Chinese settler colonization of the Uyghur homeland, these efforts to target a threat within Uyghur culture would also serve to justify increased attempts by the PRC to forcibly assimilate Uyghurs into a Han-dominant Chinese culture that was taking over their homeland. Predictably, the Uyghur response to all of these measures would involve more violent resistance, continuing and escalating the self-perpetuating cycle of repression-violence-repression that had begun in the south in 2010.

SELF-FULFILLING PROPHECIES AND UYGHUR MILITANCIES

The concept of a 'self-fulfilling prophecy' has its origins in the work of Robert Merton, an American sociologist who began his scholarly career in the 1930s. Merton discusses the 'self-fulfilling prophecy' as originating in a false assessment about a social problem that leads to social or policy actions that make that false assessment a reality. Once this false assessment becomes a reality, it further justifies the actions that facilitated its existence. As Merton writes, 'this specious validity of the self-fulfilling prophecy perpetuates a reign of error; for the prophet will cite the actual course of events as proof that he was right from the very beginning.'[7]

Merton's examples of self-fulfilling prophecies are primarily related to structural racism in the US during the 1940s. He discusses, for example, how racist beliefs in the US that black people were intellectually 'inferior' to white people led to less investment in the education of the African American population. This lack of investment subsequently led to fewer black people enrolled in colleges, justifying further claims that they were intellectually inferior and not in need of increased investment in education.[8] For Merton, the false assumptions that lead to such self-fulfilling prophecies are not innocent miscalculations or poorly formed policies. Rather, they are the product of deep-seated prejudices founded in a legacy of unequal power relations.

Merton's formulation of this concept helps us understand how PRC policies against an imagined 'terrorist threat' would facilitate an increase in Uyghur militancy and perhaps even lead to a few actual 'terrorist attacks' carried out by Uyghurs by 2013–2014. In the PRC, and in its predecessor states in modern China, Uyghurs have always been subjected to structural racism that branded them as 'inferior,' 'backward,' and 'volatile,' serving to validate modern China's paternalistic rule of colonial difference over them and its denial of their aspirations for self-determination in their homeland. However, when the PRC began characterizing all signs of Uyghur dissent and aspirations for self-determination as 'terrorism' in 2001, and had that characterization validated by the international recognition of ETIM as a 'terrorist organization' in 2002, the nature of this structural racism intensified. These actions set in motion a process that effectively stripped Uyghurs of any legitimate grievances and gradually dehumanized them as an existential threat to state and society. As the state increasingly profiled Uyghurs as a threat, kept them under constant surveillance, and marginalized them in their own homeland, it was almost inevitable that the Uyghur response to these pressures would be violent rage. In turn, the PRC could point to the evidence of this rage to justify that it had been correct from the very beginning regarding the 'terrorist threat' posed by this population. In this sense, the SUV that crashed into Tiananmen Square in October 2013 was a response to the excesses of Chinese 'counterterrorism' measures, but it would also serve to justify these measures further.

ESCALATING VIOLENCE, COUNTERTERRORISM, AND COUNTER-EXTREMISM, 2013

Before the Uyghur family crashed its SUV into Tiananmen Square in October, the Uyghur homeland had already seen an increase during 2013 in the already existent cycle of violence and repression that had been ongoing in the region over the previous three years. While this cycle's violence in 2013 included incidents in March in Korla and in May in Karghilik where Uyghur and Han citizens allegedly clashed for unclear reasons, other incidents had mostly consisted of violence between security organs and Uyghurs.[9] These included an alleged gasoline bomb thrown at a police station in March and the alleged murder of two 'community policemen,' in April, both in Khotan.[10] While almost all of these violent incidents in 2013 took place in the south of the Uyghur region, the most bloody of them took place in June in the town of Lukqun near Turpan in the north where a group of Uyghurs wielding machetes allegedly attacked a police station, local government buildings, and a construction site.[11] In the end, the Uyghur attackers had allegedly killed 17 people, and all 10 purported attackers were killed by security forces.[12] TIP issued a video praising the violence in Lukqun, which it framed again as an act of jihad, and calling Uyghurs inside the homeland to carry out more jihad operations.[13] However, it remained unclear what had happened in Lukqun and whether it was politically motivated at all.

While the Chinese state media covered this incident given its magnitude, most of the violence in the Uyghur homeland during 2013 went unreported in official media, leaving much unexplained about the circumstances in which it took place. We only know of these violent incidents' occurrence because citizens reported them on social media, and international journalists later confirmed them with local officials. However, there was one other violent incident aside from those near Turpan and in Tiananmen Square during 2013 that was reported on substantially by Chinese state media. This was the violence in Maralbeshi near Kashgar in April. State media reported that local police and 'community workers' had allegedly uncovered a 'terrorist cell' while conducting routine house-to-house searches in a rural area in Maralbeshi, leading to a clash that eventually ended in a house being burned to the ground and at least 15 police and 'community workers' killed.[14] However, much about the event remains unclear. Some reports suggested that the Uyghurs responded violently when authorities found them watching a 'terrorist' video, and others said the group was merely conducting a Qur'anic study session at the time.[15] Likewise, sources are unclear on how the house had burned down with police and 'community workers' inside and whether the fire was initiated by the Uyghurs or the police.[16] The official media's coverage of the event, which it reported as a 'terrorist attack,' was likely due to the large number of casualties suffered by security forces in the violence, but the coverage also gave the state an opportunity to 'hype' the threat posed by alleged 'terrorists' within the Uyghur population when TIP again issued a video commending the local Uyghurs involved and calling it an act of jihad.[17]

Whether or not directly linked to the violence in Lukqun and Maralbeshi, regional authorities at this time also began more earnestly seeking to link the growing violence in the region to religious ideologies they would label as 'extremism.' The PRC had generally linked religion to violent resistance in the region going back to the 1990 Baren incident, but this new effort went beyond seeking to punish those caught practicing religion outside state-mandated institutions to identify both the physical signs and cultural practices of those who might hold religious beliefs contrary to the state. According to one Chinese 'counterterrorism expert,' this effort was initiated by the regional Party's issuance of an internal classified document in May 2013 called 'Several Guiding Opinions on Further Suppressing Illegal Religious Activities and Combating the Infiltration of Religious Extremism in Accordance with Law,' known colloquially as 'Document No. 11.'[18]

The most vivid aspect of this new effort to identify what the state deemed to be 'extremist' within Uyghur cultural expressions was the 'Project Beauty' campaign during 2013 to alter Uyghur women's clothing styles by forcing Uyghur women to adopt less modest dress and 'show their beauty' by disavowing veiling and clothing styles associated with women in the Muslim world. While 'Project Beauty' was a region-wide campaign, it was unevenly implemented and was particularly pronounced in the south of the Uyghur homeland. In Kashgar, checkpoints were instituted to police women's facial coverings, and CCTV cameras were able to monitor women on the street for veils.[19] Women caught wearing veils in public were written up by authorities and forced to participate in re-education by watching propaganda films advocating for women to show the 'beauty of their faces' in public.[20]

However, the state's policing of dress and other markers of religiosity under the guise of combating 'extremism' would not be limited to public spaces. In the south around this time, authorities appear to have instituted more regular house-to-house searches to evaluate the behaviors of Uyghurs in private and to determine whether they met the state's expectations of 'extremism.' Presumably, these expectations could be met by an evaluation of the religious books in a household, by dress and décor, and even by eating and drinking habits. Furthermore, these police searches were fortified by an army of Han cadres who were deployed throughout rural areas in the Uyghur region, particularly in the south. The Party had already announced this initiative in February 2013, calling for 200,000 cadres to deploy to 9,000 villages where they were expected to live and intermingle with the local population for at least a year.[21] While these cadres claimed to be helping promote livelihoods in rural areas, they most definitely also played a role in policing behaviors, watching both local Uyghur administrators and monitoring the local population for signs of religious and cultural habits that the state had branded as 'extremist.'[22] It is probable that the 'community workers' killed in Maralbeshi were from this pool of cadres, and the violence there was likely sparked by the invasive nature of these 'routine' household searches.

Furthermore, this extensive monitoring of rural Uyghurs, especially in the south, would also include taking proactive actions against those seen as demonstrating traits deemed by the state to be 'extremist.' In particular, there were numerous incidents of massive state raids on observed gatherings of Uyghur men. The state would frequently characterize these raids as uncovering a 'terrorist cell,' but the fact that usually all of the Uyghur men targeted were killed left little evidence of what was actually transpiring. In August, for example, authorities near Karghilik killed 15 Uyghurs who were apparently surrounded while praying together in a desert location, and in Poskam county authorities killed at least 12 Uyghurs who were gathered in a rural area to allegedly 'train' in preparation for 'terrorist acts.'[23] Similar incidents around Kashgar and Yarkand reportedly killed 7 more Uyghurs in September and early October.[24] In the aftermath of these incidents, local residents reported that their towns were virtually locked down and checkpoints were set up to check the identification of all local residents. While it was evident that TIP had nothing to do with these acts of local violence, which were mostly provoked by security forces, its *Emir* would issue another video in September, which urged the people of the region to continue what he characterized as their jihad against the Chinese state.[25]

Despite the significant violence which had already transpired in 2013 prior to the SUV crash in Tiananmen Square in late October, the incident in Beijing would predictably generate the most rapid response from authorities. Soon after this incident, a joint operation by Beijing and Xinjiang police arrested five Uyghurs in Khotan, who were accused of being part of an underground 'terrorist' group that had allegedly planned the car crash.[26] Subsequently, their trial was covered in Chinese national media as a demonstration of the state's capacity in 'counterterrorism.'

However, the cycle of violence between Uyghurs and local security organs would continue in the south of the Uyghur homeland after October and into 2014. Two weeks after the incident in Tiananmen Square, nine Uyghur youth allegedly attacked a police station with axes and knives in Maralbeshi, bludgeoning to death two policemen.[27] While the nine attackers were killed by police before authorities were able to interrogate them, state security portrayed this act of violence as yet another manifestation of internationally linked 'terrorism.' This further ensured that security sweeps would continue in the name of 'counterterrorism' through the rest of 2013, leading to more Uyghur arrests and deaths. In December, an alleged police 'raid' on another group of Uyghurs in Kashgar's old city, whom authorities claimed were 'terrorists,' led to the killing of 16 Uyghurs, including 6 women.[28] Like previous incidents that the authorities characterized as 'raids' and where Uyghurs were instantly killed, it was unclear what had actually happened. According to one Kashgar resident at the time, this was not a 'raid,' but a more mundane house search that had interrupted a planning meeting for an upcoming wedding. According to this account, violence between the members of the household and the police broke out when one officer attempted to lift a woman's veil.[29]

It is difficult to know the full story behind any of the violence that took place in the Uyghur region during 2013 given the scant reliable details available about any of these incidents. Although it is possible, but unlikely, that some of the attacks may have been undertaken by aspiring jihadists and/or were inspired by access to TIP videos, it is clear that TIP itself had no direct involvement in any of the violence. As will be discussed below, TIP was likely too busy with other activities outside China in 2013 to carry out any attacks inside the country. Furthermore, most of these attacks did not look to be acts of 'terrorism' in the context of this book's definition of that term. With the exception of the SUV crash in Tiananmen Square, the nature of which was debatable, all the violence targeted police and security organs rather than innocent civilians, fueling an ongoing conflict between Uyghurs, mostly from rural villages in the south of their homeland, and Chinese security services, which would continue into 2014

THE TURNING POINT: MARCH–MAY, 2014

The first months of 2014 appeared to represent a lull in the violence that had been occurring throughout 2013 in the south of the Uyghur homeland. Although it is likely that low-level incidents of violence continued, there were no reports of major events. However, in March of that year, a significant incident did occur, again taking place outside the Uyghur region. On 1 March 2014, a group of Uyghurs appeared to have indiscriminately attacked Han civilians with long knives inside the Kunming train station in the southern Chinese province of Yunnan. According to reports, 8 attackers, including 2 women, wearing all-black outfits killed 31 people, injuring an additional 141.[30] The attack was on helpless civilians, appeared to be premeditated, and seemed to be politically motivated given that authorities allegedly found Eastern Turkistan flags at the scene of the crime.[31] As such, it was the first time since the 1997 bus bombings in Urumqi that a Uyghur-perpetrated violent act reliably appeared to be a 'terrorist attack' by the definition adopted in this book.

Expectedly, TIP released a video praising the attack and calling it an act of jihad, using the event to further threaten Chinese officials about their policies in the Uyghur homeland, but, as had been the case previously, it did not directly claim credit for the attack.[32] While this appeared to be a 'terrorist attack' by the working definition used here, it was not typical of those generally associated with international Islamic 'extremist' groups. In fact, there is no evidence that it was an act undertaken by a larger organization or that the attackers had the support of groups outside China. Rather, the attackers appeared to be acting on their own and responding to their particular situation.

According to state officials, the group had tried to leave the country through Southeast Asia to join the 'global jihad' but were unable to do so due to increased border security in the region.[33] A report by RFA also suggested that the attackers were trying to leave the country via Southeast Asia, but not necessarily for the purposes of joining a 'global jihad,' and they were subsequently stuck in Kunming without any residency documents.[34] In either scenario, it seemed clear that the attack was home-grown rather than ordered from outside the country, and the attackers were likely already on the run from police after attempting to leave the country when they decided to commit the violence.

Regardless of whether the attackers were responding to their precarious situation in Kunming, trying to make a political statement, or both, the impact of the incident on Chinese society was certainly akin to that of a 'terrorist attack,' inciting substantial fear. In this context, Han Islamophobic fear of Uyghurs in the country increased significantly, especially since the incident had occurred only five months after the SUV crash in Beijing. If the events around the Beijing Olympics and the Urumqi riots had already racially profiled Uyghurs as a 'dangerous' population, the Kunming attack led many to see that danger in the context of GWOT as an existential 'terrorist threat,' which was considered to be irrational, animalistic, and could strike anywhere and at any time, especially now that it was no longer contained in the Uyghur homeland. State officials also responded passionately and aggressively to the violence in the Kunming train station, marking a departure from the practice of not commenting on most Uyghur-perpetrated violence in the preceding two years. As Xi Jinping would announce to security officials almost immediately after the attack, you must 'severely punish in accordance with the law the violent terrorists and resolutely crack down on those who have been swollen with arrogance ... go all out to maintain social stability.'[35]

Xi's concern about the incident prompted him to take his first trip as CCP General Secretary to the Uyghur region in late April, less than two months after the attack. During his trip, Xi was cited frequently in state media discussing counterterrorism efforts. He announced a 'Strike First' campaign to stop terrorists before they perpetrated violence and applauded the efforts of law enforcement and security agencies as the 'fists and daggers' in the battle against 'terrorism.'[36] As leaked documents have recently added, he called for this campaign to be an all-out 'struggle against terrorism, infiltration and separatism' using the 'organs of dictatorship,' and showing 'absolutely no mercy.'[37] It was in this context that, as Xi was ending his trip, it was reported that a Uyghur had set off an explosion in the Urumqi train station.[38] In addition to the bomber, only one other person died, but 79 were injured. Xi Jinping was cited as telling local authorities after the attack to take 'resolute measures' and crush the 'violent terrorists.'[39]

Like the incident in Kunming, the Urumqi bombing was an act of violence deliberately carried out against civilians, and its location again in a train station seemed to lend credence to the idea that there might be an organized group of Uyghurs who were developing a signature approach to carrying out 'terrorist' acts. TIP would once again add to such speculation by issuing a video about the attack, which mysteriously featured Abdul Häq, who had been assumed dead for the last four years.[40] As is the case in most of TIP's previous videos about incidents inside China, the group does not claim responsibility for the attack, but congratulates those jihadists in their homeland on their accomplishment. However, it does begin with a dramatization of how to make a suitcase bomb and then shows CCTV footage from the train station of the actual bomber detonating his bomb, leading some western 'terrorism' experts to assume TIP had orchestrated the attack.[41] The video also called on believers in the homeland to continue their jihad, noting that it was always just to kill any Chinese civilian since they were infidels occupying a land that belonged to Muslims.[42]

Although this attack took place in Urumqi, it would lead to an escalation of security activities once again in the south, whose Uyghurs authorities assumed were the source of all instability in the region. A week after the Urumqi attack, there were reports that police had shot dead a young Uyghur in Aksu who got into an altercation with a policeman.[43] Additionally, a protest in Aksu over the authorities' detention of women and school girls for wearing conservative headscarves turned violent on 20 May as police allegedly fired into the crowd, killing several Uyghurs.[44] Subsequently, police carried out security sweeps throughout the city into the night, arresting over 100 Uyghurs for their participation in the protests.[45]

Two days after the disturbances in Aksu, another attack occurred in Urumqi, and it would take even more lives than the Kunming and Urumqi train station attacks combined. On 22 May 2014, a group of Uyghurs allegedly drove two SUVs through barricades at a morning market, which was almost exclusively frequented by Han in Urumqi and threw explosive devices as they ploughed through people on the street, with the vehicles eventually erupting into fire.[46] While it was initially reported that 31 had died, with over 90 injured, by the next day, the death toll had risen to 43.[47] The local authorities called the incident 'a serious violent terrorist incident of a particularly vile nature,' and they predictably had the city heavily patrolled in its aftermath.[48] This was the third sensational attack against civilians in three months. In total, at least 98 violent incidents were reported involving Uyghurs and police or Han civilians inside China in 2013 and 2014, resulting in between 656 and 715 deaths.[49] In response to this escalation in violence, the state was prepared to use an even heavier hand.

The week after the Urumqi market attack, Zhang Chunxian, the head of the CCP in the Uyghur region, announced the commencement of what he called the 'People's War on Terror.'[50] While it was not surprising to hear a Han political leader from the region pledging to combat 'terrorism' in the wake of the violent attacks of the previous three months, Zhang's framing of these efforts as a 'People's War' suggested a populist response evocative of the country's Maoist legacy. Indeed, this 'People's War on Terror' was to be used as a brand describing a variety of state policies that were reminiscent of past attempts at mass indoctrination and intense social pressure from Maoist times.[51] In his statement, Zhang also signaled that this 'war' would be first and foremost about ideology. As he said, the state must 'promote the eradication of extremism, further expose and criticize the "reactionary nature" of the "three forces," enhance schools' capacity to resist ideological infiltration by religious extremism, and resolutely win the ideological battle against separation and infiltration.' However, he also framed this ideological struggle in terms that evoked the growing influence of 'Second Generation Nationalities Policy' in the region, noting that 'efforts should be made to make all ethnic groups in Xinjiang identify with the great motherland, the Chinese nation, the Chinese culture and the socialist path with Chinese characteristics.'[52]

However, it would be inaccurate to suggest that these policy shifts towards a more heavy-handed and ideological war against Uyghur dissent were the initiative of Zhang's local administration alone. Rather, they probably had their foundations in the central apparatus of the Party, particularly through the preparations for the Second Xinjiang Work Forum, which took place only days after Zheng's new declaration of a 'People's War on Terror' and which would reinforce Zhang's formulation of this war. Numerous observers have noted that the Second Xinjiang Work Forum marked a departure from previous state approaches to the problems of the Uyghur region and Uyghur dissent. First, this second Work Forum stepped back from the previous focus on development and emphasized the issue of 'stability maintenance,' mostly articulated through the prism of 'counterterrorism,' and second, it highlighted overtly assimilationist goals as a constituent part of maintaining this stability, reflecting an even stronger embrace of the 'Second Generation Nationalities Policy' than had the first Work Forum.[53]

This did not mean that development in the Uyghur region was no longer important to the PRC. To the contrary, the region's development would become a major preoccupation of Xi Jinping in the coming years. Xi had unveiled his plans for an ambitious 'Silk Road Economic Belt,' the land-based portion of the 'Belt and Road Initiative' (BRI), only a year earlier in Kazakhstan.[54] It was clear that the implementation of this 'Silk Road Economic Belt,' which was part of Xi's signature foreign policy project, would require following through with the grand development plans for the Uyghur homeland, which was envisioned as the entry/exit point for all of BRI's transport infrastructure to the west and south-west. As Xi Jinping would state at the work forum, 'Xinjiang work possesses a position of special strategic significance in the work of the Party and the state ... the long-term stability of the autonomous region is vital to the whole country's reform, development and stability.'[55] If the development of the Uyghur region remained as critical, or more so, than previously to PRC objectives, the CCP had inverted its formerly declared relationship between development and stability. Development would no longer necessarily bring stability, but stability was now necessary for development, which was needed for the advancement of the PRC as a whole.

Finally, stability was now increasingly premised on a strategy of dismantling Uyghur identity, especially its Islamic aspects, and assimilating Uyghurs into a broader national identity in the name of combating 'terrorism.'[56] Setting the tone for these new assimilationist approaches to establishing and maintaining stability, Xi echoed Zhang's earlier assertion that it was critical for all residents of the region, regardless of ethnicity, to identify with China, the Chinese nation, its culture, and its form of socialism.[57] Xi further noted that it was critical to 'strengthen inter-ethnic contact, exchange and mingling' and to ensure that the people of the region became 'tightly bound together like the seeds of a pomegranate.'[58] By couching this new focus on assimilation in the context of 'counterterrorism,' the PRC was able to use the alleged threat of 'extremism' as its justification and point to 'de-radicalization' programs in the west as an analogy. Given the subjective nature of the label of 'extremism,' this gave the state a justification for attacking virtually all Muslim religious practices, many of which had become part and parcel of Uyghur identity. As such, this Second Xinjiang Work Forum was very definitely setting the stage for the Uyghur cultural genocide that was on the horizon.

THE 'PEOPLE'S WAR ON TERROR,' 2014–2016

The 'People's War on Terror,' as implemented through 2016, involved a multi-pronged attempt to cleanse Uyghurs of Islamic influences while simultaneously trying to instill in them a new form of PRC nationalism. It would, predictably, include a concerted effort to weed out and violently punish those believed to be 'extremists' and 'terrorists,' but it also involved wider efforts to alter Uyghur social behavior and cultural practices. This included further implementing the 'Project Beauty' campaign among both women and men in order to restrict the wearing of Islamic-styled clothes and facial hair, an intensification of anti-religious education, attempts to prevent Uyghurs from engaging in religious practices, and the enlistment of all citizens in a campaign to regulate each other. Furthermore, it would lay the foundations for the sophisticated surveillance system that would monitor compliance with these efforts. Overall, it was a much more culturally focused attempt to address Uyghur dissent in the region than had been adopted in the past, but it also was assimilationist in its approach, and, for pious Uyghurs, exclusionary in its practice.

This ideological campaign to address 'extremism' was itself very extreme from the start. In schools, students were actively discouraged from adopting religiosity in any form, and were encouraged to report on religious behavior among their parents. Public 'anti-extremism' campaigns led to frequent attempts to prevent Uyghurs from fasting during *Ramadan*, to promote the drinking of alcohol and the smoking of cigarettes, suggesting that abstinence from these habits was a manifestation of extremism, and to increase surveillance of mosque attendance and the religious aspects of traditional Uyghur life-cycle rituals.[59] The campaign also included attempts to mobilize Uyghur communities to help the state in policing the population for signs of religiosity. Authorities encouraged community members to report on those amongst them who publicly displayed signs of religiosity, in some cases even providing substantial monetary rewards for such reports.[60] Contests were begun throughout the region for the best 'anti-terrorism' and 'anti-extremism' murals, which became ubiquitous as anti-religious propaganda in public spaces, especially in the south.[61] In other instances, locals were trained in how to attack 'terrorists' they encountered with farm tools and were encouraged to join 'volunteer' militia to assist the police in weeding out alleged 'terrorists.'[62] Furthermore, some local administrations in the Uyghur homeland were particularly transparent with regards to the role that miscegenation could play in its efforts to change Uyghur behaviors, offering substantial monetary incentives to promote inter-marriage between Han and Uyghurs.[63]

While many of the extreme manifestations of this ideological war appeared to differ by region within the Uyghur homeland, they were not limited to rural and religious Uyghurs in the south. The campaign also targeted Uyghur intellectuals and nationalists who were not religious and not necessarily from the south of the Uyghur homeland. As evidence of this, authorities in the Uyghur region began policing the Uyghur-language internet, with even more scrutiny than before, for any content that suggested criticism of the CCP particularly targeting content that was either religious or nationalist in nature.[64] The most sensational example of this increased internet scrutiny was the arrest of Ilham Tohti, a Uyghur economics professor living in Beijing, on charges of promoting 'separatism.' Tohti likely had been the only Uyghur public intellectual able to openly criticize state policies in the Uyghur region given his residency in Beijing, but he was not a proponent of Uyghur independence from the PRC. He was well-respected among Han intellectuals, and his writings were focused on promoting the integration of Uyghurs and their homeland into the PRC, albeit on their own terms that recognized their historical relationship with their homeland.[65] However, he had created an internet forum about Uyghurs and their homeland that encouraged frank and honest discussion between Uyghurs and Han of conditions in the region. In September 2014, Tohti was convicted of 'separatism,' presumably on the basis of this internet forum, and given a life sentence in prison, a much harsher punishment than that usually given to prominent Han dissidents.[66] This event sent a message to all Uyghurs that the Chinese state would now tolerate no objections to or open debate about its policies and that the terms of the 'People's War on Terror' that had been set by the state were non-negotiable.

About a year after Tohti's sentencing, the PRC also passed a new 'Counterterrorism Law' in 2015, which would codify many of the anti-Islamic and assimilationist policies already being implemented in parts of the Uyghur homeland as a means of combating 'extremism.' With these policies now stipulated by law, it was no longer Uyghurs in specific regions who were subjected to such actions, but all Uyghurs. According to the law, 'terrorism' 'refers to propositions and actions that create social panic, endanger public safety, violate person and property, or coerce national organs or international organizations, through methods such as violence, destruction, intimidation, so as to achieve their political, ideological, or other objectives.'[67] The inclusion of 'propositions' and 'intimidation' in this definition allowed for a broad understanding of the concept, which was not limited to acts of violence, and potentially included any independent political act seeking to persuade others.

Furthermore, articles 80 and 81 of the law prohibit a variety of 'extremist activities,' most of which are completely subjective. These include the extremely vague action of 'using methods such as intimidation or harassment to interfere in the habits and ways of life of other persons,' as well as a number of activities regarding the promotion of religion writ large and actions meant to discourage people from living or interacting with those of other ethnic groups and faiths.[68] As the international coverage of this new law pointed out, these articles particularly targeted parents for actions they might take in the course of parenting their children, effectively seeking to drive a wedge between the older and younger generation of Uyghurs.[69]

This law was further reinforced in the Uyghur homeland by the initiation of new 'Religious Affairs Regulations' that were intended to distinguish between legal and illegal expressions of Islam. These regulations were likely instituted as a means to codify many of the anti-religion policies being undertaken in the region, but they remained extremely vague and highly subjective, especially with regards to the definition of 'extremist' activities and attire, both of which were prohibited. Article 38, for example, prohibited people from adopting an 'appearance [i.e. grooming], clothing and personal adornment, symbols, and other markings to whip up religious fanaticism, disseminate religious extremist ideologies, or coerce or force others to wear extremist clothing, religious extremist symbols, or other markings.'[70] However, it was not clear at all what constituted 'extremist' ideologies, clothing, symbols, or markings.

Both the 'Religious Affairs Regulations' and the 'Counterterrorism Law' led to a far more concerted effort than previously to pursue the ideological struggle against 'terrorism' (as that term was understood by the Party) that had been promised by the 'People's War.' In many ways, the stipulations in these legal documents had already been in effect prior to 2015 in the region, especially in the south. As one journalist would state in a report from Kashgar in 2014, it appeared that China was waging 'an all-out attack on Islam' in the region.[71] However, the new legal guidance ensured that this attack on Islam would become more systematic and extend far beyond Kashgar.

In addition to its ideological focus, the 'People's War' increased the violent policing of Uyghurs by security organs that had been steadily escalating since 2011. Almost immediately after its declaration, authorities held a public execution of 55 alleged Uyghur 'terrorists' in the town of Ghulja, and security organs conducted a massive 'counterterrorism' sweep in the region, which detained over 200 Uyghurs for alleged 'terrorist activities.'[72] By the end of 2014, it was reported that the number of arrests in the Uyghur region had nearly doubled from the previous year, largely reflective of increased detentions on vaguely defined 'terrorism' related charges.[73] In the southern rural areas of the Uyghur region, local security organs were tasked with even more regular house-to-house inspections to monitor dissident behavior, and targeted people in these communities were virtually held under house arrest.[74] As one might expect from past experience, this intensification in the monitoring of Uyghurs by security forces only spawned more violent resistance from Uyghurs, subsequently only further escalating the ongoing conflict between Uyghurs and security organs, especially in the south of the Uyghur region.

Violent incidents, whether initiated by security forces or Uyghurs, quickly increased even more after May 2014, and virtually all of them occurred in the south of the Uyghur homeland. A significant number of the violent incidents were provoked by house-to-house inspections and police 'raids,' as had been the case in the previous year.[75] Others were Uyghur attacks on police and government officials or on police stations and government buildings.[76] The violence began appearing increasingly political again in July and August of 2014, resulting in assassinations of five judicial officials in Aksu and of the Imam of Kashgar's main mosque, who had been a vocal supporter of the state's 'counterterrorism' measures in local media.[77]

However, the most brutal violence of 2014 would take place under a shroud of mystery in a village near Yarkand called Elishqu in late July. State accounts claimed that this was a mass 'terrorist' attack on a police station, while Uyghur sources asserted that it was the result of the repression of a protest in response to restrictions on Uyghurs' ability to observe *Ramadan* and to the police killings of Uyghurs during house-to-house searches.[78] According to state sources, 96 people had died in the violence, including 59 alleged 'terrorists,' but the WUC would claim that as many as 2000 Uyghurs had been killed.[79] Independent journalist accounts suggest that the violence began as authorities raided what they considered an 'illegal religious gathering,' which could have been any gathering of Uyghur men.[80] Regardless of what happened, and who the main aggressors were, the incident had obviously turned into a massacre, traumatizing the local population. Follow-up trips by international journalists to the region to find out what had actually happened were unsuccessful, but they did suggest that the area had been put under complete lockdown, even two years later.[81] In the aftermath of the incident, the CCP leader in the Uyghur region, Zhang Chunxian, responded by making clear that state efforts would only become more intense. As he noted, 'We have to hit hard, hit accurately and hit with awe-inspiring force ... to fight such evils we must aim at extermination ... to cut weeds we must dig out the roots.'[82]

There was a similar flow of violent incidents in 2015 as in 2014. Much of this violence followed the pattern of resistance to security inspections that had occurred throughout 2013 and 2014, but it now also involved numerous clashes at the checkpoints that had become common throughout the region.[83] This included three alleged suicide attacks on such inspection posts near Khotan in the towns of Lop and Karakash in May and one particularly deadly one in Kashgar in June.[84] The incident that would be the most violent in 2015 occurred in September near Aksu where Uyghurs had allegedly killed 50 some Han coal miners while they slept in their dormitories.[85] However, like most of the Uyghur-perpetrated violence inside China, the details of this incident were unknown. While state media in China did not report the mine attack for almost two months, when it did, it again suggested that this was the work of a 'terrorist' group linked to international jihadist networks.[86] Uyghurs from the region have told me that the incident was actually related to local land disputes. Regardless of the motivations, the security forces killed on the spot 28 Uyghurs whom they claimed had committed the act, without bothering to even arrest them.[87] Authorities also allegedly arrested at least two other Uyghurs accused of being involved in the incident, and state media publicly aired nationally an interview with one of them, who claimed that the killings were undertaken as an act of jihad.[88]

As a result of this intensification of violence in the southern Tarim Basin during 2014-2015, securitization in the region predictably only intensified. By 2016, there were reports that many Uyghur neighborhoods in urban areas had been fenced off from the rest of the city and were surveilled by an increased police presence as well as more numerous CCTV cameras.[89] The call to prayer was also outlawed, Uyghurs were subjected to more limits on their ability to move within their own homeland, and the state even outlawed a list of children's names that have Arabic roots and religious significance.[90] According to Zhang Chunxian, the head of the CCP in the region, these measures had greatly reduced violence in the region by March 2016, but it is likely that low-level violence continued unreported.[91]

While a few Uyghur elites living in Urumqi at this time have told me that they were prospering in this context, for most Uyghurs, especially those from rural villages, the pressure from security organs in the region was reaching a peak by the summer of 2016. As Darren Byler has noted from his research among rural migrants to Urumqi, this pressure, which included almost nightly checks on households, had completely alienated rural Uyghurs and had left substantial psychological scars on them.[92] Furthermore, the close scrutiny of residency permits at this time was serving to keep rural Uyghurs out of urban areas and to essentially quarantine them in tightly controlled rural villages.[93] This pressure had been building in southern rural regions of the Uyghur homeland since 2010, spurring much of the violence described above. However, some rural Uyghurs found another way to respond to this pressure; they abandoned their homeland entirely.

EXODUS FROM THE HOMELAND

While there are no official statistics on how many Uyghurs left China between 2010 and 2016, it was certainly in the tens of thousands and likely at least 30,000. As such, it would ultimately become the largest exodus of Uyghurs from China since May 1962 when some 60,000 Uyghurs had reportedly fled to Soviet Kazakhstan. However, the exodus between 2010 and 2016 would not take place over the course of days and involve a mass transfer of population over a single border as was the case in 1962. Instead, it would happen over the course of years and involve a series of different methods of travel and multiple borders. It would also involve both illegal and legal means of leaving China.

For most Uyghurs, since at least 2006 it has been extremely difficult to obtain passports for international travel, and it had become almost impossible for all but a small minority of Uyghurs after 2009.[94] Furthermore, for those who had passports, a practice was instituted that required them to be housed with either state travel agencies or local police, ostensibly forcing their holders to request state permission to leave the country.[95] In this situation, many Uyghurs, especially from rural regions in the south, began using human trafficking routes through Southeast Asia to flee illegally without documentation. While these routes were relatively well-established, they were largely new to Uyghurs, who had traditionally fled China via the borders of their homeland to locations in Central and South Asia. However, after the 2009 Urumqi riots, routes out of China through Southeast Asia would begin to see significant Uyghur traffic. In December 2009, Cambodia detained 18 Uyghurs, including women and children, who had apparently fled the PRC. Cambodia extradited the group back to China, and, upon their arrival, the adults amongst them were arrested, with two of them receiving life sentences.[96] Similarly, Laos extradited 7 Uyghurs in March 2010.[97] In 2011–2012, Malaysia also extradited a total of 17 Uyghurs, who were in the country without proper documents.[98] While these extraditions drew criticism from human rights groups, the international community had no idea of the extent of the exodus of Uyghurs that was transiting Southeast Asia until 2014 when Thai authorities arrested 424 Uyghur men, women, and children, some 200 of which were hiding in a single trafficking camp in Songkhla province.[99] The Uyghurs claimed to have Turkish citizenship, and Thailand was caught in a diplomatic battle between China and Turkey for the right to have these refugees sent to their country. While Thailand did send approximately 170 of the refugees, almost exclusively women and children, to Turkey, 109 men were extradited to China in July 2015.[100]

However, even this large number of refugees detained in Thailand represented a small fraction of the number of Uyghurs who likely used these human trafficking routes between 2010 and 2014 to leave China. Most Uyghurs leaving China via Southeast Asia intended to make their way to Turkey where it was known that they could receive refuge, but they also did not necessarily have a plan regarding how to do so. Uyghur activists in Turkey with whom I have spoken played an important role in facilitating the final stage of the journey from Southeast Asia to Turkey, negotiating with multiple governments in the process. While exact numbers of Uyghurs who left China through Southeast Asia between 2010 and 2014 may never be known, these activists claimed to have successfully transferred some 10,000 Uyghurs from Malaysia and Thailand to Turkey between 2012 and 2016. Others remain in detention centers in Malaysia and Thailand at the time of this book's publication, and some undoubtedly remain in these countries as undocumented immigrants.

Anecdotal evidence suggests that most of these refugees had come from the southern oases of the Uyghur homeland and primarily from rural villages. When I conducted interviews in the Turkish city of Kayseri during the summer of 2016 with Uyghurs who had fled China via Southeast Asia, all of those I met had come from the villages around Kashgar, Khotan, Yarkand, and Aksu. They mentioned that the pressure from police had been the primary factor which solidified their decision to leave, citing constant household inspections and harassment. Some also attributed their decision to flee as further motivated by their inability to peacefully practice Islam and their children's mandatory education in Chinese-language schools. These motivations for the exodus correspond with the findings of a report by the WUC, which also conducted interviews in Turkey with refugees who had fled China via Southeast Asia at this time.[101] The WUC also notes that most of the Uyghur men among the refugee families had spent time in PRC prisons and had been subsequently targeted for particular surveillance by authorities on their release.[102]

It is noteworthy that many fled with their entire families, including large numbers of children. They described a harrowing journey that brought them from the Yunnan and Guanxi Provinces of China across various borders with Laos, Vietnam, and Burma.[103] Those with whom I spoke told heartbreaking stories of the members of their groups who had died from illness or accident along the road and spoke about the difficult conditions while in the hands of traffickers.

Much remains mysterious about this mass exodus of Uyghurs through Southeast Asia. Interviewees told the WUC a variety of stories, which suggested that information about this 'underground railroad' out of China had spread via word of mouth and had likely included numerous human trafficking rings. Most of my interviewees suggested that they had learned about the opportunity to flee from friends and family, but two told me that Han traffickers had come directly to their village to ask them if they wanted to leave the country. The Chinese government never recognized the scale of the exodus, but it did finally acknowledge that it was occurring, suggesting that it was a human trafficking ring founded by Islamic 'extremists' to bring Uyghurs to fight in the global jihad. Chinese authorities made claims about this alleged jihadist smuggling ring in relation both to the Kunming train station attack in March 2014 and to the December 2014 incident where authorities arrested 21 Uyghurs and killed one for trying to cross the border in Guanxi province.[104] The Chinese state again made the same claims about the 109 Uyghur men returned to China from Thailand in 2015.[105]

It is important to note that none of the Uyghur refugees I interviewed in Turkey claimed that they had left China to join militant groups, and even 'terrorism' experts following ETIM/TIP are skeptical of this narrative.[106] However, it is evident that some of these refugees were eventually recruited by jihadist groups that were able to offer them refuge. A small number somehow came to be entangled with groups in Indonesia, including the Mujahidin Indonesia Timur, but the majority were recruited by TIP, which was preparing for its operations in Syria.[107] According to Uyghur activists who had gone to both Malaysia and Thailand to help refugees there get to Turkey, they encountered another Turkish Uyghur in Southeast Asia who was actively recruiting for TIP. It is unclear how many Uyghurs this person was able to recruit, but he likely had established an alternative route for some refugees to get to Turkey before directly moving on to Syria.

The PRC appears to have halted the flow of Uyghur refugees to Southeast Asia by late 2014, but Uyghurs were still apparently finding ways to flee the country. In November 2014, the PRC claimed to have broken up a Turkish-led ring providing Uyghurs with fake passports, once again claiming that the purpose of the operation was to send Uyghurs to join the global jihad.[108] Having resulted in the arrest of ten Turkish citizens, this incident created tension in the Turkish-Chinese diplomatic relationship, with the PRC claiming that Turkey was helping Uyghurs join 'terrorist' groups. Regardless of the actual story behind this alleged system of fake passport distribution, after this incident, it appears that most illegal routes out of China for Uyghurs, including via forged passports, had been neutralized.

Fortunately for Uyghurs, local Chinese authorities began implementing an unusual policy in August 2015, allowing all Uyghurs whose passports had been held by the state to freely get them back and encouraging others without existing passports to apply for them. Predictably, many Uyghurs took this opportunity to retrieve their existing passports or apply for new ones and leave the country legally, mostly traveling to Turkey. As a result, a significant influx of Uyghurs arrived in Turkey legally via airplane in late 2015, adding to the Uyghur diaspora population in Turkey much more than those who had arrived via Southeast Asia trafficking routes. This policy, which was uncharacteristically accommodationist, seemed to be ordered by Zhang Chuxian himself just months before he was replaced. It is unclear why Zhang would want to give Uyghurs their passports back in 2015, and the decision was not accompanied by a long and transparent paper trail that could provide clues about the policy's purpose.

However, one can speculate about possible motivations. Chinese authorities remained concerned about the potential for violent resistance to Chinese rule in the Uyghur region, and Zhang may have decided that letting dissatisfied Uyghurs leave on their own accord would help prevent future violence through a policy of 'voluntary' ethnic cleansing of territory by those deemed by the state to be infected with the 'three evils.' However, it may have also been merely an early attempt to compile data on the Uyghur population to assist in their surveillance. Residents of the Uyghur region were subjected to a far more rigorous passport application process than other Chinese citizens, requiring extensive bio-data, including voice samples, DNA collection, and a 3D image of themselves.[109] Regardless of the motivations, this policy led to the departure of thousands of additional Uyghurs during the months it was in effect. By late October 2016, the policy was once again reversed as Uyghurs' passports were gradually and systematically again confiscated by the police.[110]

As already noted briefly, a substantial number of these new Uyghur refugees in Turkey would mysteriously end up in Syria fighting with TIP, which also suddenly had a substantial and well-equipped army for the first time in its history. This was yet another aspect of the 'self-fulfilling prophecy' of China's efforts since 2001 to assert that it faced a serious 'terrorist threat' from within its Uyghur population. However, it is noteworthy that this new incarnation of TIP in Syria was not necessarily the same organization with the same allegiances as had been the case in Pakistan only a few years prior.

TIP IN SYRIA

Oh Turkistan, we have not forgotten you
We swore to free you
We have marched forth to achieve this great goal
We were once oppressed and humiliated under the disbelievers
Look now, we have all sorts of weapons in our hands
Marching forth in the battles with pride and seeking martyrdom
We are the ones who pledged to die in the path of Allah
TIP, *Jihad Otida/Love of Jihad* (October 2018)

In October 2012, the Chinese state media first claimed that Uyghurs were heading to Syria to join 'terrorist organizations,' asserting that both ETIM and a Turkey-based group, the Eastern Turkistan Education and Solidarity Association (ETESA), were working together to bring Uyghurs into Syria.[111] In July 2013, the Chinese government also claimed that they had apprehended one Uyghur coming back to the country after having fought in Syria.[112] While it was not surprising that some Uyghurs would end up in the ranks of foreign fighters in Syria, most observers at the time assumed that the number of Uyghurs doing so was very small.[113] However, by 2014, TIP was making videos inside Syria, showing a larger and better equipped army than it ever had in Afghanistan or Pakistan as well as pictures of a community that included many children.[114] A year later, in 2015, it was known that TIP had an active army in

Syria that had contributed to numerous battles in the north of the country, including critical ones in Jisr Al-Shughur, at the Al-Duhur Military Airbase, and in Qarqur.[115] It was also at this time that information began spreading about TIP having established what essentially amounted to Uyghur settlements in northern Syria near the border with Turkey comprising communities of entire families.[116] How had TIP gone from a small shell organization of Al-Qaeda engaged mostly in propaganda in the Pakistan-Afghanistan frontier to a large fighting force and settlement in Syria in a matter of three years?

Al-Qaeda and Turkey: strange bedfellows in TIP's emergence in Syria?

Much of the story about how TIP became established in Syria so quickly given its former lack of capacity and resources remains shrouded in mystery. However, it does seem clear that assistance from, and perhaps manipulation by, both Al-Qaeda and Turkey were contributing factors. As TIP already appeared to be gaining more recruits in Waziristan in 2011, it had also become more ideologically integrated into Al-Qaeda. When the former *Emir* Abdushukur was killed by a drone strike in 2012, only Abdullah Mansur and Abdul Häq, who had yet to reappear from his alleged killing, remained from the original organizers of TIP during the 2008 Olympics. Given that the organization was suddenly gaining significant numbers of new fighters, perhaps for the first time ever, it is likely that Al-Qaeda took notice of the group's potential and took greater control over the organization's leadership, which had significantly dwindled.

If this is true, it is likely that TIP began getting involved in Syria as early as 2012, at the same time that Al-Qaeda entered the country's civil war. Al-Qaeda first became active in Syria with the establishment of the *Al-Nusra Front to Protect the Levant* in January 2012.[117] By March 2013, TIP was suggesting in its Arabic-language magazine that it was already represented among the foreign fighters in Syria.[118] I have also met at least one Uyghur who was already in Syria in 2013 with TIP. He had come to the country via Turkey and had joined a small group of TIP recruits to partake in some military training and establish operations in the country. He also noted that a smaller group of Uyghurs was with Daesh at this time, which had yet to completely split with Al-Qaeda. Given the video produced in 2014 of Uyghur fighters in Syria, it would appear that the group was already fairly well established by this time and was working with Arab jihadist groups, likely linked to *Al-Nursra*.

However, it is not until 2015 that we see clear evidence of a larger TIP fighting force in the country through videos documenting their participation in key battles near Idlib.[119] TIP also made numerous recruiting videos at this time, suggesting that its numbers were continuing to grow. These videos show that TIP sought to appeal to a variety of emotions and different populations in recruiting people to come to Syria. A significant number of the recruitment videos focus on the plight of Uyghurs in China, connecting it to the struggle of Muslims globally, and stressing how joining the jihad in Syria will prepare Uyghurs to fight China.[120] Others appealed to potential Uyghur recruits by showing the strong and loving community of Uyghurs in Syria, including the many children who had come to the country with their parents.[121] However, it is also telling that TIP had transitioned to recruiting non-Uyghurs as well at this time, making videos in Turkish, Kazakh, and Kyrgyz languages in addition to those in Uyghur.[122]

If Al-Qaeda and the aligned *Al-Nursra* helped get TIP established in northern Syria, there is also plenty of anecdotal evidence of Turkish involvement in helping to funnel Uyghur refugees to join the group there. As has already been noted, an overwhelming number of Uyghur refugees, perhaps numbering as many as 30,000, arrived in Turkey around this time both via human trafficking networks through Southeast Asia and more directly and legally with passports given out to Uyghurs in China in 2015–2016. On arrival, Turkey provided them with neither official refugee status nor full citizenship. Rather, they were generally given temporary residency permits, usually without the right to work, and, at the time of this book's publication, many remained in the country under such tenuous status. While Turkey, with perhaps a few recent exceptions, has not extradited these Uyghur refugees to China, their situation in the country is tenuous at best, and they have struggled to make ends meet, especially those who have not even been afforded work permits. The uncertainty of their immigration status and their economic situation provided incentives for many among these Uyghur refugees in Turkey to go to Syria where they were promised housing, food, and schools for their children.

While a small number of the Uyghurs in Syria may already have been recruited by TIP in Southeast Asia, it appears the majority came after they had already found refuge in Turkey. From my discussions with Uyghur activists in Turkey who have tried to accommodate the many refugees arriving from their homeland in recent years, it is clear that they have needed to contend with another group of Uyghurs in Turkey who are funneling these new arrivals to join TIP in Syria. One of the few journalistic pieces to examine this question, for example, recounts one activist who encountered such TIP recruiters when he was meeting a group of refugees at Istanbul airport in 2015 with the intent of bringing them to the city.[123] Instead, these recruiters ushered the newcomers onto buses headed directly to Syria.

More often, these refugees were enticed to come to Syria after already struggling to make ends meet in Turkey. One TIP recruiter identified by my interviewees who had gone from Turkey to join TIP in Syria was a man by the name of Säyfullah, who appeared to be based in Istanbul. He told many recruits that joining TIP in Syria would be training for the group's eventual plan to wage a war of liberation in Eastern Turkistan. Activists seeking to prevent Uyghurs from going to Syria have also discussed being harassed and pressured to stop their work by thugs assumed to be serving TIP.[124] However, it remains unclear whether these recruiters and thugs are working for Al-Qaeda, for TIP in Pakistan/Afghanistan, for Turkish supporters of TIP, or for somebody else entirely. The Chinese government has also accused the Turkey-based Uyghur organization ETESA (known by Uyghurs as *Maarip*) of being involved in recruitment, but this organization has instead played an active role in discouraging Uyghurs from going to Syria. There has been some speculation that the Turkish government itself supported Uyghur refugee recruitment into TIP, but no conclusive evidence of this exists. Much of this speculation comes from partisan Middle Eastern sources, which have suggested that the Uyghur settlements in Syria are a part either of a Turkish 'colonization' of northern Syria or of a Turkish-supported plot to promote 'insurgency in Xinjiang.'[125] Despite the questionable nature of these sources and many of their suspect arguments, their assertions of state involvement are not entirely far-fetched. It has been well documented that Turkey allowed a variety of jihadist groups and their weapons to transit the country on their way to Syria, and Turkey, at least in the early years of the war, was somewhat supportive of *Al-Nusra*, which shared common enemies with the Turkey-backed Free Syrian Army.[126] Additionally, there is plenty of anecdotal evidence that Uyghurs involved with TIP have been able to move freely back and forth over the Syrian border with little to no resistance from Turkish border guards.

Who are the Uyghur jihadists of TIP?

The number of Uyghurs who have joined TIP in their battles in Syria is unknown, but it is substantial. The alleged high-level member of TIP I met in Turkey during the summer of 2019 suggested that the group represented 30,000 Uyghurs inside Syria at its peak. The Syrian ambassador to China claimed in 2017 that the number of Uyghur foreign fighters in Syria was around 5,000.[127] By contrast, Israeli intelligence at the same time published a report suggesting that TIP had 3,000 Uyghur fighters in Syria.[128] It is important to note that the Uyghurs in Syria include substantial numbers of families where only the adult males would serve as actual fighters for TIP. Thus, the number of Uyghurs in Syria may be much larger than the number of TIP fighters in the country. However, unlike Daesh, TIP does not appear to keep reliable records of their membership, and, thus, its true number in Syria is unlikely ever to be known.

Furthermore, like Häsän Mäkhsum's group in Afghanistan and

Abdul Häq's TIP in Pakistan, TIP in Syria appears to operate more like a community than a militant organization. While those from the community who participate in warfare, primarily the adult men, obviously follow a chain of command and answer to superiors, the community of TIP in the country appears much more loosely organized and independent of larger jihadist groups. People travel back and forth between the community in Syria and the Uyghur community in Turkey. They have created what amount to Uyghur villages in Syria, complete with schools, but there is little evidence that these villages live under the command of any particular individual or group. Finally, it is not even clear that those who have joined this community at different times or even participated in battles consider themselves 'members' of TIP.

Mohanad Ali Hage of the Carnegie Middle East Center, who has interviewed people in the region of Idlib where TIP has been most active, calls the Uyghurs with TIP in Syria 'a different type of jihadi.'[129] He notes that they do not appear interested in ruling over civilian populations, collecting taxes, or enforcing Sharia Law; rather, they tend to settle in abandoned towns where they keep to themselves and focus their fighting against Assad's armies and their allies.[130] Those Uyghurs I have interviewed who have been with TIP in Syria provide similar descriptions. They talk about towns and neighborhoods completely inhabited by Uyghurs with schools that teach Islam, mathematics, and a variety of other subjects.[131] While TIP videos suggest that the schools also train students in the use of weapons and the art of warfare, there is no evidence that TIP operations use child soldiers. Furthermore, TIP videos also highlight the communal nature of life for Uyghurs in Syria, showing holiday celebrations and other community gatherings in addition to the battles in which men are involved.

In this context, one can understand some of the attraction of Syria to Uyghur refugees. It offers a life lived on their own terms and by their own rules. While the rules by which this community lives are conservative, it is notable that my informants who had been part of the community suggest that they were not aggressively ruled by Sharia law. They mention, for example, being lectured by non-Uyghur jihadists about their lackadaisical approach to praying five times a day and their propensity for smoking cigarettes, both behavior that was tolerated in TIP's own community. That said, it is notable that few if any TIP videos show Uyghur women in Syria, suggesting a highly sex-segregated society.

A full account of the Uyghur community associated with TIP in Syria would be difficult to reconstruct with the fragmented information available to us. That said, one can piece together a few different types of Uyghurs who have joined TIP in Syria. All of the Uyghurs I have interviewed who have had experience with TIP in Syria have told me unequivocally that their motivation for going to Syria was to gain combat experience that would eventually be used in a war to liberate their homeland from the PRC. They have generally been in their twenties and thirties and had grown up during the 2000s in rural areas of their homeland where they had been under suspicion of being potential 'terrorists' or 'extremists' most of their teen and/ or adult life. Several had spent time in prison on crimes related to religious observation, and all of them had left China due to the intense pressure they felt from security organs. In this context, they held intense animosity towards the Chinese state and viewed it as an occupying power in their homeland, but they had no real interest in the ideals of global jihad. It is notable that all of these people had eventually left TIP's base in Syria to return to Turkey, suggesting that they had eventually become disenchanted with fighting somebody else's war. However, the number of such Uyghur returnees from Syria in Turkey at the time of this book's publication were significant. As one Uyghur resident of Istanbul suggested of his neighborhood during the summer of 2019, about one in three Uyghur men on the street had been in Syria.

A second group of Uyghurs who have been associated with TIP in Syria appear to have come there for economic reasons. This is especially true of Uyghur families who came to Turkey via Southeast Asia, having given all of their money to human traffickers. Such people were generally impoverished upon arrival in Turkey and were given little to no assistance by the Turkish state. In Syria, these people were promised housing, food, clothing, and education for their children. In other words, these Uyghurs came to Syria not to fight, but to find a peaceful and prosperous life. Unfortunately, they must also fight a war in order to receive these benefits. Finally, it is likely that a certain number of Uyghurs who came to Syria to fight with TIP have become true believers in the ideology of global jihadism. They likely joined TIP for either of the above-mentioned reasons rather than with the aspirations of contributing to global jihad, but they have stayed with the group because they have found a community of like-minded people, and they are now dedicated to the idea of fighting not only for the Uyghur nation, but also for the Muslim faith.

TIP in Syria is, in many ways, the most obvious manifestation of the 'self-fulfilling prophecy' initiated by the PRC when it began its campaign to assert the existence of a 'terrorist threat' within its Uyghur population in the early 2000s. As one Uyghur I interviewed in Turkey who had fought with TIP noted, 'why does the Turkistan Islamic Party exist? [it] profited from the Chinese oppression of our homeland; without that, it would not exist; China itself made the Turkistan Islamic Party.' The Uyghurs who have joined TIP in Syria are not the product of a cohesive history of Uyghur 'terrorist groups' or a Salafist movement inside their homeland. They are refugees from China's 'war on terror,' who have been driven to fight in a foreign war far from their homeland, either in the hope of one day using their experience to fight the Chinese state or merely as a means of survival and a sense of belonging.

THE GATHERING STORM

In many ways, the substantial army of Uyghurs with TIP in Syria is a creation of the Chinese state. It is the product of the conditions in the Uyghur homeland that, as described above, were facilitated by the narrative that the PRC had been cultivating since 2001 about the 'terrorist threat' that existed within its Uyghur population. At the same time, this army also continues to help feed that narrative and contribute to its use by the PRC against the Uyghur people. However, this point should not be confused with direct causation for the cultural genocide that was set in motion in the Uyghur home-land in 2016–2017. I do not agree, for example, with the premise of a recent academic article in the field of 'security studies,' which argues that the mass internment, invasive surveillance, and forced assimilation that Uyghurs in China have confronted since 2017 is primarily the outcome of the Chinese state's fears of TIP's active presence in Syria.[132] Rather, by 2016, there was a gathering storm of factors that were leading the state towards its subsequent policies in the Uyghur homeland, and the 'self-fulfilling prophecy' of TIP in Syria was only one component of that storm.

PRC settler colonization of the Uyghur region had been steadily intensifying since the 1990s, and it had sparked an ongoing vio-lent conflict with the indigenous population starting in 2009 that was spiraling out of control by 2016, especially in the southern Tarim Basin. This intensifying colonization of the region was also further emboldened by the state's increasing embrace of the 'Second Generation Nationalities Policy,' which provided an ideological premise for blatantly assimilationist policies vis-à-vis the region's indigenous population. Furthermore, it was also fueled after 2013 by the urgency to rapidly re-make the Uyghur homeland into a critical commercial center in Xi Jinping's flagship foreign policy project, the BRI, as well as by the leadership style of Xi himself who demonstrated that, more than any Chinese leader since Mao, he believes the Party can employ force to solve complex socio-economic issues, including ethnic tensions born of a long-term colonial relationship.

The drive to settle and colonize the Uyghur homeland and make it an integral part of the PRC would be the primary and root cause of the campaign of cultural genocide that would begin in 2017. The narrative of the 'terrorist threat' posed by Uyghurs to the PRC would be its justification and would expediate its implementation. This narrative had been used to dismiss the core causes of the violent resistance to colonization and related aggressive assimilation meas-ures that had been transpiring in rural Uyghur communities since 2011. Additionally, it had been used to justify the violent repression of the resistance, ostensibly further fueling this resistance and helping to establish the self-perpetuating cycle of violence between the state and civilians in the south of the Uyghur homeland. Finally, and perhaps most importantly, the narrative's inherently biopolitical understanding of a 'terrorist threat' as a contagion within a given population allowed the state to target all Uyghurs, and eventually Uyghur identity itself, as potentially being part of this threat and, thus, requiring quarantining or eradication.

In this context, the well-equipped and relatively robust TIP army of Uyghurs in Syria would serve as a potent means for the state to argue that the 'terrorist threat' it has long claimed to face from Uyghurs inside China is real and growing, an argument it has continually used to justify its genocidal strategies vis-à-vis the Uyghurs since 2017. While it would be difficult to categorize this army as a 'terrorist organization' per the working definition of that term used here, since it is mostly a conventional mercenary fighting force that does not deliberately target civilians, it is a jihadist group with connections to Al-Qaeda, which fulfills most people's expectations of 'terrorists' in the context of GWOT. Thus, its existence has also been powerful in deflecting international criticism of the present human rights crisis in the Uyghur homeland by positing that China indeed does face an existential threat from within its Uyghur population.

Finally, and even more importantly, the argument that this army in Syria and its influence on Uyghurs in China presents a threat to state and society in the PRC has been effective domestically in winning the support of citizens and government officials for the extreme policies implemented in the Uyghur region since 2017. Many Chinese citizens believe that this group is an existential threat, which was responsible for the violent incidents that transpired in Beijing in 2013, in Kunming and Urumqi in 2014, and even in Urumqi in 2009. Such beliefs likely also extend deep into the state bureaucracy, including many of those carrying out policies in the Uyghur homeland today. While those in the higher echelons of the Party are likely fully aware of the minor to non-existent threat that TIP actually poses to PRC national security, the belief among most Han citizens and large swaths of the government that this is a substantial and existential threat has been enough to justify any means necessary to mitigate it. These means have come to include cultural genocide and the elimination of Uyghur identity as we know it. While such inhumane measures would be unjustifiable even if the PRC had faced a significant 'terrorist threat,' they are even more disturbing given the actual minuscule threat that TIP or any Uyghur resistance to the state poses to the national security of China

6 Uyghur men sit at attention in a mass internment camp in Lop near Khotan, 2017.

6

CULTURAL GENOCIDE, 2017–2020

The term 'cultural genocide' is generally attributed to the Polish lawyer who coined the overall concept of 'genocide' in the 1940s, Raphael Lemkin. Lemkin viewed genocide as more than the mass killing of people from a given group; he defined the term as 'the destruction of a nation or of an ethnic group.'[1] In discussing how this destruction takes place, he notes that it is rarely accomplished through the 'immediate destruction' of the group, which would connote the mass murder of its members. Instead, it is almost always implemented gradually through the systematic eradication of the group's cultural distinctiveness and way of life, the 'essential foundations of the life of national groups.'[2] In characterizing the objectives of genocide, Lemkin writes that it involves the 'disintegration of the political and social institutions, of culture, language, national feelings, religion, and the economic existence of national groups, and the destruction of the personal security, liberty, health, dignity, and even the lives of the individuals belonging to such groups.'[3]

While Lemkin, who was the first to use the term, viewed genocide as a process of destroying group identity, the international community has generally interpreted it very narrowly as the mass murder of members of a nation or ethnic group with the intent of completely obliterating their gene pool. As most of the literature on the concept of cultural genocide bemoans, international conventions on genocide generally do not protect nations or ethnic groups from the intentional destruction of their cultural distinctiveness, way of life, and identity.[4] However, this same literature also asserts, in line with

Lemkin's original definition of genocide, that such cultural erasure is central to all forms of genocide. If cultural erasure is not always accompanied by the mass physical extermination of a people, it historically has been expressed through substantial violence. The history of settler colonialism is abundant with examples of such violent attempts to destroy national and ethnic cultures. These include the involuntary relegation of groups to quarantined communities or reservations, the forced assimilation of peoples through threats of violence and torture, and the explicit separation of children from families for the purposes of indoctrination in boarding schools. In the process, large numbers of people from the groups experiencing cultural genocide have often been killed, especially if they demonstrated resistance to the efforts to obliterate their culture and identity.

In many ways, the plight of the Uyghurs since 2017 is reminiscent of the fate of indigenous populations in the context of settler colonialism elsewhere in the world during the nineteenth and early twentieth centuries, only with twenty-first-century tools of electronic surveillance to assist in enforcement and coercion. Prior to 2017, Uyghurs were subjected to frequent violations of their human rights, faced discrimination on the basis of their identity, and were pressured to assimilate and restricted in their ability to practice their religion, but their identity did not face complete eradication. This situation changed over the course of 2017 as the PRC began a systematic and violent dismantling of Uyghur culture and identity that can be unequivocally described as cultural genocide.

In a mostly post-colonial world, such violent attempts to destroy identity and forcibly assimilate ethnic or national groups are generally no longer acceptable to the international community. However, the fact that the PRC has justified its actions as 'counterterrorism' in the context of GWOT has allowed them to take place, at least thus far, with impunity from the international community. As members of a community that is accused of harboring an existential 'terrorist threat,' the Uyghurs' human rights have been largely suspended in the eyes of much of the global community. They have been dehumanized, stripped of their historical grievances, and portrayed as being irrational perpetrators of senseless violence. This dehumanization of the Uyghurs as alleged 'terrorists' has allowed most countries in the world to generally accept the PRC's acts of cultural genocide as an appropriate response to an existential security threat. Furthermore, those states which have criticized the PRC over the cultural genocide faced by the Uyghurs are the same states who initiated GWOT and subsequently dehumanized and suspended the rights of alleged 'terrorists' for their own interests throughout much of the first decade of the 2000s. As such, their voice has lost its moral authority on this topic.

THE ORIGINS OF THE SYSTEMATIC ATTACK ON UYGHUR IDENTITY

In retrospect, one can see the foundations of present policies of cultural genocide emerging from the 'People's War on Terror' starting in 2014. The 'People's War' had identified the root cause of the alleged Uyghur 'terrorist threat' as emanating from Uyghur culture itself, or at least from dangerous influences that had been deemed by the state to have infected that culture. On the surface, this appeared to be a campaign against religiosity, but it was much more than that. The life sentence given to Ilham Tohti in 2014 made it clear that the 'People's War' was an ideological conflict that went beyond the role of Islam in Uyghur culture or even beyond combating Uyghur calls for independence in the region. Tohti is actually a PRC patriot who believes that the Uyghurs and their homeland belong within the Chinese state. His real crime, the one for which he is presumably being punished, was putting the fate of Uyghurs and that of the PRC on equal footing. He was not advocating for an independent Eastern Turkistan before his arrest, but for a Xinjiang where Uyghurs had more control over their destiny and were respected as equals with the Han. He was not criticizing the inclusion of his homeland in China. He was criticizing the Han settler colonization of his homeland, and his life sentence sent a message to all Uyghurs that this was an issue that was non-negotiable. The state appeared to have its own designs on the region, and if the Uyghurs' voice needed to be stifled in order to accomplish what was best for the PRC's overall progress, then that was what needed to be done.

Not only was the logic of the 'People's War,' particularly its focus on Uyghur cultural change and violent suppression of all dissenting voices, already pregnant with genocidal intentions, but many of the tools for cultural erasure were also being put into place at this time. As early as 2014, the PRC military contractor, China Electronic Technology Group, had been reported as being in the process of building a massive database of all Uyghurs to serve in a 'preventative policing' program that could predict which Uyghurs had the potential to become what the state categorized as 'terrorists' (i.e. those who were prone to resisting the power of the state).[5] This massive database could cross-reference information from a variety of sources, which could be quickly disaggregated for individual Uyghurs. In essence, this was a project to build profiles for millions of Uyghurs in order to assess their degree of loyalty to the state and Party by their movements, communications, activities, and interrelationships. With this system on-line by 2016 and legally justified by the PRC's new anti-terrorism law, which allowed the state greater access to personal data, it would become an important weapon of the expanded security apparatus in the region and allow for the immediate profiling of those with whom it came in contact.

In retrospect, the signs of future mass internment had also been visible in 2014. Adrian Zenz notes that in 2014, numerous counties in the Uyghur homeland began establishing 'transformation through re-education' programs – which had previously been limited to Falun Gong followers, drug addicts, and hardened criminals – to target alleged Islamic 'extremists'.[6] Throughout 2014 and 2015, this system became more widespread, but also appeared to be in a testing phase, where different regions employed different methods. Some of the programs appeared to be daytime 'reform schools,' others involved temporary boarding, and still others looked to involve longer term detention. This process had obviously become a part of the enforcement of the limits on public displays of religiosity in the region that were established by the 'People's War,' and local authorities freely reported the metrics of their work in public documents, noting numbers trained, classes administered, and the success rate of those who were 'transformed.'[7] This campaign appeared concentrated in the south of the region and targeted those who were particularly religious, but it was also carried out in rural areas in the north that had high Uyghur population density. Despite the successes claimed by local authorities, it did not appear that these efforts were stemming the violence in the region, which had only escalated through 2014 and 2015.

There is also evidence from this period that the re-education campaign carried with it a clear biopolitical logic articulated through a discourse inspired by Public Health, which viewed 'extremism' as an infection that needed to be managed in a scientific manner based on demographics. Zenz, for example, cites the PRC Justice Department's Party Committee Secretary in the region as suggesting in 2015 that '70% of Uyghur villagers will follow all the others, but that 30% are "polluted by religious extremism" and require "concentrated education;"' 'when the 30% are transformed ... the village is basically cleansed.'[8] He also quotes the secretary of the Khotan County's Politics and Law Committee from the same time providing a similar analysis, noting that 'about 5% belong to the hardened faction, 15% are supporters, and 80% are illiterates.'[9] As Zenz suggests, this logic of percentages was already suggestive of a biopolitical strategy that considered the portions of the population requiring 'treatment' and/or 'quarantining' in order to ensure that the alleged infection of 'extremism' did not spread to others.[10] Eventually, it would appear that this Public Health-inspired logic would additionally prescribe 'inoculation' for all through its targeting of Uyghur identity.

Thus, by 2014, the logic had been established and all of the required procedures were already being put in place for carrying out the systematic destruction of Uyghur identity we are witnessing today. A massive system of surveillance and loyalty evaluation was in advanced development, a methodology for mass internment and thought transformation was being beta tested, and the biopolitical logic had already been established for attacking Uyghur culture in the name of countering 'extremism' and 'terrorism.' It just needed the motivation for the state to definitively give up on trying to get Uyghurs to voluntarily submit to assimilation, and a political leader aggressive enough to put the system into action. Chen Quanguo, who took over the Party leadership of the Uyghur region on 29 August 2016, would have the qualities to do just that, and it did not seem to take him very long to abandon the belief that Uyghurs would voluntarily assimilate and submit to Chinese settler colonialism. Given the prior existence of the procedures required for the destruction of Uyghur identity, Chen should not be considered the architect of the Uyghurs' cultural genocide, but he certainly became its implementer.

CHEN THE ENFORCER

Chen Quanguo had made a name for himself as Party Secretary of the Tibetan Autonomous Region (TAR) between 2011 and 2016. During that time, he had significantly transformed Tibet. Despite this region's long history of resistance to Chinese rule, he was able to significantly limit public displays of Tibetan dissent during his tenure.[11] Chen's strategy for mitigating dissent in the TAR called for 'convenience police stations' in urban areas every 500 meters connected to cities' vast network of CCTV cameras.[12] Authorities called this extensive system of surveillance and police enforcement throughout urban areas 'grid-style social management' in the service of 'stability maintenance.'[13] Given the importance that Xi Jinping placed on 'stability maintenance' in the Uyghur region by 2016 and Chen's experience working in what the CCP considered to be its other 'troubled minority region,' Chen was a logical candidate to take over governance of the region when Zhang was relieved of his position during the summer of 2016.

Chen's arrival in the Uyghur region coincided with yet another incident that reified the narrative of the alleged 'terrorist threat' posed by Uyghurs. On 30 August 2016, a day after Chen took over the leadership of the Uyghur region, it was reported that an alleged suicide attack had been carried out against the Chinese embassy in Bishkek, Kyrgyzstan, reportedly by a Uyghur.[14] However, the details surrounding this incident were suspiciously nonsensical, reminiscent of the alleged ETIM plot to bomb the US Embassy in Bishkek in 2002. Within a week, the Kyrgyz authorities had claimed that the attack was carried out by a Uyghur of unknown origin who held a Tajik passport, had been ordered by a Uyghur group in Syria, and was funded by the *Al-Nursra Front*, but all five arrested in connection with the attack were Kyrgyz citizens.[15] Furthermore, nobody had ever identified the Uyghur who had allegedly carried out the attack; *Al-Nursra* was not known to carry out attacks outside Syria; and the Kyrgyz who were arrested in connection with the attack were neither known to be associated with TIP nor claimed to have any knowledge of the operation.[16] Regardless of who was actually behind the attack on the Chinese embassy in Bishkek, the PRC would use the incident to further hype the alleged 'terrorist threat' posed by Uyghurs to China. In response to the attack, the Chinese authorities blamed the phantom group ETIM and threatened to 'firmly strike' against the group in retribution.[17]

These events conveniently played into Chen's plans to step up security in the Uyghur region during his first year as Party leader. When Chen first articulated his policy agenda for the Uyghur region in September 2016, he stressed 'placing stability above all else,' and he called on security organs to employ increased proactive means for eradicating the 'three evils.'[18] In his first year, Chen advertised almost 100,680 security-related jobs, over thirteen times the average annual security-related government recruits for 2009–2015 when most of the violence involving Uyghurs inside China had allegedly occurred.[19] He also established an estimated 7,300 'convenience police stations' in urban areas around the Uyghur region based on the model he had employed in Tibet.[20] It was evident that Chen was beginning his term in office by building an unprecedented police state in the region.

If Chen's initial contribution to the region's already substantial security apparatus was his mass deployment of security personnel and the establishment of thousands of 'convenience police stations' as he had done in Tibet, he also proved to be adept at utilizing the Uyghur homeland's existing security infrastructure. This was particularly the case with regards to electronic surveillance, which he quickly weaponized as a means of social control. While, as discussed above, the state had already contracted with China Electronic Technology Group in 2014 to build a massive database that could be utilized to identify potential 'terrorists' within the Uyghur population before they committed violence, Chen appears to be the first political leader in the region to put this database to extensive use by adding data points to the system and utilizing it as a mass social evaluation tool.

The PRC's 'Counterterrorism Law' that had been passed in late 2015 already gave the state legal means for accessing a variety of information about Uyghurs, including bank accounts, social media accounts, work history, and history of travel. However, under Chen the state would collect a battery of biometric data on every Uyghur, which could be added to the program's existing data points. As Darren Byler, who was doing fieldwork in the region at the time, notes, there were a variety of efforts to provide Uyghurs with free health exams in 2016 where they were asked to provide DNA, fingerprints, voice signatures, and face signatures, all of which went into this system.[21] According to Byler, the state claimed to have collected such data for 18.8 million of the region's 21.8 million people by the end of the campaign.[22] In December 2016, the regional government adopted new internet regulations, which increased the state's ability to legally monitor all content posted by Uyghurs on the internet, allowing Chen's administration to make extensive use of Uyghurs' internet history to mine for data about 'ideological inclinations' and associations that could also be input into this database.[23] To aid in this effort, the state also criminalized the possession of VPNs (Virtual Private Networks) for the circumvention of surveillance, calling such programs 'terrorism software.'[24]

In a 2018 report, Human Rights Watch (HRW) provided much more detailed information about this program of big data collection, surveillance, and profiling of Uyghurs, which it identifies by its official name, the Integrated Joint Operations Platform (IJOP).[25] As HRW notes, additional information for the IJOP was collected via mobile apps on the phones of cadres who were sent out to regularly visit Uyghur homes, particularly in rural areas, and to ask household members for 'a range of data about their family, their "ideological situation," and relationships with neighbors.'[26] Other Uyghurs were asked at work or when engaging with the government on mundane tasks, such as obtaining licenses or registering residency, to fill out detailed questionnaires asking about their religious observation, daily habits, travel abroad, and so on, for inclusion in the IJOP. In short, the state would take every opportunity afforded it to collect both quantitative and qualitative data about each and every Uyghur, and that data was added to their profiles in the IJOP database.

However, more important than the additional data points collected for this database, was Chen's use of the IJOP as a tool of social control and, ultimately, the infrastructure of the Uyghur region's biopolitics. Under Chen, the state would use the IJOP to evaluate every Uyghur by a variety of parameters to characterize their degree of 'safeness,' hence determining the person's fate. As James Leibold has noted, this system 'sorts its citizenry into those deemed "normal" and thus trustworthy, and those who are "deviant" or "abnormal" in their thoughts or demeanour.'[27] Those determined to be 'normal' were allowed to continue their lives unfettered, albeit under continued surveillance, whereas those labeled as 'deviant' or 'abnormal' were likely to be subjected to interrogation, detention, imprisonment, or extensive political re-education.[28] While the PRC had obviously been developing these tools to track and evaluate Uyghurs for some time, it was not until Chen came to power that they were used to explicitly sort the population and target 'undesirables.'

Despite Chen's implementation of this massive campaign to step up the use of surveillance technology and bolster the region's police forces, violence had not been completely stopped in the region by the end of 2016. While there were virtually no reports of significant violence in the Uyghur homeland throughout most of 2016, in December reports emerged about a violent act perpetrated by Uyghurs, which appeared both politically motivated and premeditated. In the Karakash county near Khotan, a group of Uyghurs allegedly drove a truck into the yard of the regional CCP headquarters and blew up the truck, killing one person.[29] Declaring the incident a 'terrorist attack,' authorities immediately killed all four Uyghurs who had allegedly carried it out.[30]

This was the first major act of violence reported in the Uyghur region during 2016, but it came at the end of a year that authorities were hailing as exemplary in terms of 'counterterrorism' efforts. Furthermore, less than two months later, in mid-February 2017, another alleged attack was reported in Guma county, about half way between Khotan and Yarkand. Allegedly, three Uyghurs had entered a residential compound near a regional government headquarters in Guma and killed five people, including government officials.[31] Authorities predictably killed all three alleged attackers and placed the entire town under lockdown, with police and security reportedly standing every 10 to 20 meters on the street to keep order.[32] The alleged attack in Guma would be the last incident of violence in the Uyghur homeland up to the time of this book's publication that authorities would characterize as a 'terrorist attack,' but it would soon be followed by a violent state-led campaign of terror against Uyghurs that would be more extensive than all acts of Uyghur-led violence combined over the previous two decades.

THE HAMMER COMES DOWN: 2017

In 2017, all of the disparate aspects of China's counterterrorism efforts that had been in effect over the last few years came together to create a unified and systematic campaign to destroy Uyghur identity. It would be inaccurate to suggest that any one event triggered this campaign, especially given that its preparation had likely long been in process, but there were warning signs that the hammer was about to come down on Uyghurs in unprecedented ways. The violent incidents in Karakash and Guma in late 2016 and early 2017, while far less violent than the many incidents in 2014 and 2015, provided the perfect justification for Chen's administration to begin a re-evaluation of the state's 'counterterrorism' strategy in the region, particularly the role of ethnic Uyghur cadres in the implementation of that strategy.

Following the truck bombing of the government building in Karakash, it is noteworthy that Chen ordered an inspection of police and Party 'counterterrorism' work in the Khotan region in March 2017. Ninety-six rural cadres, assumed to all be ethnic Uyghurs, were subsequently punished for not monitoring religious behavior in the

region adequately, failing to sufficiently gather household information, poorly monitoring mosque attendance, and not examining
the religious content of traditional Uyghur life-cycle rituals for what
the state considered 'extremist' influences.[33]
At the same time, an 'open letter' campaign began to require
that high-ranking Uyghur officials issue public written statements
declaring their loyalty to China and calling on ethnic Uyghurs
throughout the region to focus their efforts on both weeding out so-
called 'terrorists' and ensuring those responsible for doing so were
not shirking their duties.[34] As one ethnic Uyghur high-ranking CCP
official in Kashgar wrote in one such letter, 'we must stand out and
reveal "two-faced" people, thoroughly seize bad elements out from
the masses, clean them out.'[35] In retrospect, this appeared to be the
initiation of a larger effort to identify and punish 'two-faced' officials
who might not be sincere in fighting Uyghur dissent. Thus, from
this point onward, even those Uyghurs who appeared loyal to the
Party, worked in the police, or were CCP members were put under
scrutiny as potential dissidents, disloyal to the state, and facilitating
the alleged 'terrorist threat.' In retrospect, this was a turning point in
the PRC's biopolitical interpretation of this threat. As far as the PRC
was concerned, the 'infection' of 'extremism' had already spread like
a cancer throughout the entirety of the Uyghur people.

As if to reassure the Han population of the region, in the wake of
the violent incidents in Karakash and Guma, the PLA also held two
massive military parades and 'anti-terrorism' exercises demonstrating the PRC's capacities of blunt force in January and February of
2017. The first, within a week of the alleged December 2016 truck
bombing on the Party headquarters in Karakash, was held in Urumqi,
with high-ranking officials, including Chen Quanguo, in attendance.[36] The demonstration of force displayed armed units trained to
fight 'terrorists,' rows of armored anti-riot vehicles, and exhibitions
of 'counterterrorism' tactics in urban environments.[37] Two days after
the violence in Guma, a similar event was orchestrated, with thousands of armed officers marching through the streets of Khotan.[38]
This was a particularly impressive show of force in a region that
demographically was still around 90% Uyghur. Similar parades and

military exhibitions would subsequently take place in major cities throughout the region for the remainder of the spring, traveling from city to city like a carnival of strength.[39]

In the context of the punishment of 'two-faced' Uyghur cadres that was taking place at the time, these parades seemed to be sending a message to the Han population that the state's central apparatus was ready to use any means necessary to eradicate the threat of Uyghur resistance even if local ethnic Uyghur cadres and police could not be trusted. To accent this point, the deputy Party chief of the region, Zhu Hailun, would state at the rally in Khotan that 'continued vigilance and high-pressure deterrence against terrorists have forced them to the end of the road, like a cornered beast driven to desperate action.'[40] In using this rhetoric, he might as well have declared the 'end of the road' for the Uyghur people.

Another sign of impending systematic cultural erasure that also appeared in March was the approval by the regional CCP of new 'de-extremification' regulations for the region. In general, these regulations represented a clarification of the PRC 'Countererrorism Law' and the 'Religious Affairs Regulations,' providing a more explicit definition of 'extremism' and 'extremist' behavior. The regulations list fifteen different manifestations of 'extremist' behaviour, which include virtually all forms of advice given to others on proper religious observation, including characterizing activities other than eating certain food as *Haram*, giving advice about the proper rituals to be used in religious ceremonies, discouraging others from marrying, living with, or intermingling with those of other ethnicities and faiths, and generally encouraging others to be religious.[41] Furthermore, it also lists as 'extremist' behavior the possession, sharing, obtainment, or distribution of materials that might encourage religiosity among others, the use of certain names of Arabic origin, and the wearing of 'irregular' beards and specific styles of clothing.[42] In short, the regulations criminalized virtually all religious behavior and any consumption of religious information that was not explicitly promoted by the state.

While many of these restrictions had already been applied in rural areas, particularly in the south of the Uyghur homeland, during the 'People's War on Terror,' the new regulations advocated a more pervasive application and one that was more explicitly assimilationist. As Article 4 of the regulations states, 'de-extremification shall persist in the basic directives of the Party's work on religion, persist in an orientation of making religion more *Chinese* and under the law, and actively guide religions to become compatible with socialist society.'[43] The regulations also adopted what the state called a 'whole of society' approach, calling for the eradication of anything deemed 'extremist' (i.e. Islamic) in any sphere of life. Article 12 of the regulations criminalized academic research on anything that could be interpreted as 'promoting extremification through research projects, social investigation, academic forums and the like.'[44] Likewise, subsequent articles outlined how manifestations of extremism must be removed from, and 'de-extremification' promoted in, the commercial sphere, the arenas of public health, education, telecommunications, media, transportation, trade unions, and virtually every area of governance and society one can imagine. In this sense, it was obvious that this new 'de-extremification' effort was to include scrutiny of all Uyghurs in all sectors and regions of society. While it was mostly focused on religion, it is noteworthy that its pervasive application suggested that it could be used to criminalize most aspects of Uyghur culture itself and especially any parenting acts that brought children in contact with religious ideas or which promoted Uyghur distinctiveness.

However, it was Article 14 of the new regulations that was perhaps the most ominous, as it laid the foundations for the soon to be established mass internment 're-education' system. It prescribes efforts to establish 'educational transformation, implementing a combination of individual and group education; combining legal education and mentoring; combining ideological education, psychological counseling, behavioral corrections, and skills training; combining educational transformation and humanistic care; and strengthening the effectiveness of educational transformation.'[45] Adrian Zenz, who was the first scholar to expose the construction of mass internment camps in the Uyghur homeland, has suggested that this particular article in the 'De-extremification Regulations' marked the beginning of these camps' establishment.

It is not surprising, therefore, that March 2017 also marked the beginning of a year-long process of accelerated state procurement for construction services focused on the building of the mass internment camps that were subsequently established throughout the region.[46] Zenz's research for the period between spring 2016 and the end of 2018 tracks a massive institutional build-up of prison-like structures around the region, equipped with substantial security features including high walls, barbed wire, monitoring systems, and guard rooms.[47] It is likely that the Party had based its decision to institute this mass system of internment centers on the experiences of the earlier smaller 're-education' programs that had existed since 2014 and which were testing different methods of reprogramming Uyghurs' consciousness. Zenz, for example, cites a local Party-led study of the 're-education' work against 'extremism' from 2014 to 2016, which recommended the establishment in all prefectures and counties of 'centralized transformation through education training centres.'[48] This is exactly what Chen's administration had decided to do by the middle of 2017, and it would dramatically change the situation in the region, essentially initiating the process of cultural genocide.

Since that time, the PRC has set in motion a systematic campaign to destroy the Uyghur identity, along with that of other indigenous Muslims of the region, and to forcibly assimilate these people into a Han dominant culture. The most headline-grabbing part of this systematic assault on ethnic identity is the network of mass internment camps, which are reminiscent of genocides past, but this is only the centerpiece of a complex of policies and measures promoting cultural destruction. In addition to the 're-education' internment camps, this system includes multiple other forms of incarceration as well as the comprehensive system of surveillance and evaluation in the region. Together, these institutions create an environment of complete fear and complicity while dismantling the social capital of Uyghur communities and breaking the spirits of individual Uyghurs. As this system of fear and spirit-breaking neutralizes all forms of Uyghur resistance, the Chinese state is also gradually cleansing the Uyghur territory of its uniquely Uyghur cultural markers through language destruction, the erasure of cultural traditions, and the razing of cultural monuments and communities. In place of these Uyghur cultural markers, the PRC is establishing a distinctly Chinese landscape both culturally and physically. At the same time, the state is instituting policies of forced assimilation, coerced residential labor, and coerced miscegenation aimed at breaking down Uyghur collective identity. In essence, this system is facilitating a process of erase and replace, erasing Uyghur culture and identity and seeking to replace it with a Han-centric Chinese culture and identity.

THE SYSTEM OF INCARCERATION AND INTERNMENT

By most accounts, the mass internment of Uyghurs and other indigenous Muslims in the region started shortly after the release of the 'De-extremification Regulations,' in April and May 2017.[49] However, it was not until the fall, the week of 11 September 2017, sixteen years after the attack that initiated GWOT, that reports were coming out in foreign media which acknowledged the widespread nature of this program. Over three successive days, reports were filed by *The Globe and Mail*, Human Rights Watch (HRW), and RFA suggesting that 're-education' in the region had transitioned, from something to which a nominal number of particularly religious Uyghurs were subjected in rural areas, to a mass phenomenon applicable to large swaths of the population.[50]

HRW reported that 're-education' internment centers, with a variety of names from 'Counterterrorism Training Centers' to 'Educational Transformation Training Centers,' had popped up throughout the region and that families had told the organization that their relatives had disappeared into them for months with no information about why they had been interned or when they would be released.[51] HRW also reported that the centers were a combination of repurposed existing public buildings and new construction.[52] Having successfully called up local Party organs and police stations in rural regions, RFA noted that the numbers of people entering these centers were significant in rural regions.[53] According to one female police officer from Akto who agreed to speak with RFA, 'five kinds of suspicious people have been detained and sent to education camps: people who throw away their mobile phone's SIM card or did not use their mobile phone after registering it; former prisoners already released from prison; blacklisted people; "suspicious people" who have some fundamental religious sentiment; and the people who have relatives abroad.'[54]

In the months between the beginning of the program in the spring and the reporting on it in September, Zenz estimates that procurements for the renovation and construction of these institutions amounted to at least 860 Million Yuan or 126 Million US dollars.[55] By spring of 2018, a Chinese ethnic Han law student studying in Canada had documented, using the satellite imagery of Google Earth, that these procurements had resulted in the building of 94 separate new re-education internment camps throughout the Uyghur homeland.[56] According to Zenz's calculations, these camps held an estimated one million Uyghurs by the spring of 2018, which he suggests equals 11.5% of the population of Uyghurs and Kazakhs in the region between 20 and 79 years old.[57] If these figures are accurate, the mass internment of Uyghurs and other indigenous Muslims in the region had quickly escalated to one of the largest ethnically profiled extra-legal mass internment of people in history.

As the existence of these mass internment camps was being revealed internationally during 2018, the PRC continued to deny their existence.[58] However, it was clear that the PRC would be unable to keep such a mass campaign against specific ethnic groups a secret, especially when they involved the new construction of almost 100 large prison-like structures. Furthermore, in May 2018, the *Associated Press* was able to interview several Uyghurs and Kazakhs who had been in camps and, by a variety means, had been able to escape to Kazakhstan.[59] This provided the first eyewitness accounts of life inside these camps, and the stories were highly disturbing. Amidst this mounting evidence, in October 2018, the Chinese government finally acknowledged the existence of the camps, but it claimed that these institutions were benign 'vocational training centers' meant to rehabilitate alleged 'extremists.'[60] A number of internees and staff who have been in these camps have had the opportunity to speak openly to international media and scholars since 2017. Their descriptions of daily life in the camps suggest that these institutions are not merely benign vocational schools, but are essentially ethnically profiled mass internment centers, deliberately intended to cleanse internees of their identities as Uyghurs and other indigenous Muslim ethnicities.

Life in the camps

There is evidence that these camps are not uniform either in whom they intern or in their conditions. In particular, it has been documented that people are not sent to these camps merely by a single list of criteria. Rather, there is solid evidence that regional administrations are given quotas for internees. An official from a village near Ghulja, for example, confirmed to RFA in March 2018 that his local government had been tasked with ensuring that at least 10% of the local population was sent to the 're-education' camps.[61] As a result, the criteria for internment differs by location as Party officials need to find a predetermined number of alleged 'extremists' in their locale. Given that the definition of 'extremist behavior' is so broad, officials have significant leeway in determining whom to intern. To highlight the many absurd reasons for which Uyghurs have been sent to these camps, *Foreign Policy* published an article in 2018 highlighting '48 Ways to Get Sent to a Chinese Concentration Camp,' including such 'suspicious behavior' as owning a tent, telling others not to swear, and refusing to smoke cigarettes or drink alcohol.[62] If the reasons for internment vary, the conditions in different camps also inevitably differ. Some are brand new buildings, while others are repurposed ones; some are seriously over-crowded, and others likely are not. However, as is the case in any mass internment camp, the most important factor determining the conditions inside them is the character of the person in charge and their staff. Unfortunately, given the lack of access by outside observers to these camps, except on public relations junkets to model internment centers, such granular information as which camps are the most oppressive has yet to come to light.

That said, it does seem that there is some uniformity in the activities to which internees are subjected region-wide. Most accounts of the camps mention a regime that involves both intensive Chinese-language training and hours of 'political education.'[63] However, neither of these activities are as benign as they appear at first glance. Teachers of language classes in the camps, for example, have suggested that their lessons were more concerned with power and intimidation than with pedagogy.[64] One teacher recounted that she taught behind bars, separated from her students, and students were required to sit upright at full attention for a four-hour language class.[65] If the students moved, nodded off, or twitched, the omni-present CCTV cameras would capture the movement, and the person monitoring the class on CCTV would warn them via loudspeaker to sit at full attention. Students who did not follow these orders would be forced to stand for the remainder of class or even be removed from class for further punishment. Furthermore, this particular teacher said that students did not have a common level of Chinese-language ability, some with better Chinese-language skills than the teacher, and others with no prior instruction in the language at all.[66] This dynamic suggests that these classes are intended less as a means of instruction and more as a powerful assertion of the now declared prominence of the Chinese language over that of Uyghur.

The political education classes are at least as torturous if not more so. After several hours of being subjected to propaganda videos and lectures about the greatness of the CCP, the internees are forced to participate in self-criticism. As Saraygul Sautbay, an ethnic Kazakh who also taught in an internment camp, recounted, 'the pupils had to think about their sins; almost everything could be considered a sin, from observing religious practices and not knowing the Chinese language or culture, to immoral behavior; inmates who did not think of sins that were severe enough or didn't make up something were punished.'[67] Another internee who escaped to Kazakhstan, Omär Bekali, notes that the repetitive nature of chanting propaganda slogans in these classes become akin to psychological torture over time.[68]

If the language and political education classes are themselves psychologically torturing, life outside the classroom involves an even graver spirit-breaking experience. Internees are not only forbidden to speak in their native language, but are not permitted to even interact among themselves or speak to each other outside the classroom. Furthermore, according to one alleged former guard at a particularly large camp, internees were not even allowed to display any emotions throughout their stay.[69] To enforce these draconian rules, ubiquitous CCTV cameras provide omni-present surveillance. Bathrooms are reported to be in open spaces in dorm rooms, and some have reported having to use buckets instead of actual toilets in their rooms.[70] Internees are also provided minimal rations of food, which accounts for the gaunt appearance of most of those who have been lucky enough to be released. These conditions have made suicide in the camps so pervasive that internees are sometimes asked to procure 'suicide-safe' clothing through relatives to prevent them from taking their lives.[71]

One of the more mysterious stories that is found in most eyewitness accounts of the camps is the mandatory administration of drugs to internees. A former guard notes that all young to middle-aged internees are forced to receive unknown shots on a monthly basis allegedly to prevent flus and other sicknesses.[72] None of the internees who have spoken about this practice believe that this is the purpose of the medicines that were provided them. It is unclear whether the drugs being administered are all the same or if different internees are given different medicines. Several female former internees have said that these drugs stopped their menstrual cycle and ultimately resulted in sterilization.[73] Others have said that they have lost cognitive abilities from the drugs they were given.

As one might expect, the most disturbing stories to have emerged from the camps are those about torture and abuse. Most eyewitness accounts discuss having either experienced or witnessed some level of torture. Many mention that the camp in which they were located had dedicated rooms for torture, and there are numerous accounts of the diverse ways that the 'Tiger Chair,' which latches ankles and wrists, is used in torture.[74] Others, such as Mihrigul Tursun, say they were subjected to electro-shock on numerous occasions.[75] In general, torture appears to be ubiquitous in these camps, but its brutality may depend upon the given camp. More recently, former female internees have also come forward to tell terrifying stories of sexual abuse and rape at the hands of camp guards.[76] While this sexual abuse is likely not condoned by the state, it seems to be tacitly allowed by at least some of the camp administrators. It is likely, given the scale of these camps and the apparent power given to guards in them, that such incidents are endemic.

One of the common statements heard from witnesses is that they feel as if their identity and nation is deliberately targeted in the camps. This is accomplished through both the content of the re-education classes and the psychological torture and physical humiliation to which internees are subjected. This was apparent even to one ethnic Kazakh with Kazakhstan citizenship who was interned for eight months in a camp without much prior knowledge of the Chinese language. While he admits to not understanding much of the content, he notes, 'what I gathered from those classes was that they just wanted to erase us as a nation, erase our identity, turn us into Chinese people.'[77]

In this context, it is important to note that many of the people who work as staff in these internment centers are themselves Uyghurs or from other indigenous Muslim groups. Accounts of teachers who have worked in camps suggest that their work is considered a sort of punishment in itself. Saraygul Sautbay claims she was forcibly sent to a camp to teach, and an account from another teacher suggests that school directors threaten to send underperforming teachers to teach in the camps. However, it appears that most Uyghurs and other Muslim guards and CCTV monitors have taken jobs of their own free will and are paid handsomely for their work. While it is likely that some of the staff from the indigenous groups sadistically enjoy the power they wield, the one unverified letter that has come to light from such a camp security staff member, an alleged ethnic Kazakh CCTV monitor, suggests that the work is traumatic for many if not most.[78] In addition to writing with disdain about the disturbing evidence he saw of sexual abuse and rape, he notes that he was frequently threatened with possible internment himself if he made any mistakes or refused to report violations.[79]

From internment to forced labor

Recent research suggests that there have been attempts since at least 2018 to marry 're-education' camps with new centers for forced labor. This is also related to another state-led program that is seeking to transform rural Uyghur farmers and Kazakh herders into factory laborers after the completion of a shorter course of 're-education.' These programs may provide insight into PRC plans for re-integrating some of the people who have been relegated to mass internment camps since 2017, as well as its more general plans for transforming the Uyghur identity and the Uyghur homeland, particularly in the still Uyghur-dominated Uyghur south.

Research by Adrian Zenz suggests that, starting in 2019, numerous camps began adding factory spaces within their encampments and have allowed companies, particularly in the textile industry, to establish operations in these new factories. According to Zenz, these companies use the internees as workers in exchange for a series of state-provided subsidies, which include using the factories free of charge for two years and at half market value subsequently, getting salary subsidies for each former internee they take on as workers, and a variety of other preferential benefits.[80] It is assumed that these workers are the 'graduates' of the camps, who have proven themselves fluent in Chinese and having a thorough knowledge of the political education they received. Furthermore, some of these workers are allowed to go home on weekends and to eventually transfer to 'satellite factories' in their home region.[81] This provides a possible endgame for the PRC in its 're-education' system, but it also allows for the long-term sustainability of the system and a means to integrate it with settler colonization by creating ethnically segregated and low-paid work for sufficiently 're-educated' Uyghurs and other indigenous Muslims in the region. Furthermore, reports that were published while this book was still in production provide evidence that some of these former internees, along with other Uyghur youth from the rural south, are being funneled into factories in inner China that produce parts and goods for major international corporations, directly impacting settler colonization by reducing the indigenous population of the Uyghur homeland's south.[82]

This system also provides propaganda cover for the PRC from international criticism of the mass internment of Uyghurs. It appears, for example, that during 2019, the aims and courses of some of the camps described above have shifted to teaching factory labor skills for eventual placement in factories, which are often adjacent to the internment camps themselves, but are sometimes elsewhere in the region or even located entirely outside the Uyghur homeland in China proper. This is most likely the case with the model camps shown to a variety of international journalists during the summer of 2019 where internees were shown doing factory work and receiving vocational training.[83] Additionally, as Zenz points out, some of these factories are hybrid production units that include both internees and non-internees, helping to further hide the existence of the mass internment system.

Equally, and perhaps even more disturbing, Zenz and others have identified several other related factory work programs that serve 'surplus rural labor.' One provides former farmers with training that includes the classes of the original 're-education' program in addition to factory labor skills, eventually placing them in the new factories that are being constructed throughout the region, both adjacent to internment camps and in industrial parks.[84] It seems that this training's implementation may be done differently in different regions, but in Kashgar, it involves at least a one-month centralized training implemented by the state, which focuses on Chinese-language instruction and political education.[85] In many ways, this can be characterized as 're-education lite,' and those who undergo such courses are frequently placed in factories mixed with former internees. As Zenz suggests, these programs are characterized by the state as 'industry-based poverty alleviation,' but they are effectively serving to quarantine large swaths of the rural population in factories where they will also be forced to use the Chinese language and follow the directives of Han foremen.[86]

A report published in Australia in March 2020 identifies a related program of coerced labor that has been in place since 2017, sending both former internees and other Uyghur youth to inner China to work in segregated and closely monitored work units within large factories supplying major international corporations including Nike and Apple. According to this report, at least 80,000 Uyghur youth, mostly from the rural south, have been a part of this labor transfer from the homeland since 2017, and they are limited in their movement as well as subjected to 're-education' during hours after work. As of this book's printing, it appears as if this program may be expanding, helping to facilitate large transfers of Uyghurs from their homeland.[87]

Another program involves the construction of small 'satellite factories' in rural areas, which usually serve no more than two villages.[88] This program explicitly targets women, who otherwise might avoid salaried work to stay at home and raise their children, seeking to integrate them into the Han-dominated and Chinese-language environment of daily factory work. To account for the care of these women's children, these 'satellite factories' have built-in daycare centers, which serve to socialize their children into Chinese society and break the generational transfer of cultural mores, which would be accomplished through child-rearing by a stay-at-home mother.

While it is unknown how recruitment is carried out for any of these 'surplus rural labor' programs, both in the region and in inner China, it is clear that participation in them cannot be considered voluntary given the present conditions in the Uyghur homeland. It is assumed, for example, that those who are asked to participate in these labor programs and deny the opportunity to do so will quickly earn themselves a potentially one-way ticket to an actual internment camp or a prison.

As Zenz points out, the program for internees and those for rural surplus labor and stay-at-home mothers are overtly political, and combine the goals of development, increasingly framed as 'poverty alleviation,' with those of 'stability maintenance' and 'counterterrorism.' In demonstrating this, Zenz cites the region's Vice-Chairman of the Political Consultative Council as saying 'satellite factories are to be built in the vocational skills education training centers (i.e. re-education internment camps), so that people affected by terrorism and extreme thoughts can learn the nation's common language, study law, and understand the right and wrong; they can also learn skills, become able to work, and increase their incomes.'[89] The labor transfer program to Inner China, which also involves 're-education,' serves a similar purpose, but it also facilitates demographic changes to the Uyghur homeland, thus directly aiding Han settler colonization. It is apparent that all of these programs are a high priority of the state given that much of the infrastructure for this coercive labor and 're-education' scheme is being funneled through the Pairing Assistance Program (PAP) that has been driving the region's development and colonization since at least 2010. In this way, these programs represent a transition of sorts from cultural genocide in the name of 'counterterrorism' to settler colonization by 'public-private partnership.'

The ways in which these coercive labor programs seamlessly blend with the mass internment camps is instructive of the actual role that mass internment and incarceration plays in the ongoing destruction of Uyghur identity. The mass indoctrination in the camps is unlikely to actually eradicate Uyghur culture by force, but the fear of internment or incarceration provides a significant incentive for those outside the camps to comply with state assimilation designs. As is suggested above for the factory labor programs targeting rural Uyghurs, the omni-present implicit threat of internment provides coercive incentives for Uyghurs who are not interned to 'voluntarily' participate in a variety of assimilationist programs, since refusal of participation would raise suspicion from the state of 'extremist' inclinations.

Imprisonment

While the stories of life in the mass internment camps are horrific, it is important to note that many other Uyghurs face even more brutal conditions in actual prisons, as the internment camps only house part of the population taken out of society since 2017. During 2017, almost 87,000 people were convicted of crimes in the Uyghur region, ten times more than in 2016, and between 2017 and 2018 the total number of convictions in the region was 230,000.[90] While not all of these convictions were against Uyghurs or other Muslims, and not all received prison terms, one would assume that the lion's share were Uyghurs and other indigenous Muslims who were subsequently incarcerated.

It is noteworthy, for example, that most Uyghur cultural figures, including professors, writers, and musicians, as well as most religious figures, appear to have received actual prison terms rather than being subjected to 're-education.' These people are likely considered too important to the production and maintenance of Uyghur culture and identity to risk allowing them to influence others in 're-education' classroom settings. Furthermore, by the logic of the 2017 'De-extremification Regulations,' which mostly criminalize those who influence others, it would follow that cultural and religious figures would be prime suspects for influencing the larger Uyghur population. In addition to such high-level cultural and religious figures, it is likely that many others whom the local authorities determine are particularly 'deviant' are arrested rather than extra-legally interned and are subsequently given lengthy prison terms. In fact, the line that distinguishes whether one is incarcerated or interned is probably determined by the limits on the state to process actual arrests and the limited physical space of prisons in the region.

Furthermore, there is evidence that suggests that 're-education' internment and prison sentences are not mutually exclusive. Poorly behaving internees may be arrested and relegated to prisons, and prisoners ending terms may be sent for 're-education.' There is also some evidence that the PRC may be using the blurred lines between the two systems as a means to cover up its mass internment in the region. Since October 2018, there have been reports of large numbers of people being transferred from the region to prisons in inner China.[91] Most of these reports mention the movement of internees from 're-education' camps to these prisons outside the region, but it is also possible that this is merely a response to over-crowded prisons in the Uyghur region or, more insidiously, that it is a gradual process of population transfer.

While there are likely substantive differences between being interned and being imprisoned in the Uyghur region, it is important to note that the number of Uyghurs who have suffered either of these two forms of punishment appears to be astronomical. This has left a chilling effect on all those who have not suffered these fates. It has created an environment of unprecedented fear that is felt throughout the Uyghur population, from poor farmers to government bureaucrats. Saying or writing the wrong thing, talking to the wrong person, owning the wrong book, or being from the wrong family can land anyone in either a mass internment camp or a prison. As a result, those outside these penal institutions do everything they can to please authorities. In this way, the threat of internment and incarceration has proven to be the most persuasive tool for the destruction of Uyghur identity outside the camps, especially when combined with the pervasive system of surveillance and evaluation being implemented throughout the region.

SURVEILLANCE OUTSIDE THE CAMPS AND THE ALGORITHM OF 'EXTREMISM'

As suggested above, the threat of arbitrary internment or incarceration has created an environment of complete fear for those left outside of penal institutions in the Uyghur homeland since 2017. Colleagues of mine who went to the region to try to do fieldwork in the summer of 2018, for example, found that they could only exchange pleasantries with friends for short periods of time in 'unwatched places' and could not engage substantively with anybody with whom they were not familiar. In essence, everybody in the region is in a constant state of self-censorship. This sense of constant fear is further reinforced by the sophisticated system of surveillance and evaluation that Chen Quanguo has succeeded in making pervasive throughout the region. This omni-present surveillance has created an 'open-air panopticon prison' that can track every Uyghur's movement, communications, biometrics, and history at the press of a button. As The Guardian suggested in spring 2017, it is the 'perfect police state.'[92]

The most striking aspect of the surveillance system outside the camps is its high-tech nature, which evokes visions of dystopian science fiction. Although the sophisticated gadgetry that goes into the region's network of electronic surveillance is novel, the network's true power comes from the way it is integrated into the

IJOP. Through the IJOP, the information collected by this network is automatically fed into an algorithm meant to evaluate one's level of exposure to influences deemed by the state to be 'extremist.'[93] Since 2017, daily life in the region's cities inevitably involves having one's IJOP profile examined multiple times. The ubiquitous checkpoints throughout public spaces require some form of identity confirmation, whether it is from one's ID card, mobile phone, iris scan, facial scan, or a combination of any of these identifiers. This immediately allows those manning the checkpoint to get notifications if an IJOP profile is determined suspicious. A state document leaked in 2020, which details personal information about 311 people from Karakash who had been interned in camps, for example, demonstrates that 38 of them had been identified for internment by such IJOP 'push notifications.'[94] Checkpoints also provide additional opportunities to collect data for the IJOP, as police officers are equipped with scanners that can check the contents of one's mobile phone. CCTV cameras equipped with state-of-the-art artificial intelligence technology and facial recognition perform similar feats by identifying those involved in suspicious behavior on the street. Any consumer product that could serve as a weapon, including kitchen utensils and farming tools, is engraved with a QR code, which must be registered to its owner and, thus, appears in their IJOP profile.

Essentially, Uyghurs' lives and loyalties are constantly monitored and evaluated. In this respect, the level of surveillance on an urban street in the region is almost as extensive as that in the mass internment camps. However, it is the threat of internment or arrest that makes this constant surveillance so frightening. A Uyghur who lived in the region in 2017 and much of 2018 told me that this fear prevented them from talking to anybody about anything beyond pleasantries. Although they lived in constant fear, they could discuss this with nobody and even sought to avoid appearing agitated around others in the event that such behavior would be deemed suspicious. They recounted being frequently visited by neighborhood committee members and asked to fill out information about habits and being constantly evaluated at work. Every night the person stayed up at night in fear that they would get a 'knock on the door' and be taken away. It was such fears that caused most people with family members abroad to ask them to cut off all contact with them in 2017, and those who retained contact adopted a sophisticated code system to speak about others' well-being by discussing the weather.

While this high-tech surveillance is less widespread in rural areas, it is also less necessary as a means of keeping track of the local population. Since 2013, Party cadres had been dispatched to rural areas, particularly in the south, to participate in house-to-house inspections and report on families' behaviors to assess their potential to become extremists or terrorists. According to Darren Byler, who has interviewed both Han who partook in these missions and Uyghurs who were the object of investigation, these interactions, while framed as assistance from the Party, were very tense for all involved.[95] According to a Xinjiang TV report, such cadres visited 24 million rural Uyghur homes between 2016 and 2018, conducting a total of 33 million interviews.[96] As such, this program must have yielded valuable data for the security apparatus in the region, leading authorities to vastly expand it in 2018 to include more than one million Party workers, who have been assigned partner families with whom they must live for extended periods of time, sometimes as often as one week each month.[97] These cadres present themselves to their Uyghur partner families as 'relatives,' but the power relationship inherent in the relationship is much more akin to paternalistic.

These cadres are tasked with both propaganda and data collection duties, collecting information about family habits and attitudes while also instructing them on proper behavior and child-rearing. In this respect, the program represents both a part of the surveillance system and a part of the CCP's outright assimilation campaign in the Uyghur homeland. The intimacy in these homestays must provoke as much fear, if not more so, than the pervasive and impersonal electronic surveillance of Uyghurs in urban areas. As Byler notes from one of his interviews with a young Uyghur man who had experienced numerous such interactions with visiting Party cadres in his home, there was a constant fear that acting the wrong way or saying the wrong thing would result in internment. Thus, following the cadres' instructions and displaying willful assimilation was a must.

The power of this pervasive surveillance throughout the region's cities and villages, especially when combined with the fear of internment, is two-fold. First, the fear it instills in the Uyghurs effectively breeds distrust within this ethnic community and breaks down the social capital that is central to their identity. It erases the opportunity for freely engaging in the collective social behavior that makes up the substance of Uyghur culture, whether that be life-cycle rituals, holiday celebrations, or other social gatherings. Second, it makes all Uyghurs in the region incapable of resisting CCP-led campaigns to promote assimilation. In essence, it ensures that participation in anything promoted by the Party cannot be voluntary since non-participation will be noted and likely result in internment or imprisonment.

WELCOME TO THE POMEGRANATE: ERASING AND REPLACING UYGHUR IDENTITY

In this context, state policies have enjoyed a free hand in implementing blatantly assimilationist policies that are meant to dismantle Uyghur culture as we know it. While most of these policies are more subtle than the violent forced assimilationism of the internment camps or the intrusive system of surveillance and evaluation, their power emerges from the threat these more brutal measures pose. Together, they form a systematic effort to destroy Uyghur identity and replace it with something more palatable to the state and in harmony with Han dominant society. Such an assimilationist strategy has been a CCP priority in state 'counterterrorism' efforts in the Uyghur homeland since 2014 when the state first identified the source of alleged 'extremism' as being within Uyghur culture itself. As Xi Jinping had stated at the Second Xinjiang Work Forum, in order to defeat 'terrorism,' the Party needed to promote the 'intermingling' of ethnic groups in the region so that they became one, 'tightly bound together like the seeds of a pomegranate.'[98]

This metaphor for assimilating the Uyghurs has been prominent in Party propaganda ever since, but, until 2017, most Uyghurs had resisted becoming seeds of the pomegranate. After 2017, resistance had become futile in the context of pervasive surveillance and the threat of internment. While this assimilation drive is being framed as 'counterterrorism' in defense of society from existential threats, its implementation appears more like an intensive and perhaps final stage of settler colonization. As a part of such colonization, it inevitably involves changing both the geographic landscape of the Uyghur homeland and the human terrain of the Uyghur people themselves.

Changing the Uyghur homeland

The PRC has been changing the landscape of the Uyghur region for decades through development efforts meant to spur economic growth, but these efforts always left some room for Uyghurs to leave their mark on their homeland. However, by 2017, it appeared that this room was rapidly shrinking and was potentially no longer tolerated. Perhaps due to the plans for the region as a commercial center in the BRI, there seemed to be an urgency to remove its last markers of 'Uyghurness.' This has included the demolition of religious sites, the destruction of graveyards, and a drive to enforce new building standards for residencies that are not based on Uyghur traditional housing structures.

Much of this effort has involved removing signs of the Islamic religion, which is in line with the PRC's general attack on the religious aspects of Uyghur identity. This began with the removal of crescent symbols on minarets, progressed towards repurposing mosques, and has culminated in destroying many of them. One investigative report done in collaboration between *The Guardian* and *Bellingcat* using satellite images found that at least 31 mosques and 2 shrine sites had been either partially or completed demolished since 2016.[99] However, a more recent report by the UHRP suggests that the number of holy sites partially or fully demolished during this time is over 100.[100] Many of the mosques and sites mentioned in the UHRP report are smaller community mosques, which remain difficult to document through satellite images, but both sources provide information regarding the demolition of major mosques of significance in Kaghilik and Keriya that have long histories. Such mosques not only hold religious significance to Uyghurs, but are viewed as part of their cultural history and are symbolic of the Uyghur nature of particular cities or towns.

However, perhaps of even more concern than the destruction of these major historical mosques are reports that the PRC has demolished critical pilgrimage sites that contain shrines of important Sufi saints of significance to the Uyghurs. Beyond their religious significance, these sites, which are generally outside major population centers, hold critical importance to Uyghurs' identity and their connection to the land. As Uyghur anthropologist Rahilä Davut, who has been either imprisoned or interned since at least 2017, has said about the cultural significance of these sites, 'if one were to remove these ... shrines, the Uyghur people would lose contact with earth; they would no longer have a personal, cultural, and spiritual history; after a few years we would not have a memory of why we live here or where we belong.'[101]

In addition to the destruction of the burial shrines to Sufi saints, there are reports that local authorities have also begun to uproot entire cemeteries unceremoniously, not bothering to rebury the dead. According to one investigative report, 30 Uyghur graveyards in the region have been completely excavated, presumably waiting for new construction. In addition to serving to desecrate the memories of family members, these acts suggest yet another manner in which the local CCP is severing the connection between Uyghurs and the land.

Beyond the religious realm, there is also evidence that the CCP administration in the Uyghur region is actively involved in altering the structure and appearance of rural Uyghur villages, especially in the south. On-going research by Timothy Grose demonstrates that this is part of a larger policy seeking to transform Uyghur villages through the promotion of the 'three news' intended to 'advocate a new lifestyle,' 'establish a new atmosphere,' and 'construct a new order.'[102] While much of this program is focused on ideologically transforming rural Uyghurs, the 'new atmosphere' portion of the campaign is deliberately focused on altering the landscape and housing of Uyghur villages. According to Grose, part of this campaign focuses on renovating houses in ways that rid them of their traditional Uyghur architectural elements, replacing them with allegedly 'modern' attributes associated with Han lifestyles.[103] Among other changes to residential properties, it advocates ridding homes of the *mahrab* niche in most houses, which indicates the direction of Mecca and governs one's positioning during prayer, demolishing traditional *supa* beds, and replacing traditional furniture, particularly the dining table, with 'modern' variants.[104] While mostly appearing benign, these architectural alterations actually directly impact Uyghur ritual behavior, which has contributed to the traditional logic of their residential spaces. In connection with the 'surplus rural labor' factory program, this effort suggests an attempt to completely transform rural areas in the Uyghur homeland.

The human terrain: changing Uyghurs

If the campaign to change aspects of the Uyghur homeland's physical landscape has sought to cleanse the territory of religious markers and more generally break the connection between Uyghurs and the land, the efforts to change the human terrain of Uyghur identity has been far more radical. In many ways, this is the central aim of the cultural genocide being carried out by the state, and it fits with the broader aims of the 'Second Generation Nationalities Policy' that seeks to erase ethnic cultural distinctiveness throughout the PRC. Some aspects of this forced assimilation have already been discussed above, such as the violent transformation of Uyghur consciousness applied in the mass internment camps and the implicit self-censorship of one's cultural distinctiveness enforced by the mass surveillance system. However, the drive to change the human terrain of Uyghurs is also promoted explicitly in a host of other state campaigns that are framed as 'modernizing' Uyghurs and promoting 'poverty alleviation.' One example is the various coercive labor programs for rural Uyghurs discussed above. However, it is worthwhile mentioning a few others that, while described by the state as 'voluntary' are likely understood by Uyghurs as being at the very least 'coerced' under the threat of internment.

One such effort is related to the aforementioned 'three news' campaign, which seeks to alter traditional thought and community behavior in rural communities through condemnation of religion, and coerced participation in events that promote Chinese culture and values. These efforts are directly reinforced by the Party cadre 'relatives' who have inserted themselves in village communities and include events to celebrate patriotic songs, flag-raising ceremonies, and celebrations of Chinese holidays. While little information is available about such efforts, they are likely widespread and sometimes coordinated on a regional level through activities termed 'national security education,' which even include a 'National Security Education Day' holiday. On that day in 2018, apparently over ten million residents of over 12,000 communities throughout the region took part in flag-raising ceremonies accompanied by speeches on obeying the law and reporting 'suspicious behavior.'[105] While such activities have a benign performative nature to them, they shape a new social environment for rural Uyghurs, which can gradually supplant traditional social relations. Furthermore, some of these activities entail partaking in practices that are explicitly in violation of being a Muslim. These include being asked to partake in the drinking of alcohol or cigarette smoking by Party cadre 'relatives' or, as Darren Byler has noted of the 2019 Chinese New Year celebration, being forced to consume pork in honor of the 'Year of the Pig.'[106] In both of these instances, refusal to participate could be quickly flagged by authorities as a sign of 'extremist' inclincations.

A more disturbing campaign to change the Uyghur human terrain involves the educational system in the Uyghur region. While the process of making the schools in the region teach exclusively in Chinese had been underway since the early 2000s, changes in 2017 served to create one education path of assimilation for a few of the brightest Uyghurs while promoting a path of marginalization for the majority. As for all students in China, Uyghurs' educational and career paths are determined by their performance on a nation-wide exam taken between eighth grade and high school. Those who pass are given a standard academic high school education, and those who do not are relegated to vocational schools. While the transition to all-Chinese-language instruction had already required Uyghur students to take this exam in Chinese and attend high school or vocational training in the Chinese language, affirmative action pro-grams encouraging the integration of Uyghurs into PRC society had long given them a 50-point advantage on their test grade. In 2017, this advantage was slashed to 15 points, thus dramatically reducing the number of Uyghurs attending academic high schools.[107]

As a result, high schools in the Uyghur region now have a much higher proportion of Han students, providing for a more assimilation-ist experience for those Uyghurs who do get admitted. Furthermore, since such schools are mostly located in urban areas, the rural Uyghur students who do get admitted must study in boarding school environments, which further separate them from their culture and language.[108] For those who do not get admitted, they are generally relegated to the new system of coerced labor connected to the intern-ment camps through the 'surplus rural labor' program and its 're-education lite' curriculum or sent to work and be simultaneously re-educated in larger factories in inner China. Thus, whichever path they are afforded, this system assumes that their future will be much less ingrained in Uyghur culture than that of their parents.

However, the situation of Uyghur children whose parents have been interned is far more dire, and the state's apparently intentional role in their fate is far more disturbing. The children of interned par-ents essentially face involuntary intergenerational separation, which has long been a hallmark of settler colonialism and cultural geno-cide. This is particularly true of children whose parents have both been interned in 're-education' camps. While there is evidence that a portion of these children have been able to remain in the care of family members, there is also substantial evidence that large num-bers of them are being raised in state-run institutions from a very early age.

Adrian Zenz has done ground-breaking research on this subject and has found that Chen Quanguo's administration may have had plans for massive forced intergenerational separation even prior to the establishment of the mass internment camps. According to Zenz, Chen had already established in his first month in office a plan to institute universal preschool for the children of the Uyghur region within the course of a year.[109] However, the actual implementation of this plan not surprisingly corresponds with 2017, the year that mass internment began. By late February 2017, the government began construction of 4,387 preschools that were intended to serve 562,900 new students, particularly in the south of the Uyghur homeland, with a completion deadline before the beginning of the 2017–2018 school year.[110] While this goal itself appeared ambitious, it is noteworthy that during the 2017–2018 school year, the number of children enrolled in preschool was far greater than this target. While the total preschool intake target for the region in fall 2017 had been around one million, the actual number enrolled was closer to 1.4 million.[111] Furthermore, Zenz suggests that a substantial number of these new preschool students appeared to attend institutions with the capacity to house boarding students from a very early age.

While there is no way to prove conclusively that this larger enrollment figure is accounted for by the children of interned parents, there are few other reasonable reasons for it. If this is the case, these children have effectively become wards of the state unless they are returned to their parents once they have 'graduated' from 're-education.' Regardless of whether or not they are reunited with their birth parents, while in the care of the state, these children are being raised ostensibly as Han children in a Chinese-language environment with Han childrearing methods adopted by the state as standard. The state itself has lauded the opportunity for children to be raised by the state and Party while their parents are being themselves 're-educated.' Zenz, for example, cites one government report that talks about a preschool adjacent to a mass internment camp in Khotan that allows the children to 'eat and live' at the school while their parents are engaged in 'carefree study.'

In general, the educational system in the region since 2017 appears to be increasingly built for the re-engineering of the next generation of Uyghurs as the region presumably prepares for a more intensive stage of settler colonialism. This includes the separation of children from parents through those parents' internment, the coerced employment of women who then are obliged to bring their children to state-run day-care, and an expansion of boarding schools at all levels of education. The parallels to settler colonialism examples from the past in the Americas and Australia barely require pointing out.

One final aspect of transforming the Uyghur human terrain that bears mentioning is the campaign of coerced miscegenation in the region. Formally, this campaign is driven by incentives provided to couples of mixed ethnic background to marry. Many of these incentives have existed since 2014 when Xi Jinping first hailed the importance of ethnic 'intermingling' and the pomegranate metaphor in the Uyghur region, leading to a variety of monetary and other incentives for such marriages.[112] In 2017, new incentives were added, which gave children of mixed marriages a 20-point advantage, higher than the 15-point concession given to Uyghurs, on school qualifying exams.[113] Furthermore, the present marriage market in the Uyghur region would naturally appear to incentivize marriages between Han men and Uyghur women since there is a dearth of Han women in China writ large due to the one-child policy, and there is presently a dearth of Uyghur men in the region due to internment and incarceration. While these various incentives may account for some of the interest of Han men in marrying Uyghur women, the reverse has generally not been true given the long-held animosities between the two groups.

However, like Uyghur participation in other assimilationist policies in the Uyghur region that are on the surface 'voluntary' or 'incentivized,' the real motivation for Uyghurs to partake since 2017 has been coercion. On this particular issue, the coercive elements are particularly intense. First, the state is heavily invested in promoting inter-ethnic marriage in the Uyghur region, and there have even been campaigns to draw Han men to the region for this purpose, showing the exotic beauty and caring nature of Uyghur women.[114] Secondly, and more importantly, refusing a Han man's hand in marriage in the present context could have grave consequences for Uyghur women and especially for their parents. The 2015 'De-extremification Regulations' that have served as the template for reasons to be sent to mass internment and imprisonment, for example, explicitly mention the prevention of others from marrying outside their ethnic group or faith as a manifestation of 'extremism.' Thus, if Uyghur parents were to refuse to offer their daughter's hand in marriage to a Han, it would be an almost automatic relegation to internment or imprisonment. Furthermore, if a Uyghur woman was to refuse a Han proposal, it may result in the internment or imprisonment of both her and her parents. As an interview with a Uyghur woman on the subject by Darren Byler points out, many Uyghur women are presently resigning themselves to marrying Han men, only seeking to stall the process as long as possible. Again, the comparisons to other settler colonial circumstances in history are obvious.

BREAK THEIR ROOTS

PRC policy in the Uyghur homeland today is a systematic attempt to destroy this ethnic group's collective identity and its cultural markers. It is violent, calculated, and shockingly transparent. This effort continues to be couched as an attempt to eradicate a 'terrorist threat' within the Uyghur population, but it is painfully obvious that this is not its real goal. Given that Uyghur-led violence had already markedly diminished in 2016 before the campaign began, and has presumably been absent from the region's life ever since, the 'counterterrorism' slogans still used to justify this state-led erasure of Uyghur culture must sound like a cruel joke to most Uyghurs in the region today. Rather, the cultural genocide taking place against the Uyghurs in China is very much like the many other examples of this phenomenon from the past history of settler colonialism. As in many of these examples from colonialism's past, at the center of the experience is a network of mass internment concentration camps. The intent of these camps with regards to the indigenous population, in the words of one local Han official, is to 'break their lineage, break their roots, break their connections, and break their origins.'[115] It is unclear if that can be completely accomplished by the camps alone, but in conjunction with the other policies discussed in this chapter, it seems that this is exactly what authorities are trying to systematically do to the Uyghur people. Unfortunately, for the time being, they seem to be succeeding.

CONCLUSION

What is happening to the Uyghurs inside China is a blatant act of cultural genocide and a human tragedy. It is neither the first of its kind in history nor perhaps even the worst of the human tragedies that have occurred thus far in the twenty-first century. However, it is a tragedy of global proportions that begs for a global response. In concluding this book's account of how this tragedy has unfolded through a combination of colonialism and 'counterterrorism,' which together have amounted to a full-out state-led war on the Uyghurs, I will try to answer three critical questions about its future trajectory: 1) what is the logical conclusion of the Uyghur cultural genocide? 2) what are the implications of this tragedy for the future of GWOT? and 3) what can be done to stop this tragedy from getting any worse?

WHAT IS THE LOGICAL CONCLUSION OF THE UYGHUR CULTURAL GENOCIDE?

It is first important to speculate about the PRC's own endgame in carrying out acts of cultural genocide against the Uyghurs. There are a variety of motivations for what the state is doing in the region. It demonstrates the power of the Party to resolve complex problems, in this instance the perceived problem of alleged 'terrorism,' effectively and forcefully, also sending a cautionary message to other dissenting actors throughout China. It asserts the territorial integrity of PRC sovereignty, and it may even serve as an example for a new state conception of ethnic identity. However, I believe that the primary driver of this state-led cultural genocide is the settler colonization of the Uyghur homeland. The PRC wants, once and for all, to integrate the Uyghur homeland into a more homogeneous, Han-centric state, leaving it open for unfettered re-development. Arguably, this had been the goal of the Party in the region since at least the late 1990s, but especially since the early 2000s, and it had poured billions of dollars into the region's development for this purpose. In the face of this development, which was accompanied by assimilationist policies, Han in-migration, and an ever-increasing securitization, many Uyghurs responded with sporadic resistance, sometimes violently. As this resistance became increasingly violent in 2013–2015, the state had decided it needed to take drastic measures to completely neutralize the population so that it could go about its work of developing the region unfettered as an integral part of China.

While the motivation has never been about eradicating a perceived 'terrorist threat' in the region, the narrative that a 'terrorist threat' within the Uyghur population existed has been and continues to be central to implementing cultural genocide. The characterization of the region's violence as emerging from an irrational 'extremist' and international 'terrorist threat' had helped to justify a continually violent and biopolitical response from the state to any and all Uyghur resistance. Thus, it should be kept in mind that many implementing and supporting the cultural genocide in the Uyghur homeland today fully believe that it is a response to an existential 'terrorist threat' posed by an 'extremist' virus that has infected the Uyghur culture and people. That said, the state's endgame and its true motivations have little to nothing to do with 'terrorism.' The goal is to strip this region of its Uyghur characteristics so that it can be developed as part of a larger and unified concept of Chinese society.

In this context, it is very difficult to imagine an accommodationist way out of the present situation that would appeal to both Uyghurs and the PRC. Contemplating the elevation of Uyghurs in shared governance, as had been the case during the coalition government that briefly ruled the region in the late 1940s, or even the allowance of the cultural and religious liberties of the 1980s seem almost unimaginable in the present context. Likewise, it is highly unlikely that the state will suddenly release all of the Uyghurs presently in mass internment camps or in prisons on political charges, as it would unleash a very angry population with even less to lose than in 2014–2015 when violence in the region was at its peak. Recent reports do suggest that the situation has begun to soften in the region since the summer of 2019, but this should not be confused with accommodation or an abandonment of cultural genocide.

In August 2019, international journalists were shown some closed camps and were allowed to interview a few hand-picked released 'graduates' from the camps, but they also saw that other camps still exist and that the 'graduates' with whom they spoke were visibly terrified to misspeak.[1] By early 2020, reports suggested that in addition to camp closings, there has been efforts to minimize the presence of obvious securitization in urban areas. According to one account, many of the checkpoints in urban centers had been dismantled, some convenience police stations had been closed, and more Uyghur men were present on the street.[2] However, these reports also suggested that surveillance remained very active, that nobody on the street would willingly engage in a discussion of the camps, and bearded men and headscarves were virtually non-existent.

This softening of the complete police state that had been in place since 2017, if it continues, likely reflects a new normal, where the same pressures of coercion exist on the indigenous population, but are better hidden from view and more palatable to tourists. In this sense, it may be that the arbitrary internment of substantial percentages of the population is gradually being replaced with a system where the continued threat of 're-education' and imprisonment is now the means of control and pacification. Those who have refused to submit to the whitewashing of their culture and either willful assimilation or self-marginalization likely will remain incarcerated indefinitely. Meanwhile, those allowed to live outside have implicitly agreed to the terms of the state with regards to the colonization of their homeland and the destruction of their culture. If they begin to show signs of resistance to the state's plans for the region, it is most likely that they will join those who remain interned or imprisoned. Under such a regime of control, which can possibly continue indefinitely, there is no reason to believe that efforts at cultural genocide will cease, and there is little that can stop it, short of a complete purge of PRC state leadership and a mea-culpa to the Uyghur people. Given the actions that the state is presently taking and the experience of past settler colonies, one can envision what the outcome of this cultural genocide might look like. The region would no longer be termed the Xinjiang Uyghur Autonomous Region, but merely Xinjiang, and it would be overwhelmingly Han in its demographics. Traditionally Uyghur cities like Kashgar would become primarily populated by Han and completely indistinguishable from generic Chinese urban spaces elsewhere in China, being virtually cleansed of any signs of Uyghur historical habitation except where retained for tourism purposes. A greatly depleted and traumatized Uyghur population would survive, but it would be marginalized in its own homeland, detached from its history, culture, and language. Perhaps, they would be relegated to depressed communities in unhospitable conditions that are tied to low wage labor in adjacent 'satellite factories,' or maybe they would ultimately be quarantined on 'reservations.' While token members of the group might succeed through education and perseverance to rise up enough to enter the Han-dominant middle-class and even elite, this would be accomplished only by fully assimilating into Han culture. The remainder would become part of an ethnically profiled underclass. Such an endgame is imaginable and possible, but it would also likely require many more years of the status quo involving further state violence and a concerted effort to silence outside critics.

Unfortunately for the Uyghurs inside China, there is little they can do in the present context to resist such outcomes. However, Uyghurs outside China may be able to complicate PRC designs on the erasure of their culture and identity. The Uyghur diaspora around the world has grown significantly since 2009, and a broader segment of these exiles has become politically motivated as most have family members who have been either interned or imprisoned. They now provide the only viable sources of Uyghur resistance to the cultural genocide taking place in their homeland. It is also for this reason that they have been targeted for harassment by the PRC despite their location outside China's borders.[3] However, depending upon where they are located, the Chinese state may not be able to silence them entirely.

The largest segments of this diaspora, in the Central Asian states of Kazakhstan and Kyrgyzstan, have mostly been neutralized given that their host states are already significantly dependent economically on the PRC, on which they border. However, there is also a significant ethnic Kazakh population from China in Kazakhstan, which has been very vocal in publicizing information about the situation in the Uyghur homeland, creating an organization called *Ata-Jurt* dedicated to this purpose. *Ata-Jurt* has helped get stories out to the international media from former internees, mostly Kazakhstan citizens, who were interned when visiting China. While Kazakhstan authorities arrested the leader of *Ata-Jurt* and forced him to step down in an attempt to silence the group, it continues to operate given that it has support from Kazakh nationalists in the country who prevent the government from closing it down entirely. As activists on the border with the Uyghur region, *Ata Jurt* may continue to be a critical source of information about what is happening to Uyghurs and Kazakhs in China, keeping the issue in the international spotlight. Furthermore, it may even be successful in forcing the Kazakhstan government to express more concern over the issue with neighboring China.

The Uyghur diaspora in Turkey, while still smaller than in Central Asia, has grown substantially since 2012, but their advocacy capacities are limited by the fact that many of them have only tenuous residency status in the country. Furthermore, Turkey's increasingly close economic ties to the PRC hamper their ability to be vocal, and China's increased disinformation about its treatment of Uyghurs for Turkish audiences at least partially mitigates the efforts of the country's Uyghurs to gain public support for their cause from the larger citizenry.[4] Nonetheless, Uyghur exiles in Turkey, especially those with citizenship, retain strong political capital within the country, especially among nationalists and *Pan-Turkists*, which makes it difficult for the government to completely silence them. As such, this diaspora could play a critical role in maintaining attention to the Uyghur plight, especially within the Muslim world.

The diaspora in the US, Canada, Europe, and Australia is much smaller, but it has been particularly active in keeping the situation of the Uyghurs on the agenda of liberal democracies and in the western media. While they have also received threats from PRC officials, it is more difficult for China to use intimidation to silence Uyghurs living in these countries. In the current context, this community's activism has expanded significantly, including among Uyghur youth who have grown up in the US and Europe and have become savvy about how to mobilize people in the west. While this movement is largely de-centralized, it has the power, not only to bring significant public attention to the fate of the Uyghurs, but to help spur more grassroots advocacy movements that can assert pressure on the PRC.

The most unpredictable part of the Uyghur diaspora is the Turkistan Islamic Party (TIP), which still exists and now has more fighters than ever in its decade-long history. However, much mystery still surrounds this group, especially regarding its sources of funding and its patrons. Furthermore, recent video statements from the group suggest that TIP in Syria and TIP in Afghanistan have developed into two completely different groups, albeit apparently still identifying with each other. This may mean that they actually represent two different power sources among Uyghur militant religious nationalists in exile with completely separate patrons and goals.

In an August 2019 video statement, Abdul Häq, who still identifies as the group's *Emir*, notes that his group has now completely moved from Waziristan to Afghanistan, most likely to Badakhshan and closer to the Chinese border than ever before.[5] In the video, Häq addresses the present situation in the Uyghur homeland, stating that those seeking political solutions to what is happening to Uyghurs through protests and advocacy are misguided. Instead, he says that the only way to fight China's aggression towards Uyghurs is through armed struggle. Interestingly, he also mentions that the group has abandoned the generic black flag of jihad and has returned to the blue *kök bayraq* of Häsän Mäkhsum and the First ETR, suggesting that it may be adopting a stronger nationalist orientation that is less associated with global jihadism. It has also changed the logo of its video production company *Islam Awazi* by removing the black flag of jihad from it, clearly delineating its videos from those of TIP in Syria. This last video message from Abdul Häq and the change of its flag seems to suggest that the group may be reviving Häsän Mäkhsum's more nationalist vision for an insurgency inside China. However, it is difficult to believe that any group could achieve such a feat today when the Uyghur region is under complete lockdown and ethnic Uyghurs elsewhere in China can be easily tracked. Furthermore, the capacity of this group in Afghanistan is likely meager at best, and has a long history of issuing threats against the PRC without carrying out any actions. Thus, its future and its capacity to influence the situation are questionable.

The future of TIP in Syria likewise remains uncertain at this time. It has a new website, produces a weekly news segment that provides its own interpretation of world events, and appears to be one of the few groups still fighting Russia and the Assad regime in the country's last opposition stronghold of Idlib. Its videos now identity itself separately as Turkistan Islam Partisi Sham Shûbisi (Turkistan Islamic Party Sham Branch), continuing to use its black flag and its old video logo, clearly distinguishing itself from Abdul Häq's group in Afghanistan. While this group has far more resources than the group in Afghanistan, its allegiances and patrons are unknown, as are its patrons' attitudes towards China. Finally, it is unclear if TIP in Syria will ultimately be destroyed during the opposition's last stand against the Assad regime in Idlib, if its members will eventually flee to Turkey, or if its present patrons will use them in another proxy war elsewhere in the world.

However, the survival of either of these groups is also not a necessity for the persistence of a Uyghur militant response to what is happening in the Uyghur homeland. I have spoken with several Uyghurs who had gained combat experience in Syria and still hope to use that experience against the Chinese state. They have told me that they are just waiting for somebody to organize a group with a viable plan to attack China. When I asked one such former fighter if he was afraid of dying in an attempt to fight against a state as strong as China, he said that his entire family in the homeland had already disappeared into camps or prisons, and he had nothing left to live for anyway. I assume the numbers of people like him are not insignificant, and it would not be surprising to see them create new militant groups in the coming years. Although such fighters would unlikely find their way back into China under the present circumstances, they could do damage to Chinese interests abroad, which are increasingly widespread around the world. However, the real question is whether that would do anything to help the Uyghurs suffering inside China. In fact, it may only make things worse by providing proof for the PRC of the imminence of the alleged 'terrorist threat' posed by Uyghurs, hence only justifying its cultural genocide in the name of 'counterterrorism.'

Although the full realization of China's settler colonialization of the Uyghur homeland appears to be the direction in which the present crisis is headed, it is important to note that the Uyghur people are extremely resilient. In fact, that is part of the reason that the Chinese state has gone to such lengths to break their spirit as a people. They have not faced a systematic cultural genocide before, but I am also not entirely convinced that they cannot weather even the extreme situation they face today. Given the recent mobilization of Uyghurs and Kazakhs in exile around the current situation in the Uyghur homeland, these exiles may indeed serve as a deterrence to at least China's most extreme designs on the region. Thus, while the present prognosis for the future trajectory of the cultural genocide in the Uyghur homeland is very grim, there is still some hope that its impact can be mitigated and its violent erasure of Uyghur culture can be stemmed.

WHAT ARE THE IMPLICATIONS OF THIS TRAGEDY FOR THE FUTURE OF GWOT?

One of the arguments that this book has made consistently is that the Uyghur cultural genocide, while not a response to a real or perceived 'terrorist threat' within the Uyghur population, has been facilitated and expedited by the narrative that such a threat exists. However, it is reasonable to ask the counterfactual question of whether the state's complete dismantling of Uyghur identity would be happening now whether or not GWOT had ever been declared. After all, the cultural genocide perpetrated against the Uyghurs today is more about China's colonization of the Uyghur homeland than it is about 'terrorism.' While this is true, I don't think the situation could have so readily escalated to genocidal extremes without China framing Uyghurs as a 'terrorist threat' and Uyghur culture as having been infected by 'extremism.' These assertions about the alleged 'terrorist threat' posed by the Uyghurs have greatly assisted the PRC in deflecting international criticism of its actions and has helped inform how it could carry out cultural genocide with impunity.

In October 2019, the UN General Assembly considered a non-binding statement presented by the UK and supported by 23 states condemning the PRC's actions in the Uyghur homeland as gross violations of human rights.[6] In an immediate response, 54 countries backed a statement presented by Belarus that applauded the PRC's human rights record, noting that its actions in its Uyghur region were an appropriate and even humane approach to combating a dangerous Islamic 'extremist' and 'terrorist' threat.[7] I doubt that many, if any, of the UN representatives from these 54 countries believed that this was true. They were defending China for a myriad of other self-interested reasons. However, they would have had much more difficulty doing so if it had not been for the GWOT narrative and its implicit assumption that the fight against 'terrorism' justifies the suspension of human rights.

Additionally, the biopolitical nature of GWOT's logic has been influential in the ways that the PRC has carried out this cultural genocide. By asserting that it faces a 'terrorist threat' from within the Uyghur population, the logic of GWOT has allowed the Chinese state to target this entire ethnic group as suspected 'terrorists,' for whom rights are justifiably suspended. Furthermore, by using the logic of GWOT to locate the foundations of the threat in the vaguely defined ideology of religious 'extremism,' the Chinese state has enjoyed the ability to target and criminalize Uyghur culture itself, especially its religious aspects, as allegedly having been infected by 'extremist' influences.

This has led the state down an explicitly genocidal path rather than encouraging a more gradualist approach to settler colonization, which could eventually overwhelm and marginalize Uyghurs by a market driven in-migration of Han settlers. This had been the direction of China's engagement of the Uyghurs and their homeland in the late 1990s and early 2000s and could have remained so if the PRC had not been seduced by GWOT's logic of dehumanization and cultural/ethnic profiling, which lends itself almost inherently to genocidal strategies. Thus, while the PRC would likely have sought to colonize the Uyghur homeland regardless of the presence of GWOT, it is difficult to imagine that this could have taken place so rapidly and so violently without the benefit of the narrative that GWOT created around the label of 'terrorism.'

In this context, one could say that the crisis facing Uyghurs inside China today is a prime example of the mutations that GWOT has gone through over time and space. GWOT has never really been about 'terrorism.' It has always been about finding a justification for the pursuance of other interests. Over the course of the war's history, it has justified regime change in Afghanistan and Iraq, and it has been used countless times as a means to delegitimize and violently suppress domestic opposition in a variety of countries, whether in civil wars such as Syria and Yemen or in authoritarian regimes such as those in Russia, Central Asia, Ethiopia, and Egypt. Almost two decades into this amorphous war, it appears that the narrative of GWOT is now evolving into a tried and tested tool for new efforts at settler colonization, ethnic cleansing, and cultural genocide. This was the case with the Rohingya in Myanmar; it is the case with the Uyghurs in China; and it may be evolving into the case for Kashmiris in India. This observation alone should be enough to realize that this loosely defined and persistent war must come to a conclusion.

The only way to end the war is for the international community to reimagine the concept of 'terrorism' itself. This would require adopting an internationally recognized and objective definition of how 'terrorism' should be defined and how it should be identified. Doing so would neutralize the term's instrumental use and would establish rules of engagement for future wars involving non-state militant actors. In my opinion, the working definition employed in this book, that which was proposed by Boaz Garnor at GWOT's commencement in 2002, is the perfect place to begin discussions of what such a definition should look like. It is certainly possible that forging an international consensus on what constitutes 'terrorism' proves to be impossible in today's world, but not addressing this issue almost guarantees that it will be a 'forever war' that will continue to fuel human atrocities.

WHAT CAN BE DONE TO STOP THE UYGHUR CRISIS FROM GETTING ANY WORSE?

While ending GWOT could go a long way towards preventing future tragedies like that facing Uyghurs today, it will unfortunately have little impact on the cultural genocide presently underway in the Uyghur homeland. Stemming the tide of this cultural genocide will require concerted and persistent pressure on the PRC. Unfortunately, most states have thus far been either unwilling to criticize China publicly about its treatment of the Uyghurs or ineffective in getting acknowledgment of the criticisms that they have aired publicly. This is mostly due to the international economic power that the PRC presently projects around the world. It is noteworthy, for example, that no Muslim country has made an official statement of concern about what is happening to Uyghurs inside China. Even Kazakhstan and Kyrgyzstan, whose citizens and co-ethnics have been documented as being sent to camps, have been silent. While Turkish officials have made some critical statements about the issue, the government has not taken any substantive or official diplomatic actions to back up these statements. Furthermore, the UN and its member states have been unsuccessful in starting a serious discussion on the issue as the above-mentioned votes in the UN General Assembly indicate. This is particularly true given that the PRC has become increasingly adept at UN processes, using them to prevent sustained criticism of Chinese policies and actions.

The only states that have spoken out about the situation of the Uyghurs in China have been liberal democracies. The US, many

CONCLUSION

European states, Australia, Japan, and several other liberal democracies have all voiced substantial concern about the situation ongoing in the Uyghur homeland. Unfortunately, these states have also proven ineffective in applying any pressure on China regarding this issue for multiple reasons. First, these countries' involvement in the early period of GWOT was also riddled with human rights abuses related to 'counterterrorism' practices. This is particularly true of the US about whom China can easily engage in 'whataboutisms' regarding the treatment of suspected terrorists and extremists: Guantanamo Bay Detention Center was also an extra-legal internment camp; the National Security Agency also engaged in invasive surveillance of ethnically profiled communities; killing suspected 'terrorists' by drones is less humane than 're-education,' and so on. In this context, the US and its allies in GWOT are left with little moral authority to criticize China's extreme approach to eradicating alleged 'terrorism' because they have also justified reprehensible behavior in the name of 'counterterrorism' and set the precedent for doing so. Secondly, the soft power of the US and Europe, particularly in the developing world, is waning and becoming eclipsed by that of China and its economic power. As a result, the liberal democracies no longer have the ability to isolate China from either the global economy or from international political legitimacy. Finally, liberal democracies do not want to use the only leverage they do have over China, which is economic engagement, since disengagement could be equally damaging for both parties.

Given this situation, one should not expect that other states will be able or willing to pressure China to change its course of actions in the Uyghur homeland unless they are pushed to do so by their citizens. Thus, the only real action that can put significant pressure on China at the moment must come from the grassroots, and it must target the PRC in the only way that can create real leverage, economically. There is a precedent for such action in the anti-apartheid movement of the 1980s. Citizens from around the world engaged in concerted advocacy to boycott the South African government for its apartheid policies, forcing universities and pension funds to divest from South African companies and pressuring international companies to stop their operations in the country. While a complete boycott of Chinese goods is difficult to mobilize in today's global economy, which is largely built around Chinese production, an attempt to do so may begin to have results. Likewise, an effort to get major funds and institutional investors to divest from Chinese stocks could have an impact, especially if it is a worldwide movement. Such efforts can also target international businesses working in China and especially those with operations in the Uyghur homeland or whose supply chains employ coerced Uyghur laborers. Finally, such a grassroots movement needs to alert people to the fact that action on this issue is not only about the fate of Uyghurs. It is also about the precedent the Uyghur cultural genocide sets for their own fate in a world where the values of human rights, privacy, and diversity are under siege.

FINAL WORDS: FIRST THEY CAME FOR THE UYGHURS ...

One of the reasons that the Uyghurs' situation in China has garnered so much attention from international journalists and academics is that those paying attention to the Uyghur cultural genocide can see omens of their own future as well as of the future of the world as a whole. In part, this is because it is happening in China, the second largest economy in the world and a state that is gaining power and influence globally. However, the cautionary tale told by the fate of the Uyghurs is about more than a rising China that is authoritarian, disrespectful of human rights, and capable of human atrocities. It is also about a post-liberal world where the power of the state is increasingly absolute; where universal values are losing their currency; where personal privacy has become a commodity; and where intolerance to difference is on the rise. While this does not mean that we will all soon be living the 'Orwellian' nightmare being experienced by the Uyghurs, it does suggest that the same forces that have inspired and facilitated the Uyghur cultural genocide have the potential to impact our lives. One could frame these forces as three emerging global trends that have facilitated China's actions against Uyghurs and that should be very disturbing to those who value diversity, human rights, and privacy.

The most imminent of these trends is that towards a 'post-privacy world.' The technology involved in the Uyghur cultural genocide is founded on big data collection and analysis, which has become a ubiquitous part of people's lives around the world whether we are aware of it or not. The IJOP, which has served as the means for identifying those Uyghurs who must be 're-educated' and culturally cleansed in internment camps or quarantined in prisons, runs on the same principals of 'surveillance capitalism' as those adopted by the companies driving the high-tech economy everywhere now, including Google, Facebook, and so on.[8] In fact, such companies, with which people around the world engage on a daily basis when they participate in social media or search the internet, collaborate with the same Chinese companies that have built the infrastructure for the Uyghurs' repression. In this context, most states in the world today, especially in partnership with powerful private technology companies, already have the capacity to replicate what China is presently doing to the Uyghurs. Those who do not have such capacity as of yet are quickly gaining it by buying the needed technology from Chinese companies or getting it provided free of charge through development programs lauding the convenience of 'Smart Cities.' In this context, the Uyghurs will likely not be the last people to experience state-led violence and genocide fueled by big data.

However, the Uyghur cultural genocide has not been facilitated by technology alone. It also benefits from a more general trend towards a 'post-rights world.' Since the advent of GWOT, respect for human rights globally has been on a steady decline. This is partly because states around the world have used the alleged existential threat of 'terrorism' to advocate for the suspension of rights in the interest of security. Furthermore, the US, which had positioned itself as a global defender of human rights, was probably the worst offender of the global rights regime during GWOT's first years. It forged alliances with dictatorial regimes to facilitate interrogations of alleged terrorists using torture, it ran a massive surveillance program of its own citizens in search of 'terrorists', and it carried out extra-judicial killings of alleged 'terrorists' via drone strikes. These actions taken by the alleged global 'protector' of human rights have contributed to a general global cynicism about the concept of universal human rights and a 'rules-based international order' more generally. However, the advent of a 'post-rights world' is also the product of shifting geopolitical power relations. As the US begins to acknowledge its waning hegemony in the world, it has also stepped back from its role in promoting the ideals of democracy and human rights globally, especially at the UN. At the same time, both China and Russia are seeking to play greater roles in defining global discourses on human rights to fill the vacuum left by an increasingly isolationist US. In this role, Russia and China both appear poised to weaken the international concepts of human rights, which they perceive as an encroachment on their sovereignty, and push for an International order, particularly through the UN, where human rights are seen as subjective and country dependent.

Finally, one could also argue that the Uyghur cultural genocide reflects a broader trend towards a world in which the racist logic of settler colonialism is re-emerging within the borders of nation-states, as intolerance of difference and parochial nationalism are on the rise. It is telling that the world has witnessed at least four different instances over the last few years where states have been assertive in settler colonial drives within their borders. In Brazil, Jair Bolsonaro has launched a campaign to reclaim and develop areas of the Amazon rainforest where indigenous populations previously had been given particular rights over this land and powers of autonomous self-governance within its territory. In India, Narendra Modi has re-asserted control over Kashmir, which had previously enjoyed autonomy as a disputed territory. In Israel, Benjamin Netanyahu, with the encouragement of Donald Trump, is reasserting his control over Palestinian lands, perhaps ending the possibilities for a two-state solution. And, in China, of course, the state appears to be in the process of carrying out cultural genocide in the Uyghur homeland, which it is actively settling and colonizing. Other, less violent signs of this trend are apparent in the rise of xenophobic and populist nationalist politics throughout western democracies, whether that is reflected in Trump's rise in the US, Brexit in the UK, or the power of Victor Orban in Hungary.

CONCLUSION

In this context, the Uyghur cultural genocide may not be as exceptional as it seems, but is instead a symptom of a greater malaise in the world. Along these lines, historians may look back at the circumstances of the Uyghurs since 2017 as one of the most visible nails in the coffin of that briefly held ideal of a 'rules-based international order' that is meant to protect the principles of human rights, personal privacy, and the human dignity of all people in the world. This is not to say that the UN has ever been effective in implementing its intended rules-based system for the world, but in the past, one would have expected a more vigorous debate on the UN floor about the appropriateness of blatant crimes against humanity. What is notable about the Uyghur case is the deafening sound of silence from most of the world on the issue. Is this a sign that blatant and violent state-led cultural genocide can be expected to be a part of the new normal again throughout the world? Will we be soon looking back with fond nostalgia at the late twentieth century when the world seemed to at least hold up a façade of consensus on universal human rights, remorse for past atrocities, and protections for the disenfranchised and marginalized? If so, some will likely point to the decline of the US and the rise of China as the key event signaling this transformation of the world system. However, as this book tries to point out, the decline of our present imperfect 'rules-based international order,' of which the Uyghur cultural genocide is just one symptom, is much more aptly attributed to the processes that began with the declaration of the Global War on Terror.

These global trends and their ramifications should make apparent the urgency of action needed to stem the violent cultural genocide in the Uyghur homeland. If the people of the world do not speak out about what is happening to Uyghurs today and put pressure on the PRC to change its course, it will set a very dangerous precedent for states' rights to implement mass repression and ethnically profiled population control on the basis of the sanctity of sovereignty. If what is happening to the Uyghurs today goes on unaddressed, many others may find themselves in similar situations in the future thinking they should have done something when 'first they came for the Uyghurs ...'

A NOTE ON METHODOLOGY

In many ways, this book reads like a historical narrative, albeit one reflecting on relatively recent history. After summarizing the first 250 years of the colonial relationship between modern China and Uyghurs in the first chapter, the book wades through the last nineteen years of history in an effort to understand the subsequent impact of China's persistent assertions since 2001 that it has long faced an existential 'terrorist threat' from Uyghurs. This historical perspective is also meant to contextualize the current human tragedy of cultural genocide taking place in the Uyghur homeland and to examine how the present extreme nature of Chinese state policies towards the Uyghurs evolved. If the book's content is largely historical, as an anthropologist, my analysis inevitably benefits from an ethnographic lens that draws from my experiences doing fieldwork among Uyghurs over the last 25 years. In particular, this perspective allows me to tell a story that is not just about state policies, but also about Uyghur responses to these policies and the fundamental disconnect between the two.

However, fieldwork among Uyghurs inherently presents methodological challenges. Conducting ethnographic research inside the Uyghur region has always been politically sensitive. Foreign researchers have long been monitored, especially when traveling outside the region's capital city of Urumqi, and interviewing informants about anything sensitive could place them in harm's way, especially if there exists recorded evidence of conversations. Furthermore, it has been virtually impossible for foreign researchers to live with a

Uyghur family for an extended period of time in rural areas with dense Uyghur populations, precluding long-term participant observation outside urban contexts.

When doing research for my dissertation during the mid and late 1990s, I dealt with these challenges by basing myself in Kazakhstan where I lived with a Uyghur family in a densely populated Uyghur community. There, I could more freely conduct participant observation in local Uyghur communities and record unfettered interviews with Uyghurs from China who came to Kazakhstan to visit relatives or trade at the local bazaars. During that time, I would also frequently take month-long trips to the Uyghur region to conduct research there, but I would refrain from engaging in any recorded interviews, which could put those with whom I spoke in harm's way. This provided me with plenty of data for my dissertation on cross-border relations between the Uyghurs of Kazakhstan and China, but my personal fieldwork challenges were to become significantly more daunting after finishing my dissertation.

While finishing my dissertation, I wrote a chapter for an edited volume on the Uyghurs and their homeland, entitled *Xinjiang: China's Muslim Borderland*, which was to become extremely controversial inside China.[1] The manuscript presented an overview of issues relating to the region, including the history and present situation of the long tense relationship between Uyghurs and modern Chinese states. While the book was an academic text with chapters written by many of the top scholars on Uyghurs and their homeland in the US, Chinese authorities reacted to its publication by suggesting that the volume was a US government project intended to promote Uyghur 'separatism.'[2] Subsequently, the contributors to this volume have consistently been denied visas to travel and conduct research in China, earning them the ominous title of the 'Xinjiang thirteen.' As a result, my last fieldwork in the Uyghur homeland was conducted in the summer of 2000, just prior to my return to the US to write up my dissertation. This lack of access to the region, while largely beyond my control, represents the most significant limitation on my research

Admittedly, I never applied for another Chinese visa. As I watched my colleagues go to great lengths to gain access to China with only nominal success, I opted to focus my research on the Central Asian region more broadly, relegating my study of Uyghur communities to those who had left their homeland for other countries at different times historically. While living in Kazakhstan and Kyrgyzstan between 2001 and 2006, I was able to continue my research with the local Uyghur communities in these countries, including Uyghurs from China who were visiting the region. More recently, I have spent numerous summer months in Turkey over the last twelve years, conducting research within the Uyghur refugee community that has grown in that country throughout the 2000s, and especially after 2009. Additionally, I have engaged with Uyghur refugees in the US and Europe on a regular basis.

Through these experiences, I have been able to gather a substantial number of interviews with Uyghurs, many of whom lived in the Uyghur homeland as recently as 2016. Furthermore, since these interviews were conducted outside China, the interviewees have been particularly candid about their experiences. Nonetheless, given the present sensitive predicament of Uyghurs globally, but especially in their homeland, I refrain from identifying in the book the names or any personal details of those whom I interviewed throughout this research. The only exceptions are Uyghur public figures who are well known and politically active.

While I have not physically been in the Uyghur region of China since 2000, I have compensated for this absence by seeking out subsequent waves of Uyghur refugees who have left their homeland and were able to recount important aspects of their lives there during different periods. Additionally, the book's analysis benefits extensively from the works of, and my personal communications with, scholars who continued to enjoy access to the Uyghur region. This includes scholars, such as Joanne Smith-Finley and Rachel Harris, whose long-term ethnographic research had taken place during roughly the same time that I had access to the region, but who were able to subsequently return there on a regular basis over the last two decades. Additionally, it includes an important group of younger scholars whose long-term fieldwork in the region took place at different times throughout the 2000s, including Rian Thum, David Tobin,

A NOTE ON METHODOLOGY

David Brophy, Sandrine Catris, Elise Marie Anderson, Sarah Tynen, Darren Byler, and Timothy Grose.

If interviews with exiles and engagement with the work of other scholars helped me piece together the experiences of Uyghurs inside their homeland during the last two decades despite my lack of access to the region, my research on Uyghur militant groups outside China, who have been identified as 'terrorists,' presented particularly vexing challenges. First, the secondary literature on these groups tends to be speculative and written by those who are neither experts on Uyghur culture and history nor speak or read the Uyghur language. As a result, this literature often includes factual errors and asserts questionable conclusions based on comparative studies of 'terrorist' groups without any local contextualization. Second, doing ethnographic research among Uyghur militants where they have been based in Afghanistan, Waziristan, or Syria is almost impossible or at least extremely dangerous.

Fortunately, I have been able to interview several Uyghurs who have been associated with militant groups in these regions and have heard their own accounts of the reasons they ended up with these groups, the conditions in which these groups operate, and the activities they carry out. In addition, I have supplemented these interviews by watching hundreds of videos produced in the Uyghur language by the Turkistan Islamic Party (TIP), the primary Uyghur militant group active since 2008 and the main justification used by the PRC for its claims that it faces a 'terrorist threat' from within its Uyghur population. While 'terrorism experts,' almost all of whom lack the Uyghur language skills to sufficiently analyze such sources, often look at such videos for indications of leadership changes, alliances with larger jihadist organizations, or claims of responsibility for specific attacks, I watched them more as a means of trying to understand the group's daily life, aspirations, and history as well as the nature of its community. Of particular usefulness in this regard are the videos honoring martyrs, which provide detailed biographies of those who have joined TIP, including stories of the repression they experienced inside China, their birthplace, and education. Given the sheer volume of videos made by TIP since 2008, watching them chronologically provides something of a visual ethnography of the group's history. As a result of this research, I would suggest that the book's account of Uyghur militant religious nationalist groups since 1998 represents the manuscript's most original research and provides a new perspective on the myths and realities of the PRC's claims that it faces a 'terrorist threat' from Uyghurs.

TRANSLITERATION AND PLACE NAMES

Place names and transliteration are perennial problems for nations without states whose native language is not written in the Latin alphabet. This is especially true for the Uyghurs, who have used a variety of scripts in their written language historically. This book generally employs the American Library Association/Library of Congress (ALA-LC) standard to transliterate Uyghur words and proper names from the Arabic script spelling used inside China today. However, when referring to Uyghur activists, scholars, journalists, and so on, in exile outside China, it uses the transliteration that these people use in their country of settlement (i.e. 'Rabiya Kadeer' instead of 'Rabiyä Qadir,' 'Isa Alptekin' instead of 'Äysa Alptekin,' etc.). For Uyghurs in militant groups abroad, the book uses the ALA-LC direct transliteration of their names as spelled in their own documents and videos, which at times may reflect Arabic bastardizations of Uyghur names. For place names inside the Uyghur region, the book uses the Uyghur names exclusively rather than the Chinese versions (i.e. 'Ghulja' instead of 'Yining,' 'Guma' instead of 'Pishan,' etc.). Furthermore, it generally adopts a modified version of the standard used by the UN Group of Experts on Geographic Names in spelling. This system in Uyghur does not distinguish between long and short vowels, with the exception of the short 'ü,' does not distinguish between the regular 'k' and the guttural 'q,' uses 'q' for the 'ch' sound, and 'x' for the 'sh' sound. To reflect most maps and references in the English language, the book's modified version of this system does not distinguish between short and long 'u' (i.e. 'Urumqi' instead of 'Ürümqi') and employs 'sh' instead of 'x' (i.e. 'Karakash' instead of 'Karakax'). However, in some instances, I have chosen to use the version of the place name most recognizable to readers (e.g. 'Kashgar' instead of 'Kashkar').

FIGURES

ABBREVIATIONS

APEC	Asia-Pacific Economic Cooperation
BRI	Belt and Road Initiative
CCP	Chinese Communist Party
ETESA	Eastern Turkistan Education and Solidarity Association
ETIM	Eastern Turkistan Islamic Movement
ETIP	East Turkistan Islamic Party
ETLO	Eastern Turkistan Liberation Organization
ETPRP	Eastern Turkistan People's Revolutionary Party
ETR	Eastern Turkistan Republic
FDD	Foundation for the Defense of Democracy
GLF	Great Leap Forward
GMD	Guomindang
GPCR	Great Proletarian Cultural Revolution
GWOT	'Global War on Terror'
HRW	Human Rights Watch
IJOP	Integrated Joint Operations Platform
IMU	Islamic Movement of Uzbekistan
ISI	Pakistan's Inter-Service Intelligence
PAP	Pairing Assistant Program
PLA	People's Liberation Army
PRC	People's Republic of China
RFA	Radio Free Asia
SCIOPRC	State Council Information Office of the PRC
SCO	Shanghai Cooperation Organization
SETA	Special Economic Trading Area

ABBREVIATIONS

TAR	Tibetan Autonomous Region
TIP	Turkistan Islamic Party
UHRP	Uyghur Human Rights Project
UNSC	United Nations Security Council
USSR	Union of Soviet Socialist Republics
XPCC	Xinjiang Production and Construction Corps
XUAR	Xinjiang Uyghur Autonomous Region
WUC	World Uyghur Congress

ACKNOWLEDGMENTS

It has become a cliché to refer to the writing of a book as a journey, but in writing this manuscript, I now understand why this is a well-worn metaphor. As my first book, I can honestly say that the work that went into it draws from my entire three-decade career in studying the Uyghur people. The book's content has been informed by fieldwork I conducted for my dissertation among Uyghurs in Kazakhstan and the Uyghur region of China in the 1990s as much as it has by my last fieldwork in Turkey during the summer of 2019 and everything in between.

Given that, at least indirectly, this work is the product of 30 years of studying the Uyghur people, I feel obliged to thank an army of people who have all played a part in facilitating its research and writing. To begin, I must thank my graduate school advisors who welcomed my enthusiasm for studying the Uyghur people while I was at the University of Southern California. This includes Ayse-Azade Rorlich, who taught me the importance of wading through sources in Turkic languages and cultivated my inner historian, as well as the recently deceased Eugene Cooper, whose wisdom and humor kept me sane and inspired. I also must thank the entire Uyghur community of Kazakhstan who welcomed me into their lives between 1994 and 2000. In particular, I owe great appreciation to my adopted *Yärliq* father Savut Mollaudov and my adopted *Kitäiliq* father Abbas Aliyev. I wish they had both lived to read this book, but I am also glad that they are unable to witness the destruction of Uyghur culture in their homeland today. In addition, I owe a great debt of gratitude to my adopted *Yärliq* sister Sayinur Dautova and my adopted *Kitäiliq* sister Dilyanur Kasymova, who helped me endlessly during my fieldwork in Kazakhstan. I also must thank the Elliott School of International Affairs for their support of my more recent research. I thank both Michael Brown and Reuben Brigety as successive Deans at the Elliott School for their support in this project and patience with its completion. I also want to acknowledge the support of both the Sigur Center for Asian Studies and the Institute for European, Russian, and Eurasian Studies (IERES) for their direct support of this research. The Sigur Center provided me with a research assistant for a semester when I first began the project and financed my final research for the book in Turkey during the summer of 2019. IERES has also provided me with a research assistant for two semesters over the last two years, which has been critical to the completion of the project, and has always worked with me to organize events and symposia on Uyghur-related topics. Additionally, I must thank my colleagues in the Program on New Approaches to Research and Security in Eurasia (PONARS) for providing me with endless intellectual stimulation and feedback on my work over the years. In particular, this book's initial conception emerged from a working paper I presented to these colleagues at a PONARS workshop in 2012, and their subsequent encouragement helped me undertake this project. Finally, I want to thank my research assistants over the last few years, who have helped me by digging up sources, transcribing interviews, and serving as critical sounding boards for my ideas. This includes Shirin Arslan, Allison Quatrini, and especially Bekzat Otep-Qizy, without whose assistance I would never have gotten this done. I hope all of you can see your work in the finished product.

I also must thank the many Uyghurs in the US, in Europe, and in Turkey, who graciously helped me with various parts of my research. They were always willing to share contacts, provide information, facilitate introductions, and frequently offer hospitality. While many of these people must go unnamed for their own protection, there are some whom I can acknowledge given that they are already outspoken public figures. These include Abduwali Ayup,

Tahir Imin, Rabiya Kadeer, Omer Kanat, Alim Seytoff, and Seyit Tumturk. These people, and all the others who will go unnamed, have been very gracious with their time and assistance. While he is not a member of the Uyghur community, I also want to thank Ben Venzke from IntelCenter for his willingness to offer me discounted access to his organization's treasure trove of videos made by the Turkistan Islamic Party, which have been critical to deciphering this group's history.

I owe a debt of gratitude to the ever-growing international community of scholars who study Uyghur issues. While I have gained great insight from all of the scholars whose works are cited here, I owe particular thanks to those who have read drafts of chapters and provided extremely helpful feedback, including David Brophy, Joanne Smith-Finley, James Millward, and Rian Thum. Additionally, I want to thank Michael Clarke and Darren Byler for their feedback on other writings that fed into the ideas expressed in this book, as well as James Leibold for encouraging me to undertake the project. I must especially thank the anonymous reviewers of the draft manuscript, who are inevitably also members of the Uyghur studies community, for their expeditious and meticulous review and extremely useful recommendations. To the many others in this community with whom I have spent hours discussing Uyghur culture and history, I thank you for your insights, work, and friendship. I imagine there are few other scholarly communities in academia that are as welcoming and collegial.

Since writing a book requires dedicating extensive personal time, it should also go without saying that I owe a great deal of gratitude to my family for having patience with me as I put this manuscript together. In particular, I thank my wife, Asel, for giving me the space to finish the manuscript, especially during its final weeks of production, and I thank my daughter, Aideen, for the inspiration she provided my writing through her enthusiasm for life. I dedicate this book to these two strong Kazakh-American women – my 'A-Team' at home.

Although I am writing this before I have taken full advantage of the work they will inevitably put into the final manuscript, I also want to thank the teams at Manchester University Press and Princeton University Press for their hard work in getting this manuscript ready for publication. In particular, I especially want to thank Jonathan de Peyer for his dedication to this project from the start and patience with lapsed deadlines, as well as Fred Appel for his enthusiasm and confidence in the project.

Finally, I want to thank the many Uyghurs I have interviewed over the years in Kazakhstan, Kyrgyzstan, Turkey, Europe, and the US. With the exception of those who have very public profiles, I have refrained from naming these inspirational people or providing much identifying information about them to ensure their anonymity and safety. However, please know that without your willingness to talk with me, this book would not exist. I am in awe of your resilience in the face of tragedy, and I wish you and the entire Uyghur nation a much brighter future.

NOTES

PREFACE

1 Mamatjan Juma and Alim Seytoff, 'Xinjiang Authorities Sending Uyghurs to Work in China's Factories, Despite Coronavirus Risks,' *Radio Free Asia* (27 February 2020).

2 SCMP Reporters, 'China Plans to Send Uygur Muslims from Xinjiang Re-Education Camps to Work in Other Parts of Country,' *South China Morning Post* (2 May 2020).

3 Keegan Elmer, 'China says it will 'Normalise' Xinjiang Camps as Beijing Continues Drive to Defend Policies in Mainly Muslim Region,' *South China Morning Post* (9 December 2019).

4 Erkin, 'Boarding Preschools For Uyghur Children "Clearly a Step Towards a Policy of Assimilation"': Expert,' *Radio Free Asia* (6 May 2020).

5 Gulchehre Hoja, 'Subsidies For Han Settlers "Engineering Demographics" in Uyghur-Majority Southern Xinjiang,' *Radio Free Asia* (13 April 2020).

INTRODUCTION

1 Emily Feng, 'China Targets Muslim Uyghurs Studying Abroad,' *Financial Times* (1 August 2017).

2 See Adrian Zenz and James Leibold, 'Xinjiang's Rapidly Evolving Security State,' *Jamestown Foundation China Brief* (14 March 2017); Magha Rajagopalan, 'This is What a 21st Century Police State Really Looks Like,' *Buzzfeed News* (17 October 2017).

3 Adrian Zenz and James Leibold, 'Chen Quanguo: The Strongman Behind Beijing's Securitization Strategy in Tibet and Xinjiang,' *Jamestown Foundation China Brief* (21 September 2017).

4 Nathan VanderKlippe, 'Frontier Injustice: Inside China's Campaign to "Re-educate" Uyghurs,' *The Globe and Mail* (9 September 2017); HRW, 'China: Free Xinjiang "Political Education" Detainees' (10 September 2017); Eset Sulaiman, 'China Runs Region-wide Re-education Camps in Xinjiang for Uyghurs and Other Muslims,' *RFA* (11 September 2017).

NOTES

5 Alexia Fernandez Campbell, 'China's Reeducation Camps are Beginning to Look Like Concentration Camps,' *Vox* (24 October 2018).

6 See 'Inside the Camps Where China Tries to Brainwash Muslims Until They Love the Party and Hate Their Own Culture,' *Associated Press* (17 May 2018); David Stavrou, 'A Million People Are Jailed at China's Gulags. I Managed to Escape. Here's What Really Goes on Inside,' *Haaretz* (17 October 2019).

7 See Amie Ferris-Rotman, 'Abortions, IUDs and Sexual Humiliation: Muslim Women who Fled China for Kazakhstan Recount Ordeals,' *Washington Post* (5 October 2019); Eli Meixler, '"I Begged Them to Kill Me." Uighur Woman Tells Congress of Torture in Chinese Internment Camps,' *TIME* (30 November 2018); Ben Mauk, 'Untold Stories from China's Gulag State,' *The Believer* (1 October 2019).

8 Shoret Hoshur 'Nearly Half of Uyghurs in Xinjiang's Hotan Targetted for Re-education Camps,' *RFA* (9 October 2017).

9 Sean R. Roberts, 'Fear and Loathing in Xinjiang: Ethnic Cleansing in the 21st Century,' *Fair Observer* (17 December 2018).

10 See Zenz and Leibold, 'Xinjiang's Rapidly Evolving Security State.'

11 Roberts, 'Fear and Loathing in Xinjiang.'

12 Darren Byler, 'China's Nightmare Homestay,' *Foreign Policy* (26 October 2018); Steven Jiang, 'Chinese Uyghurs Forced to Welcome Communist Party Into Their Homes,' *CNN* (14 May 2018).

13 James Leibold, 'Surveillance in China's Xinjiang Region: Ethnic Sorting, Coercion, and Inducement,' *Journal of Contemporary China* (2019).

14 Darren Byler, 'Xinjiang Education Reform and The Eradication of Uyghur-Language Books,' *SupChina* (2 October 2019); Lily Kuo, 'Revealed: New Evidence of China's Mission to Raze the Mosques of Xinjiang,' *The Guardian* (6 May 2019); Bahram Sintash and UHRP, 'Demolishing Faith: The Destruction and Desecration of Uyghur Mosques and Shrines' (28 October 2019); Sui-Lee Wee and Paul Mozur, 'China uses DNA to Map Faces with Help from the West,' *The New York Times* (3 December 2019).

15 Adrian Zenz, 'Beyond the Camps: Beijing's Grand Scheme of Forced Labor, Poverty Alleviation and Social Control in Xinjiang,' *SocArxiv Papers* (12 July 2019).

16 See Darren Byler, 'Uyghur Love in a Time of Interethnic Marriage,' *SupChina* (7 August 2019); Adrian Zenz, 'Break Their Roots: Evidence for China's Parent-Child Separation Campaign in Xinjiang,' *The Journal of Political Risk*, 7:7 (July 2019).

17 Chris Buckley and Austin Ramzy, 'Facing Criticism Over Muslim Camps, China Says: What's the Problem?' *The New York Times* (9 December 2019).

18 Statistical Bureau of Xinjiang Uygur Autonomous Region 'National Population by Region, State, City and County' (15 March, 2017).

19 For more on the nomadic/settled cultural divide in Central Asia, see Elizabeth Bacon, *Central Asians Under Russian Rule: A Study in Culture Change* (Ithaca, NY: Cornell University Press, 1980).

20 For more on the local traditions of Islam among Uyghurs, see Rian Thum, *The Sacred Routes of Uyghur History* (Cambridge, MA: Harvard University Press, 2014) and Ildiko Beller-Hann, *Community Matters in Xinjiang, 1880–1949: Towards a Historical Anthropology of the Uyghur* (Leiden: Brill, 2008).

21 For more on the ancient Uyghur Empire, see Colin Mackerras, *The Uighur Empire According to T'ang Dynastic Histories: A Study in Sino-Uighur Relations, 744–840* (Columbia, SC: University of South Carolina Press, 1973).

22 See James Millward, *Eurasian Crossroads: A History of Xinjiang* (New York: Columbia University Press, 2007), pp. 1–77.

23 See Laura Newby, '"Us and Them" in 18th and 19th Century Xinjiang,' in I. Beller-Hann, M. Cesàro, and J. Finley (eds), *Situating the Uyghurs Between China and Central Asia* (Hampshire, UK: Ashgate, 2007); Beller-Hann, *Community Matters in Xinjiang*; Thum, *The Sacred Routes of Uyghur History*.

24 UN Permanent Forum on Indigenous Issues, 'Indigenous Peoples, Indigenous Voices: Who are Indigenous Peoples?' *United Nations* (2006).

25 For official government accounts of the history of the XUAR and the Uyghurs, see State Council Information Office of the PRC (SCIOPRC), *Full Text of White Paper on History and Development of Xinjiang* (26 May 2003); *White Paper: Historical Matters Concerning Xinjiang* (22 July 2019).

26 Personal communication with Elise Marie Anderson, 2019.

27 Walter Laqueur, *Terrorism* (London: Weidenfeld and Nicolson, 1977), p. 179.

28 Gerald Seymour, *Harry's Game: A Thriller* (New York: Random House, 1975).

29 Boaz Garnor, 'Defining Terrorism: Is One Man's Terrorist Another Man's Freedom Fighter?' *Policy Practice and Research*, 3:4 (2002), p. 288.

30 Ibid., pp. 294–296.

31 United States Department of State, *Patterns of Global Terrorism, 2003*, April 2004, p. xii.

32 Slavoj Zizek, *Welcome to the Desert of the Real* (London: Verso, 2002), p. 93.

33 Ibid., p. 93. Emphasis in the original.

34 Michel Foucault, *'Society Must Be Defended': Lectures at the College De France, 1975–76* (London: Picador, 1997), p. 32.

35 Ibid., p. 256.

36 For more on the concept of *homo sacer*, see Giorgio Agamben, *Homo Sacer: Sovereign Power and Bare Life* (Stanford: Stanford University Press, 1998).

37 Zizek, *Welcome to the Desert of the Real*, p. 93.

38 See Stuart Elden, 'Terror and Territory,' *Antipode: A Radical Journal of Geography* 39:5 (2007), 781–955.

39 See Kumar Ramakrishna, 'The Rise of Trump and Its Global Implications; "Radical Islamic Terrorism": What's in a Name?' *RSIS Commentaries*, No. 23 (Singapore: Nanyang Technological University, 2017); Hilal Evar,

'Racializing Islam Before and After 9/11: From Melting Pot to Islamophobia,' *Transnational Law and Contemporary Problems*, 21:119 (2012), 119–174.

1 COLONIALISM, 1759–2001

1 James Millward, *Beyond the Pass: Economy, Ethnicity, and Empire in Qing Central Asia, 1759–1864* (Stanford: Stanford University Press, 1998), p. 17.
2 Justin M. Jacobs, *Xinjiang and the Modern Chinese State (Studies on Ethnic Groups in China)* (Seattle, WA: University of Washington Press, 2016), pp. 10–11.
3 See Rian Thum, et al., 'The Rise of Xinjiang Studies: A New Author Forum,' *The Journal of Asian Studies*, 77:1 (2018), 7–18.
4 Max Oidtmann, *Forging the Golden Urn: The Qing Empire and the Politics of Reincarnation in Tibet* (New York: Columbia University Press, 2018).
5 Dibyesh Anand, 'Colonization with Chinese Characteristics: Politics of (In) security in Xinjiang and Tibet,' *Central Asian Survey*, 38:1 (2019) 129–147, p. 130.
6 Ibid., pp. 131–133.
7 Partha Chatterjee, *The Nation and Its Fragments* (Princeton, NJ: Princeton University Press, 1993), pp. 16–18.
8 Lorenzo Veracini, 'Understanding Colonialism and Settler Colonialism as Distinct Formations,' *Interventions*, 16:5 (2014), 615–633.
9 Ibid., p. 623.
10 For official government accounts of the history of the XUAR and the Uyghurs, see SCIOPRC, *Full Text of White Paper on History and Development of Xinjiang* (26 May 2003); *White Paper: Historical Matters Concerning Xinjiang* (22 July 2019).
11 Millward, *Eurasian Crossroads*, p. 92.
12 Ibid., p. 92.
13 Lazar I. Duman, 'Feodal'nyi institut iantsii v. Vostochnom Turkestane v XVIII veke,' *Zapiski Instituta Vostokovedenia Akademii Nauk SSSR* (Moscow, 1935) (Russian), p. 90; Duman, 'Agrarnaia Politika Tsinskogo (Manchzhurskogo) Pravitel'stva v Sin'tsziane v Kontse XVIII Veka,' *Izd-vo Akademii nauk SSSR* (Moscow, 1936) (Russian), p. 156; Vasily V. Radlov, *Narechiya Tyurkskikh Plemen, Zhivushchikh v Yuzhnoi Siberii I Dzhungarskoi Stepi* (St Petersburg: Tipografiy Imperatorskoi Akademii Nauk, 1866) (Russian), p. 15.
14 Rian Thum, 'The Uyghurs in Modern China,' *Oxford Encyclopedia of Asian History* (Oxford: Oxford University Press, 2018), p. 4.
15 Millward, *Beyond the Pass*, p. 35.
16 For more on the ambiguous relationship between local Muslims and Yakub Beg's state, see Eric Schluessel, 'An Uyghur History of Turn-of-the-Century Chinese Central Asia,' *Maydan* (10 July 2019).
17 See Millward, *Beyond the Pass*; S.C.M. Paine, *Imperial Rivals: China, Russia, and Their Disputed Frontiers* (Armonk, NY: M.E. Sharpe, 1996).

NOTES

18 See B. Gurevich, *Mezhdunarodnye Otnoshenija v Central'noi Azii v XVII – pervoi polovine XIX v.* (Moscow: Izdatel´stvo Nauka Glavnaia Redakciia Vostocnoi Literatury, 1983) (Russian).

19 Malik Kabirov, *Pereselenie Iliiskikh Uigur v Semirech'e* (Alma-Ata: Izdat. AN Kaz. SSR, 1951) (Russian)

20 Millward, *Eurasian Crossroads*, p. 136.

21 Ibid., pp. 140–141.

22 Cited in ibid., p. 142.

23 Ibid., pp. 144–145.

24 For a description of the *usul-i-jadid* educational system, see Adeeb Khalid, *The Politics of Muslim Cultural Reform: Jadidism in Central Asia* (Berkeley, CA: University of California Press, 1999).

25 Jacobs, *Xinjiang and the Modern Chinese State*, p. 9.

26 Cf. Andrew Forbes, *Warlords and Muslims in Chinese Central Asia: A Political History of Republican Sinkiang, 1911–1949* (Cambridge: Cambridge University Press, 1986), pp. 13–33; Lars-Erik Nyman, *Great Britain and Chinese, Russian and Japanese interests in Sinkiang, 1918–1934* (Stockholm: Esselte Studium, 1977), pp. 19–26; Jacobs, *Xinjiang and the Modern Chinese State*, pp. 17–75.

27 Cited in Jacobs, *Xinjiang and the Modern Chinese State*, p. 7.

28 David Brophy, *Uyghur Nation: Reform and Revolution on the Russia-China Frontier* (Cambridge, MA: Harvard University Press, 2016).

29 See Millward, *Eurasian Crossroads*; Newby, '"Us and Them" in 18th and 19th Century Xinjiang'; Beller-Hann, *Community Matters in Xinjiang*; Thum, *The Sacred Routes of Uyghur History*.

30 Brophy, *Uyghur Nation*.

31 Sean R. Roberts, 'Imagining Uyghurstan: Re-evaluating the Birth of the Modern Uyghur Nation,' *Central Asian Survey*, 28:4, pp. 361–381 (2009).

32 See Brophy, *Uyghur Nation*, pp. 217–219.

33 Jacobs, *Xinjiang and the Modern Chinese State*, pp. 27–29.

34 See ibid., pp. 75–78.

35 Forbes, *Warlords and Muslims in Chinese Central Asia*, pp. 40–41.

36 Ibid., p. 39.

37 Cf. ibid., p. 42; Jacobs, *Xinjiang and the Modern Chinese State*, pp. 79–82.

38 Forbes, *Warlords and Muslims in Chinese Central Asia*, pp. 44–46.

39 Jacobs, *Xinjiang and the Modern Chinese State*, p. 86.

40 Brophy, *Uyghur Nation*, pp. 242–243.

41 Ibid., p. 247.

42 Older works, which characterized this as being inspired exclusively by Islam, tended to call it The Islamic Republic of East Turkistan (or TIRET). See Forbes, *Warlords and Muslims in Chinese Central Asia*; Linda Benson, *The Ili Rebellion: The Moslem Challenge to Chinese Authority in Xinjiang, 1944–1949* (New York, M.E. Sharpe, 1990). However, as Millward (*Eurasian Crossroads*, p. 204) points out, the constitution of the Republic referred to the state only as the Eastern Turkistan Republic (ETR).

43 Jacobs, *Xinjiang and the Modern Chinese State*, p. 86.

44 Forbes, *Warlords and Muslims in Chinese Central Asia*, pp. 121–123.
45 See Allen S. Whiting, *Sinkiang: Pawn or Pivot?* (East Lansing, MI: Michigan State University Press. 1958), pp. 21–45; Forbes, *Warlords and Muslims in Chinese Central Asia*, pp. 128–158.
46 Jacobs, *Xinjiang and the Modern Chinese State*, pp. 103–110.
47 See Brophy, *Uyghur Nation*, pp. 254–255.
48 See V.A. Barmin, *Sinziyan v Sovetsko-Kitayskikh Otnosheniyakh 1941–1949 gg* (Barnaul, Russia: Barnaul'skii Gosudarstvenniy Pedagogicheskii Universitet, 1999) (Russian), p. 144.
49 For more on the Soviet policies of *Korenizatsiia*, see George Liber, 'Korenizatsiia: Restructuring Soviet Nationality Policy in the 1920s,' *Ethnic and Racial Studies*, 14:1 (1991), 15–23.
50 Brophy, *Uyghur Nation*, pp. 256–257.
51 See Forbes, *Warlords and Muslims in Chinese Central Asia*, p. 139; Brophy, *Uyghur Nation*, p. 261.
52 Forbes, *Warlords and Muslims in Chinese Central Asia*, pp. 140–142.
53 Brophy, *Uyghur Nation*, pp. 263–264.
54 Ibid., p. 254.
55 Forbes, *Warlords and Muslims in Chinese Central Asia*, pp. 157–158.
56 Cf. ibid., pp. 158–159; Barmin, *Sinziyan v Sovetsko-Kitayskikh Otnosheniyakh 1941–1949 gg*, p. 21.
57 Barmin, *Sinziyan v Sovetsko-Kitayskikh Otnosheniyakh 1941–1949 gg*, pp. 20–23.
58 Ibid., p. 71. There is also evidence that Soviet agents were sent to Xinjiang to seek out such local resistance groups to support at the same time. In 1946, several Soviet agents of the MVD and KGB were given awards for 'fulfilling the mission of the Central Committee of the Soviet Communist Party in Xinjiang since May 4, 1943' (ibid., p. 75).
59 Jacobs, *Xinjiang and the Modern Chinese State*, pp. 133–135.
60 Benson, *The Ili Rebellion*, p. 3.
61 Ibid., p. 52.
62 See *Shinjang Uch Villyät Inqilabi*. (Ürümchi: Shinjang Güz.l Säniät-Foto Sürät Näshriyati, 1994).
63 See the journals *Kuräsh* (Ghulja, 1945–1948) and *Itifaq* (Ghulja, 1948–1949).
64 See Linda Benson, 'Uygur Politicians of the 1940s: Mehmet Emin Bugra, Isa Yusuf Alptekin, and Mesut Sabri,' *Central Asian Survey*, 10:4 (1991), 87–113.
65 See Benson, *The Ili Rebellion*.
66 Ibid., pp. 97–98.
67 Ibid., pp. 100–103.
68 Ibid., p. 109.
69 Barmin, *Sinziyan v Sovetsko-Kitayskikh Otnosheniyakh 1941–1949 gg*, p. 180.
70 See Benson, *The Ili Rebellion*, pp. 175–176; Barmin, *Sinziyan v Sovetsko-Kitayskikh Otnosheniyakh 1941–1949 gg*, p. 180.
71 Donald H. McMillan, *Chinese Communist Power and Policy in Xinjiang, 1949–1977* (Boulder, CO: Westview Press, 1979), pp. 8–9.

72 Ibid., pp. 46–47.
73 Cited in J.T. Dreyer, *China's Forty Millions: Minority Nationalities and National Integration in the People's Republic of China* (Cambridge, MA: Harvard University Press, 1976), p. 94.
74 Thum, 'The Uyghurs in Modern China,' p. 11.
75 Rasma Silde-Karklins, 'The Uighurs Between China and the USSR,' *Canadian Slavonic Papers*, 17:2–3 (1975), pp. 354–355.
76 McMillan, *Chinese Communist Power and Policy in Xinjiang, 1949–1977*, p. 92.
77 Millward, *Eurasian Crossroads*, p. 258.
78 Ibid., pp. 251–252.
79 Ibid., p. 252.
80 Ibid., p. 253.
81 Thum, 'The Uyghurs in Modern China,' p. 12.
82 Linda Benson and Ingvar Svanberg, *China's Last Nomads: History and Culture of China's Kazaks: History and Culture of China's Kazaks* (New York: ME Sharpe, 1998), p. 136; Millward, *Eurasian Crossroads*, p. 261.
83 James Millward and Nabijan Tursun, 'Political History and Strategies of Control, 1884–1978,' in S.F. Starr (ed.), *Xinjiang: China's Muslim Borderland* (New York: M.E. Sharpe, 2004), p. 94.
84 Sean R. Roberts, 'The Uyghurs of the Kazakhstan Borderlands: Migration and the Nation,' *Nationalities Papers*, 26:3 (1998), pp. 513–514.
85 See J.T. Dreyer, 'Ethnic Minorities in the Sino-Soviet Dispute,' in William McCagg and Brian D. Silver (eds), *Soviet Asian Ethnic Frontiers* (New York: Pergamon Press, 1979), pp. 195–226, p. 209; Malik Sadirov, 'Beguna Tokulgän Qanlar,' *Yengi Hayat* (4 June 1994).
86 Cf. Dreyer, 'Ethnic Minorities in the Sino-Soviet Dispute,' pp. 208–209; Sadirov, 'Beguna Tokulgän Qanlar'; Shämsidin Abdurehim-Ughli, 'Yeqin Otmushning Qanliq Khatirsi,' *Yengi Hayat* (28 May 1994).
87 Abdurehim-Ughli, 'Yeqin Otmushning Qanliq Khatirsi.'
88 Millward, *Eurasian Crossroads*, pp. 264–265.
89 Cf. McMillan, *Chinese Communist Power and Policy in Xinjiang, 1949–1977*, pp. 181–252; Millward and Tursun, 'Political History and Strategies of Control, 1884–1978,' pp. 96–98.
90 McMillan, *Chinese Communist Power and Policy in Xinjiang, 1949–1977*, p. 196.
91 Millward and Tursun, 'Political History and Strategies of Control, 1884–1978,' p. 97.
92 See Sandrine E. Catris, *The Cultural Revolution from The Edge: Violence and Revolutionary Spirit in Xinjiang, 1966–1976* (Bloomington, IN: Indiana University; Ann Arbor, MI: ProQuest, UMI Dissertations Publishing, 2015).
93 Ibid., pp. 115–118.
94 See Sabit Uyghuri, *Uyghur Namä* (Almaty: Nash Mir, 2005), pp. 5–6.
95 Catris, *The Cultural Revolution from The Edge*, p. 181.
96 See ibid.; Uyghuri, *Uyghur Namä*, p. 6.
97 Silde-Karklins, 'The Uighurs Between China and the USSR' provides the

estimate of the Han population in 1967, and Stanley Toops, 'The Population Landscape of Xinjiang/East Turkestan,' *Inner Asia*, 2:2 (2000), 155–170 provides the official data from 1953 and 1982.

98 See Sean R. Roberts, 'Development with Chinese Characteristics in Xinjiang: A Solution to Ethnic Tension or Part of the Problem?' in M. Clarke and D. Smith (eds), *China's Frontier Regions: Ethnicity, Economic Integration and Foreign Relations* (London: I.B. Tauris, 2016).

99 Gardner Bovingdon, *The Uyghurs: Strangers in Their Own Land* (New York: Colombia University Press, 2010), pp. 52–53.

100 See Abdurehim Tileshüp Ötkür, *Iz* (Ürümchi: Xinjiang Khälq Näshriyati, 1985); Turghun Almas, *Uyghurlar* (Ürümchi: Xinjiang Yashlar-Ösmürluar Näshriyati, 1989).

101 See Millward, *Eurasian Crossroads*, pp. 327–328.

102 See ibid., pp. 325–327. Some reports supporting this view also note that the uprising was only ended by a substantial bombing campaign in the region, which killed scores of local people. See Marika Vicziany, 'State Responses to Islamic Terrorism in Western China and their Impact on South Asia,' *Contemporary South Asia*, 12:2 (2003), 243–262, p. 249.

103 See John Kohut, 'Xinjiang Separatist Organization's Extent Examined,' *South China Sunday Morning Post* (23 February 1992).

104 Millward, *Eurasian Crossroads*, p. 328.

105 Bovingdon, *The Uyghurs*, p. 56.

106 'Record of the Meeting of the Standing Committee of the Political Bureau of the Chinese Communist Party concerning the maintenance of Stability in Xinjiang (Document No. 7)' (1996).

107 Ibid.

108 Ibid.

109 Ibid.

110 See Sean R. Roberts, 'Locality, Islam, and National Culture in a Changing Borderlands: The Revival of the Mäshräp Ritual Among Young Uighur Men in the Ili Valley,' *Central Asian Survey*, 17:4 (1998), pp. 673–700; J. Dautcher, *Down a Narrow Road: Identity and Masculinity in a Uyghur Community in Xinjiang China* (Boston, MA: Harvard University Asia Center, 2009).

111 Millward, *Eurasian Crossroads*, p. 333.

112 Ibid., p. 333.

113 See Amnesty International, *People's Republic of China: Gross Human Rights Violations in the Xinjiang Uighur Autonomous Region* (1999) pp. 127–129.

114 See Sean R. Roberts, 'Toasting the Nation: Negotiating Stateless Nationalism in Transnational Ritual Space,' *The Journal of Ritual Studies*, 18:2 (2004), 86–105.

115 Joanne Smith-Finley, *The Art of Symbolic Resistance: Uyghur Identities and Uyghur-Han Relations in Contemporary Xinjiang* (Leiden: Brill, 2013).

116 Ibid., pp. 235–293.

117 Bovingdon, *The Uyghurs*, pp. 184–188.

118 Toops, *Demographics and Development in Xinjiang after 1949*, p. 20.
119 See Smith-Finley, *The Art of Symbolic Resistance*.

2 How the Uyghurs became a 'terrorist threat'

1 George W. Bush, 'Address to a Joint Session of Congress (20 September 2001),' *Our Mission and Our Moment: Speeches Since the Attacks of September 11* (Washington: White House), p. 11.
2 Ibid., p. 10.
3 'President Delivers State of the Union Address,' *WhiteHouse.gov* (29 January 2002).
4 See UN Office of Drugs and Crime, 'Introduction to International Terrorism (Module 1),' *University Module Series: Counter-Terrorism* (2018), p. 10.
5 Lee Jarvis and Tim Legrand (2018), 'The Proscription or Listing of Terrorist Organisations: Understanding, Assessment, and International Comparisons,' *Terrorism and Political Violence*, 30:2 (2018), 199–215, p. 201.
6 Ibid.
7 See H. Zhao, 'Security Building in Central Asia and the Shanghai Cooperation Organization,' in A. Iwashita and Sh. Tabata (eds), *Slavic Eurasia's Integration into the World Economy and Community* (Sapporo: Slavic Research Center, Hokkaido University, 2004), p. 283.
8 Akihiro Iwashita, 'The Shanghai Cooperation Organization and Its Implications for Eurasian Security: A New Dimension of "Partnership" after the Post-Cold War Period,' in Iwashita and Tabata (eds), *Slavic Eurasia's Integration into the World Economy and Community*, p. 264.
9 'The Shanghai Convention on Combating Terrorism, Separatism and Extremism,' *SCO Secretariat* (2001).
10 Bates Gill, 'Shanghai Five: An Attempt to Counter US Influence in Asia?' *Newsweek Korea* (4 May 2001).
11 'China Pledges to Battle Internal "Terrorism,"' *Agence France-Press* (11 November 2001).
12 Ministry of Foreign Affairs of PRC, 'Spokesperson on East Turkistan National Conference's Seminar Held on EP's premises' (19 October 2001).
13 'No Double Standards in Anti-terror Fight, Says China of Domestic Unrest,' *Agence France-Press* (11 October 2001).
14 Permanent Mission of the PRC to the United Nations (PMPRCUN), 'Statement by H.E. Mr. Tang Jiaxuan, Minister of Foreign Affairs and Head of Delegation of The People's Republic of China, At the 56th Session of the UN General Assembly' (11 November 2001).
15 This document, which is prominently dated 29 November 2001, is both on the webpage of the PRC Mission to the UN and in a journalistic account of the Uyghur terrorist threat (see J. Todd Reed and D. Raschke, *The ETIM: China's Islamic Militants and the Global Terrorist Threat* (Santa Barbara, CA: Praeger Publishers, 2010)). Neither source provides the provenance of the document, but its presence on the webpage of the PRC Mission to the UN suggests its origin is the PMPRCUN. It may also have come from the Ministry of Foreign Affairs or the State Council Information Office.

16 PMPRCUN, *Terrorist Activities Perpetrated by 'Eastern Turkistan' Organizations and Their Links with Osama bin Laden and the Taliban* (29 November 2001).

17 Ibid.

18 Ibid.

19 Ibid.

20 Ibid.

21 As evidence of the PRC's dedication to getting Uyghurs recognized as an international 'terrorist threat', the Ministry of Foreign Affairs website lists an impressive number of meetings and statements it made about international terrorism in the two months following 11 September 2001. See Ministry of Foreign Affairs of PR, 'China Opposes Terrorism' (2015), www.fmprc.gov.cn/mfa_eng/topics_665678/3712_665976/, last accessed 19 February 2020.

22 SCIOPRC, *'East Turkistan' Terrorist Forces Cannot Get Away With Impunity'* (January 2002).

23 Ibid. For a later articulation of this same historical narrative, see SCIOPRC, *White Paper: The Fight Against Terrorism and Extremism and Human Rights Protection in Xinjiang* (18 March 2019).

24 SCIOPRC, *'East Turkistan' Terrorist Forces Cannot Get Away With Impunity.*

25 Ibid.

26 It is noteworthy that the two incidents of bus bombings in Urumqi also constituted the bulk of casualties from all of the explosions described in the document. The bus bombings in Urumqi allegedly killed 12 people combined, and all other explosions taken together allegedly only accounted for 3 deaths.

27 SCIOPRC, *'East Turkistan' Terrorist Forces Cannot Get Away With Impunity.*

28 Most of the 22 Uyghurs who were transferred to Guantanamo Bay in 2002 from Pakistan and Afghanistan had originally been detained in late 2001. See Richard Bernstein, 'When China Convinced the US That Uighurs Were Waging Jihad,' *The Atlantic* (19 March 2019).

29 See Shirley Kan, 'US-China Counter-Terrorism Cooperation: Issues for US Policy,' *Report for Congress, RS21995, Congressional Research Service* (Washington, DC: The Library of Congress, 2004), p. 2.

30 Qiang Chen and Qian Hu, 'Chinese Practice in International Law: 2001,' *Chinese Journal of International Law* (2002), 328–386, p. 334.

31 Dewardric L. McNeal and Kerry Dumbaugh, 'China's Relations with Central Asian States and Problems with Terrorism,' *Report for Congress, RL31213, Congressional Research Service* (Washington, DC: The Library of Congress, 2002), p. 5.

32 See Kan, 'US-China Counter-Terrorism Cooperation,' p. 4.

33 US Department of State Country Report on Human Rights Practices 2001 – China (Includes Hong Kong and Macau), *DOS* (4 March 2002).

34 Bernstein, 'When China Convinced the US That Uighurs Were Waging Jihad.'

35 'Determination Pursuant to Section 1(b) of Executive Order 13224 Relating to the Eastern Turkistan Islamic Movement (ETIM)' [FR Doc. 02-22737], *Federal Register*, 63:173 (19 August 2002), p. 57054.

36 Philipp Pan, 'US Warns of Plot by Group in W. China,' *Washington Post* (29 August 2002).

37 Ibid.

38 Ibid.

39 Ibid.

40 See Bovingdon, *The Uyghurs*, p. 136.

41 J.A. Kelly, 'US-East Asia Policy: Three Aspects, 2002 East Asian and Pacific Affairs Remarks, Testimony, and Speeches,' *US Department of State Archive* (11 December 2002).

42 House Committee on Foreign Affairs, 'Exploring the Nature of Uighur Nationalism: Freedom Fighters or Terrorists?' 111th Congress, 1st Session, GPO Document Source: CHRG-111hhrg50504 (16 June 2009), pp. 20–22.

43 See 'The Guantanamo Docket – A History of the Detainee Population,' *The New York Times* (last data changed 2 May 2018).

44 Pan, 'US Warns of Plot by Group in W. China.'

45 See 'President Delivers State of the Union Address,' and Jason M. Breslow, 'Colin Powell: U.N. Speech "Was a Great Intelligence Failure,"' *PBS* (17 May 2016).

46 See Erik Eckholm, 'US Labeling of Group in China as Terrorist is Criticized,' *The New York Times* (13 September 2002); James Dao, 'Threats and Responses: Diplomacy; Closer Ties With China May Help US on Iraq,' *The New York Times* (4 October 2002); Karen DeYoung, 'US and China Ask UN to List Separatists as Terror Group,' *Washington Post* (11 September 2002).

47 Philip T. Reeker, 'Designation of the Eastern Turkistan Islamic Movement Under UNSC Resolutions 1267 and 1390,' *Homeland Security Digital Library* (11 September 2002).

48 'Press Statement on the UN Designation of the Eastern Turkistan Islamic Movement,' *US Department of the Treasury* (11 September 2002).

49 'China Seeks Cooperation Worldwide to Fight "East Turkistan" Terrorists,' *Xinhua* (15 December 2003).

50 'Interpol Lifts Wanted Alert for Exiled Uygur Leader, Angering China,' *Reuters* (24 February 2018).

51 Robert Malley and Jon Finer, 'The Long Shadow of 9/11: How Counter-terrorism Warps US Foreign Policy,' *Foreign Affairs*, 97 (2018), p. 58.

52 A 2010 Congressional Research Services report [see S. Kan, 'US-China Counterterrorism Cooperation: Issues for US Policy,' RL33001, *Congressional Research Service* (Washington, DC: The Library of Congress, 15 July 2010] claims that a Russian newspaper mentioned ETIM in an article as early as 2000. However, in checking this article's text (Ibragimov, 'Pugayuschii Lik Ekstremizma,' *Nezavisimaya Gazeta* (3 February 2000)), I found it only mentions that money was given by a wealthy Uyghur in Saudi Arabia to the *Islamic Movement of Uzbekistan* with the stipulation

that part of the money be shared with Uyghur militants in Afghanistan, nowhere referring to an organization called ETIM.

53 Council on Foreign Relations, *East Turkestan Islamic Movement (ETIM)* (24 September 2001); Center for Defense Information, *In the Spotlight: East Turkestan Islamic Movement (ETIM)* (9 December 2002).
54 Center for Defense Information, *In the Spotlight*.
55 McNeal and Dumbaugh, 'China's Relations with Central Asian States and Problems with Terrorism,' p. 8.
56 Gunaratna has been embroiled in multiple scandals regarding his analysis of different 'terrorist' threats, especially during the first years after 2001. In particular, he has been criticized for his lack of due diligence in sourcing and his unsubstantiated speculations. See 'Rohan Gunaratna,' *SourceWatch: Your Guide to the Names Behind the News*, www.sourcewatch.org/index. php?title=Rohan_Gunaratna, last accessed 21 August 2019.
57 Rohan Gunaratna, *Inside Al Qaeda: Global Network of Terror* (New York: Columbia University Press, 2002), p. 173.
58 Ibid.
59 The two sources on which Gunaratna draws are *Jane's Intelligence Review* (Rahul Bedi, 'The Chinese Connection,' *Jane's Intelligence Review*, 14:2 (February 2002)) and an unlocatable report from the Middle East Institute (presumably a longer version of Julie Sirrs, 'The Taliban's International Ambitions,' *Middle East Quarterly*, 8:3 (2001), 61–71). In looking at these two sources, it is difficult to understand how Gunaratna came to his conclusions from them when they actually both only offer minimal information about a handful of Uyghur militants in Afghanistan.
60 J. Wang, 'Eastern Turkistan Islamic Movement: A Case Study of a New Terrorist Organization in China,' *International Journal of Offender Therapy and Comparative Criminology*, 47:5 (2003), 568–584, p. 569.
61 James Millward, *Violent Separatism in Xinjiang: A Critical Assessment (Policy Studies No. 6)* (Washington, DC: East-West Center, 2004).
62 See Yitzhak Shichor, 'Blow Up: Internal and External Challenges of Uyghur Separatism and Islamic Radicalism to Chinese rule in Xinjiang,' *Asian Affairs*, 32:2 (2005), 119–136; Davide Giglio, 'Separatism and the War on Terror in China's Xinjiang Uighur Autonomous Region' (PhD Thesis, United Nations Institute for Peace Support Operations, 2004).
63 See Joshua Kurlantzick, 'Unnecessary Evil: China's Muslims Aren't Terrorists. So Why Did the Bush Administration Give Beijing the Green Light to Oppress Them?' *Washington Quarterly*, 34:12 (2002), 26–32; Dru Gladney, 'Xinjiang: China's Future West Bank?' *Current History* 101 (2002), 267–270; Denny Roy, 'China and the War on Terrorism,' *Orbis*, 46:3 (2002), 511–521; Michael Dillon, 'We Have Terrorists Too,' *The World Today*, 58:1 (2002), 25–27.
64 See Adam Wolfe, 'China's Uyghurs Trapped in Guantanamo,' *Asia Times* (4 November 2004).
65 'Chinese Militant "Shot Dead,"' *BBC* (23 December 2003).
66 See Council on Foreign Relations, 'Background Q&A: Eastern Turkestan Islamic Movement (China, Separatists)' (2005).

67 'Albania takes Guantanamo Uighurs,' *BBC* (6 May 2006).
68 TIP, *Islam Yolvasi: Häsän Mäkhsum* (Arabic) (21 May 2004).
69 Ibid.; TIP *Jihad Lands: Turkestan* (9 August 2004).
70 Turkistan, *A Message of Incitement to Jihad from a Mujahid to the Muslims of East Turkestan* (Arabic) (2006).
71 N. Swanstrom (ed.) 'Special Issue: Terrorism,' *The China and Eurasia Forum Quarterly*, 4:2 (May 2006).
72 Cf. Yitzhak Shichor, 'Fact and Fiction: A Chinese Documentary on Eastern Turkestan,' Terrorism,' *The China and Eurasia Forum Quarterly*, 4:2 (May 2006), 89–108; C.P. Chung, 'Confronting Terrorism and Other Evils in China: All Quiet on the Western Front?,' 75–88; G. Pan, 'East Turkestan Terrorism and the Terrorist Arc: China's Post-9/11 Anti-Terror Strategy,' 19–24; Rohan Gunaratna and Kenneth Pereire, 'An Al-Qaeda Associate Group Operating in China?' pp. 55–62, all in Swanstrom (ed.) 'Special Issue: Terrorism,' *The China and Eurasia Forum Quarterly*, 4:2 (May 2006)
73 Gunaratna and Pereire, 'An Al-Qaeda Associate Group Operating in China?' p. 61.
74 Kenneth Pereire, 'Jihad in China? Rise of the East Turkestan Islamic Movement (ETIM),' *RSIS Commentary* (Singapore: Nanyang Technological University, 2006).
75 Liza Steele and Raymond Kuo, 'Terrorism in Xinjiang?' *Ethnopolitics*, 6:1 (2007), 1–19, p. 17.
76 Martin Wayne, *China's War on Terrorism: Counter-Insurgency, Politics and Internal Security* (London: Routledge, 2008).
77 Ibid., pp. 31–54.
78 Ibid., p. 41.
79 TIP, [untitled] – (Abdul Häq's statement on the Olympics) (1 March 2008).
80 Jake Hooker and Jim Yardley, 'China Says Plane and Olympic Plots Halted,' *The New York Times* (10 March 2008).
81 W.G. Cheng, 'Terror Arrests in China Draw Concern About Crackdown on Dissent,' *Bloomberg* (14 March 2008).
82 Elizabeth Van Wie Davis, 'Terrorism and the Beijing Olympics: Uyghur Discontent,' *Jamestown Foundation China Brief*, 8:8 (2008).
83 Ibid.
84 See *StratFor Series*: 'China: Shining a Spotlight on ETIM,' 'China: The Evolution of ETIM' and 'China: ETIM and the Olympic Games' (May 2008).
85 *StratFor*, 'China: ETIM and the Olympic Games.'
86 TIP, *Yunandiki Mubarak Jihadimiz* (23 July 2008); TIP, *Duniya Musulmanlargha Umumi Murajät* (August 2008).
87 See Andrew Jacobs 'Ambush in China Raises Concerns as Olympics Near,' *The New York Times* (5 August 2008); Jonathan Watts, 'Eight Dead After Bombings in Western China Mars Olympic Opening Weekend,' *The Guardian* (10 August 2008).
88 See Thomas Joscelyn, 'The Uighurs in Their Own Words,' *The Long War Journal* (21 April 2009); Thomas Joscelyn 'Obama's Uighur Problem,'

Washington Examiner (21 April 2009); Thomas Joscelyn, 'Rep. Rohrabacher is Wrong About the Uighurs at Gitmo,' *Washington Examiner* (18 June 2009).

89 'China Identifies Alleged "Eastern Turkistan" Terrorists,' *Xinhua* (21 October 2008).

90 Shaykh Bashir, 'Why Are We Fighting China?' *The NEFA Foundation* (July 2008); 'The Chinese and Pakistani Media are Full of Lies and Accusations,' *NEFA* (1 May 2009); 'On the Occasion of the Communists' Massacre of Our Muslim Nation in China and in Urumqi (East Turkistan)' *NEFA* (9 July 2009); 'The History of the Movement and its Development (interview with Abdul Häq),' *NEFA* (14 March 2009); IntelCenter, 'TIP-Threat Awareness Wall Chart' (2008).

91 US Treasury, 'Treasury Targets Leader of Group Tied to Al Qaida' (20 April 2009).

92 Andrew McGregor, 'Will Xinjiang's Turkistani Islamic Party Survive the Drone Missile Death of its Leader?' *Jamestown Foundation Terrorism Monitor*, 8:10 (11 March 2010), 7–10.

93 See TIP, *Turkistan-al Islamiyyah* (Arabic) (2008); Kirk H. Sowell, 'The Turkistani Islamic Party in Arabic Jihadist Media,' *Sky News* (1 August 2010), 1–23. In a commissioned report for Sky News that surveys the content and popularity of this magazine, Sowell suggests that it has been developed primarily to bring attention to the cause of Uyghur independence from China and for fundraising purposes, but he also suggests it has not been very successful in either case. A similar conclusion is reached by Jacob Zenn ('Jihad in China? Marketing the Turkistan Islamic Party,' *Jamestown Foundation Terrorism Monitor* (17 March 2011)).

94 IntelCenter, 'Turkistan Islamic Party (TIP) Dramatically Steps Up Messaging Efforts' (1 July 2013).

95 Karolina Wojtasik, 'How and Why Do Terrorist Organizations Use the Internet?' *Polish Political Science Yearbook*, 46:2 (2017), 105–117.

96 See Tania Branigan, 'Al-Qaida Threatens to Target Chinese over Muslim Deaths in Urumqi,' *The Guardian* (14 July 2009), Chris Zambelis, 'Uighur Dissent and Militancy in China's Xinjiang Province,' *CTC Sentinel*, 3:1 (2010), 16–19.

97 'Urumqi Riots: Weapons Prepared Beforehand, Division of Tasks Clear,' *Xinhua* (21 July 2009).

98 See Raffaello Pantucci, 'Turkistan Islamic Party Video Attempts to Explain Uyghur Militancy to Chinese,' *Jamestown Foundation Terrorism Monitor*, 9:25 (23 June 2010); Peter Nesser and Brynjar Lia, 'Lessons Learned from the July 2010 Norwegian Terrorist Plot,' *CTC Sentinel*, 3:8 (2010).

99 Reed and Raschke, *The ETIM*.

100 R. Gunaratna, A. Acharya, and P. Wang, *Ethnic Identity and National Conflict in China* (New York: Palgrave Macmillan, 2010).

101 Ibid.

102 For moderating voices from regional experts, see Chris Cunningham, 'Counterterrorism in Xinjiang: The ETIM, China, and the Uyghurs,' *International Journal on World Peace*, 29:3 (2012), 7–50; Michael Clarke, 'Widening the Net: China's Anti-terror Laws and Human Rights in the

NOTES

Xinjiang Uyghur Autonomous Region,' *International Journal of Human Rights*, 14:4 (2010), 542–558.

103 Cf: David Kerr and Laura Swinton, 'Xinjiang, and the Transnational Security of Central Asia,' *Critical Asian Studies*, 40:1 (2008), 89–112; Bhavna Singh, 'Ethnicity, Separatism and Terrorism in Xinjiang China's Triple Conundrum,' *Institute of Peace and Conflict Studies Special Report*, No. 96 (2010); Philip B.K. Potter, 'Terrorism in China: Growing Threats with Global Implications,' *Strategic Studies Quarterly*, 7:4 (2013), 70–92. These articles all have wildly different characterizations of the evolution of ETIM/TIP, which pick and choose from characterizations of these organizations' history in earlier sources.

3 MYTHS AND REALITIES OF THE ALLEGED 'TERRORIST THREAT' ASSOCIATED WITH UYGHURS

1 UN Security Council, 'UN Consolidated List of Terrorist Individuals and Entities, res. 1267/1989/2253' (2019).

2 US State Department, 'Terrorist Exclusion List' (2004).

3 Recording of interview with Häsän Mäkhsum by Omär Kanat (January 2001).

4 For articulations of this argument, see Gunaratna, *Inside Al Qaeda*; Gunaratna, Acharya, and Wang, *Ethnic Identity and National Conflict in China*; Martin Wayne, 'Inside China's war on terrorism,' *Journal of Contemporary China*, 18:59 (2009), 249–261. The assertion that the PRC trained Uyghurs to join the mujahidin is most extensively promoted in John Cooley's book *Unholy Wars: Afghanistan, America, and International Terrorism* (London: Pluto Press, 2002), but the author gives no sources for this argument. Gunaratna's 2002 book on Al-Qaeda that echoes this assertion does so with reference to one brief report from a 2002 *Jane's Intelligence Review* report (Bedi, 'The Chinese Connection'), which cites none of its sources.

5 See TIP, *Jihad Lands*. It should be noted that the inspiration Mäkhsum received from Abdulhäkim Mäkhsum, who is described in early TIP documents as the founder of the 'movement,' has led many sources to erroneously suggest that ETIM was founded by Abdulhäkim Mäkhsum in the 1940s. See, for example, Reed and Raschke: *The ETIM*, p. 47.

6 For a description of a wider reformist movement in the XUAR at this time and its connections to *Jadid* traditions see Edmund Waite, 'The Emergence of Muslim Reformism in Contemporary Xinjiang: Implications for the Uyghurs' Positioning Between a Central Asian and Chinese Context,' in I. Beller-Hann, M. Cesàro, and J. Finley (eds) *Situating the Uyghurs Between China and Central Asia* (Hampshire, UK: Ashgate, 2007).

7 For more on the *Jadid* traditions of Central Asia, see Khalid, *The Politics of Muslim Cultural Reform*.

8 TIP, *Jihad Lands*.

9 Ibid.

10 Recording of interview with Häsän Mäkhsum by Omer Kanat (January

2001); 'Uyghur Separatist Denies Links to Taliban, Al-Qaeda,' *RFA* (27 January 2002).

11 See TIP, *Jihad Lands*.

12 Ibid.

13 Ibid.

14 Ibid.

15 These details are from an interview with Omer Kanat, who interviewed Qarahaji for almost ten hours in 2004. Kanat was the interpreter for David Cloud who interviewed Qarahaji for *The Wall Street Journal* (see David Cloud and Ian Johnson, 'In Post-9/11 World, Chinese Dissidents Pose US Dilemma,' *The Wall Street Journal* (3 Aug 2004)).

16 Ibid.

17 Ibid.

18 'Uyghur Separatist Denies Links to Taliban, Al-Qaeda,' *RFA*.

19 Cloud and Johnson, 'In Post-9/11 World, Chinese Dissidents Pose US Dilemma.'

20 Ibid.

21 TIP, *Turkistan Mujahidliri Arkhipliridin 36* (October 2017).

22 TIP, *Biz vä Jihad Hazirlighi* (2009); TIP, *Jännät Ashiqliri 5* (2010).

23 TIP, 'The Structure of the Turkistan Islamic Party' (10 August 2004).

24 Cloud and Johnson, 'In Post-9/11 World, Chinese Dissidents Pose US Dilemma.' It should be noted that the article that appeared in *The Wall Street Journal* said they had traveled to Kandahar to explicitly meet with Osama bin Laden, but as translator, Kanat remembers the interview differently. He notes that they went to a large meeting with numerous groups in attendance, and Osama bin Laden had been one of the speakers.

25 Omer Kanat, personal communication (August 2019).

26 There is a brief snippet of video footage of Mäkhsum sitting with bin Laden at what appears to be a large feast, and this footage has been reproduced in many TIP videos to emphasize the importance of Mäkhsum. It is likely that this took place at the aforementioned Kandahar meeting of militant groups.

27 For a discussion of Kazakhstan's use of the 'Uyghur card' to obtain concessions from China on a variety of issues, see Sean R. Roberts, 'A Land of Borderlands: Implications of Xinjiang's Trans-Border Interactions,' in S. Frederick Starr, ed, *Xinjiang: China's Muslim Borderlands* (Armonk, NY: ME Sharpe, 2004), pp. 232–234.

28 Ahmed Rashid, 'Taliban Temptation,' *Far Eastern Economic Review* (11 March 1999).

29 Kariyatil Krishnadas, 'Chinese Telecom Company Accused of Aiding Taliban,' *EE Times* (12 December 2001).

30 Andrew Small, 'China's Man in the Taliban,' *Foreign Policy* (3 August 2015).

31 See Charles Hutzler, 'Attack On America: China Engages Taliban While Others Turn Away,' *The Wall Street Journal* (2001); Rashid, 'Taliban Temptation.'

32 Small, 'China's Man in the Taliban.'

33 Omär Kanat, personal communication (August 2019).

34 Ibid.
35 See Guantanamo Docket, GTMO Detainee Reports: 'Arkin Mahmud ISN103,' 'Ahmed Tourson ISN 20l,' 'Adel Noori ISN 584,' 'Abdul Razak ISN 219,' *The New York Times* (2005)
36 'Summary of Unsworn Detainee Statement, Ahmed Tourson, ISN 201,' p. 4.
37 Several of the detainees do acknowledge that Häsän Mäkhsum and Abdul Häq were associated with the 'camp' in Jalalabad where they stayed. See, for example, 'Summary of Administrative Review Board Proceedings for Bahtiyar Mahnut ISN 277,' pp. 3–4; 'Summary of Unsworn Detainee Statement, Abdul Ghappar Abdul Rahman ISN 281,' p. 4; 'Summary of Unsworn Detainee Statement, Ahmad Muhamman Yaqub ISN 328,' pp. 7–8.
38 It is possible that these Uyghurs had been sent to this location to revive the remnants of the original site for Mäkhsum's community prior to being moved to Khost.
39 'Summary of Unsworn Detainee Statement, Akhdar Qasem Basit ISN 276,' p. 3.
40 See Sean R. Roberts, 'The Uyghurs of the Kazakstan Borderlands: Migration and the Nation,' *Nationalities Papers*, 26:3 (1998), 511–530.
41 TIP, *Jännät Ashiqliri 5* (2010).
42 TIP, *Turkistan Mujahidliri Arkhipliridin 36* (October 2017).
43 Recording of interview with Häsän Mäkhsum by Omer Kanat (January 2001).
44 Omer Kanat, Personal communication (August 2019).
45 Ibid.
46 See 'Death of a Militant: Boon for Beijing? *StratFor* (2003); 'Chinese Militant "Shot Dead,"' *BBC* (23 December 2003).
47 TIP, *Jihad Lands.*
48 'Uyghur Separatist Denies Links to Taliban, Al-Qaeda,' *RFA.*
49 TIP, *Islam Yolvasi* (2004).
50 Turkistan, *A Message of Incitement to Jihad from a Mujahid to the Muslims of East Turkestan* (Arabic) (2006).
51 The suspect document, which is dated 2003 [see TIP, *Häsän Mäkhsumning Shahadit Munasiviti Bilän* (2003)], is from a 2010 website that TIP itself suggests is a 'phising' trap likely established by the Chinese government to track would-be Uyghur jihadists [see TIP, *Barliq Tor Ziyarätchiliri Sämigä* (2010)].
52 See 'China Identifies Alleged "Eastern Turkistan" Terrorists,' *Xinhua* (2008) for the Chinese government's official biography of Häq, including his given name. For the 2003 list, see 'China Seeks Cooperation Worldwide to Fight "East Turkistan" Terrorists,' *Xinhua* (2003).
53 TIP, 'Sheykh Abdul Haq: "The History of the Movement and its Development,"' *Islamic Turkistan* (Translation from NEFA Foundation) (2009).
54 Ibid. It is also possible that Häq only claimed this connection to Salafism to benefit the intended readership of his Arabic-language magazine, which was obviously intended for Arab Salafis.
55 Ibid.
56 US Treasury, 'Treasury Targets Leader of Group Tied to Al Qaida.'

57 Waliullah Rahmani, 'Has al-Qaeda Picked a Leader for Operations in China?' *Jamestown Foundation Terrorism Focus*, 5:41 (2008), 8–9.

58 TIP, *Jännät Ashiqliri 13* (September 2014). This film includes a posthumous biography of Abdulshukur.

59 Ibid. In the film, which honors Abdulshakur, Mansur talks about coming to Afghanistan with the latter in 1994.

60 TIP, *Jännät Ashiqliri 8* (2012).

61 Jacob Zenn, 'The Turkistan Islamic Party in Double-Exile: Geographic and Organizational Divisions in Uighur Jihadism,' *Jamestown Foundation Terrorism Monitor*, 16:17 (2018), 8–11.

62 TIP, *Imani Burch vä Nursrät* (June 2009) and TIP, *Biz vä Jihad Hazirligi* (2009).

63 TIP, *Zalim Qankhur Khitay Komunistlirining Ilip Barghan Qanliq Qirgichiliq Munasiviti Bilän, 2009–Yili, 7–Ayning, 8–Kuni* (July 2009).

64 See TIP, *Imani Burch vä Nursrät* (June 2009) and TIP, *Khitay Täshviqäti – Zähärlik Täshviqat: Abdullah Mansur Söbät Bilän* (September 2009).

65 TIP, 'Barbaric Massacres of China Will Not Go Unanswered' (Arabic) (31 July 2009).

66 Raffaello Pantucci and Edward Schwarck, 'Transition in Afghanistan: Filling the Security Vacuum – The Expansion of Uighur Extremism?' *CIDOB Policy Research Project*, Barcelona Center for International Affairs (2014), p. 11.

67 It appears that Abduläziz was named on China's most wanted terrorist list in 2012 and that his given name is Abdulkuyum Kurban. See 'Police Names 6 Wanted Terrorists,' *Xinhua* (6 April 2012). Apparently, he was killed by a drone strike in 2012, see TIP, *Muminlärning Sayahiti 8* (September 2013).

68 See TIP, *Muhim Mäsililär Ustidä* (June 2011); TIP, *Ämir Mäiruf Abduläzizning Talanma Dävätliridin 1–4* (2011); TIP, *Firayliq Toghrisida* (2011); TIP, *Jamaät Bolup Uyushush vä Yalghuz Jihad Qilishning Hökmi* (March 2012); TIP, *Muminlärning Sayahiti 3* (February 2012); TIP, *Jamaät, Hijrät, vä Jihad Häqqidä Qisqichä Chushänchä* (June 2012).

69 On Turkish fighters, see TIP, *Tükiye'deki Müsülman Kardeshlerimizde Nashihat* (Turkish) (July 2012); TIP, *Savasin Aslanlari* (Turkish) (December 2012); TIP, *Horasan'da Kurban Bayrami Cihad Meydanlarinda* (Turkish) (November 2012). On Caucasian fighters, see TIP, *Nasha Obitel' Khorasan 1–2* (Russian) (2012) and TIP, *Kavkaz Mujahidlirighä Mäktub* (2012).

70 See TIP, *Jännät Ashiqliri 4* (2010).

71 For more on the significance of using the name *Khorasan* for these people's collective place in the global *Jihad*, see Adam Taylor, 'The Strange Story Behind the "Khorasan" Group's Name', *Washington Post* (25 September 2014).

72 See TIP, *Äziz Vätän Turkistan* (May 2012) and TIP, *Turkistan Oghlanliri* (2012).

73 TIP, *Yeqinda Khotän vä Qäshqärdâ Elip Berilghan Jihad Härikätlär Munasiviti Bilän* (7 September 2011).

74 'Türkistan Islam Çemaati Mücahidi Sehit Muhammed Türkistanin'in Hayati' (Turkish) *Dogu Türkistan Bulteni* (31 March 2016).

75 TIP, *Muminlärning Sayahiti 1* (3 October 2011).
76 TIP, *Turkistan Mujahidliridin Khitay Khälqigä Khät* (May 2011).
77 Pantucci and Schwarck, 'Transition in Afghanistan,' p. 10.
78 See Nesser and Lia, 'Lessons Learned from the July 2010 Norwegian Terrorist Plot.'
79 Raffaelo Pantucci, 'Uyghurs Convicted in East Turkestan Islamic Movement Plot in Dubai' *Jamestown Foundation Terrorism Monitor*, 8:29 (2010), 5–6.
80 See TIP, *Shähid Bulsam* (December 2012); TIP, *Berding* (27 April 2012); TIP, *Shärqi Turkistan Musulman Qerindashlirimizgha Näsihät* (August 2012); TIP, *Äziz Vätän Turkistan* (21 April 2012)
81 TIP, *Jännät Ashiqliri 13* (2014).
82 TIP, *Jännät Ashiqliri 8* (2012).

4 Colonialism meets counterterrorism, 2002–2012

1 Amnesty International, 'China's Anti-terrorism Legislation and Repression in the Xinjiang Uyghur Autonomous Region,' *Amnesty International* (2002), 1–34.
2 Ibid., pp. 19–22. Drawing from unofficial reports, Amnesty documents the criminal sentencing of over 100 Uyghurs on terrorism charges between September and November of 2001, with at least nine receiving death sentences, but it also cites Uyghur diaspora sources claiming that some 3,000 Uyghurs were detained during this period with 20 of them executed and scores more incarcerated.
3 Ibid., pp. 14–15.
4 Ibid., p. 16.
5 UHRP, 'Prosecution of Uyghurs in the Era of the "War on Terror"' (16 October 2007), pp. 6–7.
6 See Stanley Toops, *Demographics and Development in Xinjiang after 1949 (Policy Studies, No. 1)* (Washington, DC: East-West Center, 2004), p. 20.
7 While not without skepticism, Joanne Smith Finley points out this trend in international scholarship on Uyghurs in the early 2000s. See Smith-Finley, *The Art of Symbolic Resistance*, pp. 393–394.
8 Toops, *Demographics and Development in Xinjiang after 1949*.
9 Ibid., p. 20.
10 Doris Ma and Tim Summers, 'Is China's Growth Moving Inland? A Decade of "Develop the West,"' *Asia Programme Paper: ASP PP 2009/02* (London: Chatham House, 2009), p. 5.
11 See Scott Radnitz and Sean Roberts, 'Why the Carrot Isn't Working, Either,' *Foreign Policy* (13 November 2013); Roberts, 'Development with Chinese Characteristics in Xinjiang.'
12 This argument was famously asserted by Walt Whitman Rostow (*The Stages of Economic Growth: A Non-Communist Manifesto* (Cambridge: Cambridge University Press, 1960)) in his capitalist response to the Communist Manifesto. Rostow's logic followed the same modernist logic as Marx employed, suggesting that the new economic relations fostered by economic growth would lead to a withering of cultural differences.

13 Nicolas Becquelin, 'Staged Development in Xinjiang,' *The China Quarterly*, 178 (June 2004), 358–378, pp. 364–365.

14 Ibid., p. 370.

15 Ibid., p. 359

16 For international reaction, see UNESCO Mission to The Chinese Silk Road as World Cultural Heritage Route, 'Mission Report: A Systematic Approach to Identification and Nomination,' *UNESCO* (2003), p. 25; Ross Perlin, 'The Silk Road Unravels,' *Open Democracy: Free Thinking for the World* (29 July 2009).

17 UHRP, 'Living on the Margins: The Chinese State's Demolition of Uyghur Communities' (30 March 2012), p. 37.

18 See *The Erdaoqiao Bazaar of Urumqi Guide*, www.itourbeijing.com (www.itourbeijing.com/china-travel/the-silk-road-guide/the-erdaoqiao-bazaar-of-urumqi.htm), last accessed 10 November 2014.

19 Ildiko Beller-Hann, 'The Bulldozer State: Chinese Socialist Development in Xinjiang,' in M. Reeves, J. Rasanayagam, and J. Beyer (eds), *Ethnographies of the State in Central Asia: Performing Politics* (Bloomington, IN: Indiana University Press, 2014), pp. 173–197.

20 UHRP, 'Uyghur Language Under Attack: The Myth of "Bilingual" Education in the Republic of China' (24 July 2007).

21 Ibid.

22 Arienne Dwyer, *The Xinjiang Conflict: Uyghur Identity, Language Policy, and Political Discourse (Policy Studies No. 15)* (Washington, DC: East-West Center, 2005), pp. 37–41.

23 Ibid., pp. 46–50.

24 These twelve four-year schools, modeled on similar institutions established far earlier for Tibetans, initially enrolled 1,000 Uyghur students per year, with the intention of having a steady enrollment of 5,000 by 2007. See Yan and Song, 'Difficulties Encountered by Students During Cross-cultural Studies Pertaining to the Ethnic Minority Education Model of Running Schools in "Other Places" and Countermeasures,' *Chinese Education and Society*, 43:3 (2010), 10–21.

25 UHRP, 'Uyghur Language Under Attack,' p. 6.

26 Timothy Grose, '(Re)Embracing Islam in Neidi: the "Xinjiang Class" and the Dynamics of Uyghur Ethno-national Identity,' *Journal of Contemporary China*, 24:91 (2015), 101–118.

27 Ibid., 110–111.

28 Ibid.

29 UHRP, 'Deception, Pressure, and Threats: The Transfer of Young Uyghur Women to Eastern China' (8 February 2008).

30 Ibid.

31 Ibid., p. 3.

32 Jennifer Tayman, who has studied Chinese-educated Uyghur youth in Urumqi, notes that they felt estranged from others in their ethnic group, but 'like the rest of the Uyghur community, the *Min Kao Han* … in Xinjiang were not supportive of the Han presence in the region.' Jennifer Taynen, 'Interpreters, Arbiters or Outsiders: The Role of the Min Kao

Han in Xinjiang Society,' *Journal of Muslim Minority Affairs*, 26:1 (2006), 46.

33 Justin Hastings, 'Charting the Course of Uyghur Unrest,' *The China Quarterly*, 208 (2011), 893–912.

34 Bovingdon, *The Uyghurs: Strangers in their Own Land.*

35 Simon Elegant, 'China's Curious Olympic Terror Threat,' *TIME* (10 March 2008).

36 Hastings, 'Charting the Course of Uyghur Unrest.'

37 TIP, 'Untitled' (Abdul Häq's statement on the Olympics) (1 March 2008).

38 Elegant, 'China's Curious Olympic Terror Threat.'

39 Hastings, 'Charting the Course of Uyghur Unrest,' p. 910.

40 Elegant, 'China's Curious Olympic Terror Threat.'

41 Hastings, 'Charting the Course of Uyghur Unrest,' p. 911.

42 Wang Zhengua, '3 Killed, 12 Injured in Shanghai Bus Explosions,' *China Daily* (5 May 2008); Gordon Fairclough, 'Bus Blasts Kill Two in China,' *Wall Street Journal* (21 July 2008); TIP, *Yunandiki Mubarak Jihadimiz* (2008).

43 See 'China Dismisses Bus Bombs Claim,' *BBC* (26 July 2008) for more on the official state denial of Uyghur involvement in the bombings.

44 Geoffrey York, 'Beijing Busy Welcoming the World as it Turns Away its Ethnic Minorities,' *The Globe and Mail* (18 July 2008).

45 Ibid.

46 Hastings, 'Charting the Course of Uyghur Unrest,' p. 911.

47 Edward Wong, 'Doubt Arises in Account of an Attack in China,' *The New York Times* (29 September 2008).

48 Ibid.

49 Hastings, 'Charting the Course of Uyghur Unrest,' p. 911.

50 Ibid.

51 UHRP, 'Deception, Pressure, and Threats,' p. 2.

52 Ibid., p. 6.

53 UHRP, 'Massive Rise in State Security Arrests in East Turkestan in 2008' (6 January 2009), p. 14.

54 Tania Branigan, 'Ethnic Violence in China leaves 140 dead,' *The Guardian* (6 July 2009).

55 Angel Ryono and Matthew Galway, 'Xinjiang Under China: Reflections on the Multiple Dimensions of the 2009 Urumqi Uprising,' *Asian Ethnicity*, 16:2 (2015), 235–255, pp. 235–236.

56 'Urumqi Riots: Weapons Prepared Beforehand, Division of Tasks Clear,' *Xinhua* (21 July 2009).

57 Jane Macartney, 'Hundreds Die in Bloodiest Clashes since Tiananmen Crackdown,' *The Times* (7 July 2009).

58 See Peter Foster, 'Eyewitness: Tensions High on the Streets of Urumqi,' *The Telegraph* (7 July 2009); UHRP, 'A City Ruled by Fear and Silence: Urumqi, Two Years On' (2011), p. 15.

59 Rian Thum, 'The Ethnicization of Discontent in Xinjiang,' *The China Beat Blog* (2 October 2009).

60 Thomas Cliff, 'The Partnership of Stability in Xinjiang: State-Society

Interactions Following the July 2009 Unrest,' *The China Journal*, 68 (2012), 79–105.

61 HRW, 'Enforced Disappearances in the Wake of Xinjiang's Protests' (20 October 2009).

62 Kathrin Hille, 'Xinjiang Widens Crackdown on Uighurs,' *Financial Times* (19 July 2009).

63 UHRP, 'Can Anyone Hear Us? Voices from the 2009 Unrest in Urumqi' (2010) pp. 42–43.

64 HRW, 'Enforced Disappearances in the Wake of Xinjiang's Protests.'

65 UHRP, 'Can Anyone Hear Us?' p. 19.

66 UHRP, 'Sacred Right Defiled: China's Iron-fisted Repression of Uyghur Religious Freedom' (8 March 2013).

67 Shan Wei and Weng Cuifen, 'China's New Policy in Xinjiang and its Challenges,' *East Asian Policy*, 2:3 (2010), p. 61.

68 Cui Jia, 'New Measures to Boost Xinjiang Livelihoods,' *China Daily* (28 May 2010).

69 Wei and Cuifen, 'China's New Policy in Xinjiang and its Challenges,' p. 62.

70 Cui Jia, 'Xinjiang Takes a Leaf out of Sichuan's Book,' *China Daily* (21 May 2010); Lisa Zeng Sommer, 'Xinjiang Enticements,' *Energy Tribune* (21 July 2010).

71 Cliff, 'The partnership of stability in Xinjiang,' p. 99.

72 Michael Clarke, 'China's Integration of Xinjiang with Central Asia: Securing a "Silk Road" to Great Power Status?' *China and Eurasia Forum Quarterly*, 6:2 (2008), p. 89.

73 UHRP, 'Uyghur Homeland; Chinese Frontier: The Xinjiang Work Forum' (27 June 2012), p. 16.

74 Amy Regar, 'From Kashgar to Kashi: The Chinese Remaking of Kashgar,' *Huffington Post* (17 April 2012).

75 UHRP, 'Uyghur Homeland; Chinese Frontier,' p. 19.

76 Andrew Jacobs, 'Economic Aid Fuels Change of Fortune on Silk Road,' *The New York Times* (14 November 2010).

77 Alessandro Rippa and Rune Steenberg, 'Development For All? State Schemes, Security, and Marginalization in Kashgar, Xinjiang,' *Critical Asian Studies*, 51:2 (2019), 274–295.

78 UHRP, 'Uyghur Homeland; Chinese Frontier,' pp. 3–6.

79 Ibid., p. 17.

80 UHRP, 'Living on the Margins,' p. 29.

81 UHRP, 'Uyghur Homeland; Chinese Frontier,' p. 15.

82 Grose, '(Re)Embracing Islam in Neidi,' p. 106.

83 Becquelin, 'Staged Development in Xinjiang.'

84 Cliff, 'The Partnership of Stability in Xinjiang,' p 82.

85 James Leibold, 'Toward a Second Generation of Ethnic Policies,' *Jamestown Foundation China Brief*, 12:13 (6 July 2012).

86 Ibid.

87 Jonathan Watts, 'China Raises Xinjiang Police Station Death Toll to 18' *The Guardian* (20 July 2011).

NOTES

88 Gulchehra Hoja, 'Uyghurs "Fenced In" to Neighborhoods in China's Xinjiang Region,' *RFA* (19 August 2016).

89 See UHRP, 'Sacred Right Defiled.'

90 For a revealing timeline of how violence escalated at this time and further in coming years, see *RFA*, 'The Uyghurs: The Fate of a Troubled Minority' (2015), www.rfa.org/english/news/special/uyghurtroubled/home.html, last accessed 26 February 2020.

91 Watts, 'China Raises Xinjiang Police Station Death Toll to 18.'

92 Choi Chi-yuk, 'Ban on Islamic Dress Sparked Uygur Attack,' *South China Morning Post* (2011).

93 Watts, 'China Raises Xinjiang Police Station Death Toll to 18.'

94 Michael Dillon, 'Death on the Silk Road: Violence in Xinjiang,' *BBC* (3 August 2011).

95 Jason Dean and Jeremy Page, 'Beijing Points to Pakistan After Ethnic Violence,' *The Wall Street Journal* (1 August 2011).

96 TIP, *Yeqinda Khotän vä Qäshqärdä Elip Berilghan Jihadi Härikätlär Munisiviti Bilän* (August 2011).

97 Ibid.

98 Dean and Page, 'Beijing Points to Pakistan After Ethnic Violence.'

99 Ibid.

100 Ibid.

101 'At Least Eight Uyghurs Shot Dead by Chinese Authorities in Xinjiang,' *RFA* (19 June 2012).

102 UHRP, 'Uyghurs Shot to Death in Guma County, Amid Intense State-led Repression' (29 December 2011).

103 'Immigration Tensions Led to Attack,' *RFA* (19 February 2012).

104 Ibid.

105 '"Hijack Attempt Foiled" in China's Xinjiang,' *BBC* (29 June 2012); Alexa Olesen, 'Chinese Police Raid Religious School; 12 Kids Hurt,' *Associated Press* (6 June 2012).

106 'China Jails 20 on Jihad, Separatism Charges in Restive Xinjiang,' *Reuters* (27 March 2013).

107 Qiao Long, 'Korla Under Tight Security After Police Confirm Attacks,' *RFA* (7 March 2013); Shohret Hoshur, 'Suicide Attack on National Day,' *RFA* (12 October 2012).

108 See 'China Official Vows "Iron Fist" Crackdown in Xinjiang,' *BBC* (5 July 2012).

109 See for example Alexander Evans, 'China Cracks Down on Ramadan in Xinjiang,' *Foreign Policy* (2 August 2012) and Kathrin Hille 'China Bans Religious Activities in Xinjiang,' *Financial Times* (2 August 2012).

5 THE SELF-FULFILLING PROPHECY AND THE 'PEOPLE'S WAR ON TERROR,' 2013–2016

1 William Wan, 'Chinese Police Say Tiananmen Square Crash Was "Premeditated, Violent, Terrorist Attack,"' *Washington Post* (30 October 2013).

2 See Sean Roberts, 'Tiananmen Crash: Terrorism or Cry of Desperation?' *CNN.com* (31 October 2013).

3 'CNN Disrespects Itself with Terror Sympathy,' *Global Times* (4 November 2013); 'CNN恶意报道北京"10·28"暴力恐怖袭击案　中国网友群起反击' (Chinese) *CCTV* (3 November 2013).

4 Li Qi, 'Why 140,000 Chinese People Want to Kick Out CNN,' *Washington Post* (8 November 2013).

5 TIP, *Beijing Tiänänmen Mäydanda Elip Berilghan Jihadi Ämäliyät Toghrisida Bayanat* (1 November 2013).

6 Raffaelo Pantucci, 'Tiananmen Attack: Islamist Terror or Chinese Protest?' *Jamestown Foundation China Brief*, 14:1 (2014), 6–8.

7 Robert K. Merton, 'The Self-fulfilling Prophecy,' *The Antioch Review* (1948), p. 185.

8 Ibid., p. 190.

9 Qiao Long, 'Korla Under Tight Security After Police Confirm Attacks'; Shohret Hoshur, 'Fresh Clashes Hit Kashgar,' *RFA* (26 May 2013)

10 'Gasoline Bomb Attack on Police Station in Hotan,' *RFA* (12 March 2013); Hai Nan, 'Second Clash Reported in Xinjiang,' *RFA* (26 April 2013).

11 Chris Buckley, '27 Die in Rioting in Western China, *The New York Times* (26 June 2013).

12 Ibid.

13 TIP, *Turpan Lukchundä Elip Berilghan Jihadi Ämiliyät Toghrisida Bayanat* (July 2013).

14 '21 Dead in Xinjiang Terrorist Clashes,' *CNTV* (24 April 2013); 'China's Xinjiang Hit by Deadly Clashes,' *BBC* (24 April 2013).

15 'Overview of the Maralbeshi Incident on 23 April 2013,' *World Uyghur Congress* (May 2013), p. 1.

16 Ibid.

17 TIP, *Maralbeshi Seriqboyida Elip Berilghan Jihadi Ämäliyät Toghrisida* (May 2013).

18 Zunyou Zhou, 'Chinese Strategy for De-radicalization,' *Terrorism and Political Violence*, 31:6 (2017), 1187–1209.

19 Catherine Traywick, 'Chinese Officials ask Muslim Women to Unveil in the Name of Beauty,' *Foreign Policy* (26 November 2013).

20 Ibid.

21 Leibold, *Surveillance in China's Xinjiang Region: Ethnic Sorting, Coercion, and Inducement*, p. 8.

22 Ibid., pp. 8–9.

23 Shohret Hoshur, 'At Least 15 Uyghurs Killed in Police Shootout in Xinjiang,' *RFA* (25 August 2013) and 'Up to 12 Uyghurs Shot Dead in Raid on Xinjiang "Munitions Center,"' *RFA* (17 September 2013).

24 Qiao Long, 'Chinese Police Shoot Dead Seven Uyghurs in Kashgar: Group,' *RFA* (7 October 2013).

25 TIP, *Shärqi Turkistanda Elip Berilghan Jihadi Ämäliyätlär Toghrisida* (September 2013).

26 Steven Jiang and Katie Hunt, 'Five Arrested in Tiananmen Square Incident, Deemed a Terrorist Attack,' *CNN* (30 October 2013).

27 'China Says 11 Killed in Attack on Xinjiang Police Station,' *Agence France-Press* (17 November 2013).

28 Shohret Hoshur, 'Six Women Among Uyghurs Shot Dead in Xinjiang Violence,' *RFA* (18 December 2013).

29 Ibid.

30 Edward Wong, 'China Executes 3 Over Deadly Knife Attack at Train Station in 2014,' *The New York Times* (15 March 2015).

31 Shohret Hoshur, 'China Train Station Attackers May Have Acted "in Desperation,"' *RFA* (3 March 2014).

32 TIP, *Kunmingdiki 2-Qetimliq Jihadi Ämäliyät Munisiviti Bilän: Khitaygha Ochuq Khät* (March 2014).

33 'Train Station Attackers Were Trying to Leave China for Jihad: Official,' *VOA News* (5 March 2014).

34 Hoshur, 'China Train Station Attackers May Have Acted "in Desperation."'

35 Tania Branigan and Jonathan Kaiman, 'Kunming Knife Attack: Xinjiang Separatists Blamed for "Chinese 9/11,"' *The Guardian* (2 March 2014).

36 Hannah Beech, 'In China, Deadly Bomb and Knife Attack Rocks Xinjiang Capital,' *TIME* (1 May 2014).

37 Austin Ramzy and Chris Buckley, 'The Xinjiang Papers: "Absolutely No Mercy" – Leaked Files Show How China Organized Mass Detentions of Muslims,' *The New York Times* (16 November 2019).

38 Li Jing and Adrian Wan, 'Security Tightened After Three Killed in Bomb, Knife Attack at Urumqi Train Station,' *South China Morning Post* (1 May 2014).

39 Ibid.

40 TIP, *Ürümchi Jänubi Vokzalda Elip Berilghan Pidaiyliq Ämäliyiti Toghrisida Bayanat* (1 May 2014).

41 Ibid.

42 Ibid.

43 Yang Fan, 'Uyghur Shot Dead by Police in New Attack in Xinjiang,' *RFA* (8 May 2014).

44 Shohret Hoshur, 'Over 100 Detained After Xinjiang Police Open Fire on Protesters,' *RFA* (23 May 2014).

45 Ibid.

46 Simon Denyer, 'Terrorist Attack on Market in China's Restive Xinjiang Region Kills More Than 30,' *Washington Post* (22 May 2014).

47 Andew Jacobs, 'In China's Far West, a City Struggles to Move On,' *The New York Times* (24 May 2014).

48 'Urumqi Car and Bomb Attack Kills Dozens,' *Associated Press* (22 May 2014); Jacobs, 'In China's Far West, a City Struggles to Move On.'

49 UHRP, 'Legitimizing Repression: China's "War on Terror" Under Xi Jinping and State Policy in East Turkestan' (3 March 2015), p. 7.

50 'Xinjiang's Party Chief Wages "People's War" Against Terrorism,' *Xinhua* (26 May 2014).

51 See Susan Traveskes, 'Using Mao to Package Criminal Justice Discourse in 21st-century China,' *The China Quarterly*, 226 (2016), 299–318.

NOTES

52 Ibid.

53 Ondrej Kilmeš, 'Advancing "Ethnic Unity" and "De-extremization": Ideational Governance in Xinjiang under "New Circumstances" (2012–2017),' *Journal of Chinese Political Science*, 23:3 (2018), 413–436, p. 418; James Leibold, 'Xinjiang Forum Marks New Policy of "Ethnic Mingling,"' *Jamestown Foundation China Brief*, 14:12 (2014).

54 'President Xi Jinping Delivers Important Speech and Proposes to Build a Silk Road Economic Belt with Central Asian Countries,' *Ministry of Foreign Affairs of the PRC* (7 September 2013)

55 Leibold, 'Xinjiang Forum Marks New Policy of "Ethnic Mingling."'

56 Ibid.

57 Zhou, 'Chinese Strategy for De-radicalization,' p. 4.

58 Ibid.

59 See Gisela Grieger 'China: Assimilating or Radicalising Uighurs?' *European Parliament Research Service* (2014); Ishaan Tharoor, 'China's War on Ramadan sees Muslim Students Forced to Breakfast,' *Washington Post* (11 July 2014); Barbera Demick, 'China Imposes Intrusive Rules on Uighurs in Xinjiang,' *Los Angeles Times* (5 August 2014).

60 Shannon Tiezzi, 'China's "People's War" Against Terrorism,' *The Diplomat* (2 August 2014); Wong Chun Han, '"People's War" on Terrorism in China Turns Lucrative with One Million Yuan Rewards,' *The Wall Street Journal* (11 September 2014).

61 'The Colourful Propaganda of Xinjiang,' *BBC* (12 January 2015).

62 See Tiezzi, 'China's "People's War" Against Terrorism'; Demick, 'China Imposes Intrusive Rules on Uighurs in Xinjiang.'

63 Edward Wong, 'To Temper Unrest in Western China, Officials Offer Money for Intermarriage,' *The New York Times* (2 September 2014).

64 See Isobel Cokerell, 'Inside China's Massive Surveillance Operation,' *WIRED* (9 May 2019).

65 See Ilham Tohti, 'Present-day Ethnic Problems in Xinjiang Uighur Autonomous Region: Overview and Recommendations,' *ChinaChange.org* (2013), trans. Cindy Carter.

66 Edward Wong, China Sentences Uighur Scholar to Life,' *The New York Times* (24 September 2014).

67 'Counter-Terrorism Law' *China Law Translate* (27 December 2015).

68 Ibid.

69 Kavitha Surana, 'China Tells Citizens to Inform on Parents who "Lure" Kids into Religion,' *Foreign Policy* (12 October 2016).

70 Julia Famularo, 'Chinese Religious Regulations in the Xinjiang Uyghur Autonomous Region: A Veiled Threat to Turkic Muslims?' *Project 2049 Institute* (8 April 2015), 1–16, p. 5.

71 Denyer, 'Terrorist Attack on Market in China's Restive Xinjiang Region Kills More Than 30.'

72 Tom Phillips, 'Beijing Assembles People's Army to Crush China Terrorists With an Iron Fist,' *The Telegraph* (20 July 2014); Tania Branigan, 'China Detains More than 200 Suspected Separatists in Xinjiang, State Media Says,' *The Guardian* (26 May 2014).

73 'Arrests in China's Xinjiang "Nearly Doubled in 2014,"' *Agence France-Press* (23 January 2015).

74 See Darren Byler, 'Spirit Breaking: Uyghur Dispossession, Culture Work and Terror Capitalism in a Chinese Global City', (PhD Thesis, University of Washington, 2018), p. 124.

75 See Shohret Hoshur, 'Four Killed in New Violence, Nine Sentenced to Death in Xinjiang,' *RFA* (5 June 2014); 'Six Killed, Two Injured in Fresh Xinjiang Clashes,' *RFA* (11 June 2014), 'Five Uyghurs Killed in Connection with Raid on Xinjiang Suspect,' *RFA* (7 July 2014), 'Police Officer Stabbed to Death, Another Wounded in Xinjiang Attack,' *RFA* (25 June 2014).

76 See Shohret Hoshur, 'Five Police Officers Killed in Attack on Xinjiang Security Checkpoint,' *RFA* (22 June 2014).

77 *RFA*, 'The Uyghurs: The Fate of a Troubled Minority'.

78 See Emily Rauhala, 'China Now Says Almost 100 Were Killed in Xinjiang Violence,' *TIME* (4 August 2014).

79 Cf. Rauhala, 'China Now Says Almost 100 Were Killed in Xinjiang Violence' and Shohret Hoshur, 'At Least 2,000 Uyghurs Killed' in Yarkand Violence: Exile Leader,' *RFA* (5 August 2014).

80 Barbera Demick, 'Deadly Clash in China: An Ambush by Uighurs or a Government Massacre?' *Los Angeles Times* (7 August 2014).

81 Bob Woodruff and Karson Yiu, 'What Happened When I Went to the Alleged ISIS Breeding Ground in China,' *ABC News* (29 May 2016).

82 Rauhala, 'China Now Says Almost 100 Were Killed in Xinjiang Violence.'

83 Shohret Hoshur, 'Five Dead After Security Checkpoint Clash in Xinjiang's Hotan Prefecture,' *RFA* (30 January 2015);'Uyghur Man Draws Knife, is Shot Dead by Police,' *RFA* (19 February 2015); 'Hacking, Shooting Incident Leaves 17 Dead in Xinjiang's Aksu Prefecture,' *RFA* (20 February 2015);'Chinese Authorities Shoot "Suspicious" Uyghurs Dead in Xinjiang Restaurant,' *RFA* (13 March 2015);'Six Uyghurs Die in Village Police Operation in Xinjiang,' *RFA* (1 May 2015); 'At Least Eight Uyghurs Shot Dead by Chinese Authorities in Xinjiang,' *RFA* (19 June 2015); Lee Sui-Wee, 'Police in China Shoot Dead Six in Restive Xinjiang,' *Reuters* (12 January 2015);'Chinese Police Shoot Seven Uyghurs Dead Following Fatal Xinjiang Knife Attack,' *RFA* (18 March 2015).

84 Shohret Hoshur, 'Six Dead, Four Injured in Two Successive Suicide Attacks in China's Xinjiang,' *RFA* (13 May 2015); Eset Sulaiman, 'Chinese Police Shoot Two Uyghurs Dead in Xinjiang Bomb Attack,' *RFA* (28 May 2015); Michael Martina and Ben Blanchard, 'At Least 18 Chinese are Dead in China's Western Xinjiang Province after a Ramadan Attack on Police,' *Reuters* (23 June 2015).

85 Ben Blanchard, 'At Least 50 Reported to Have Died in Attack on Coalmine in Xinjiang in September,' *Reuters* (1 October 2015).

86 Michael Forsythe, 'Suspect in Xinjiang Mine Attack Spoke of Jihad, Chinese News Reports Say,' *The New York Times* (17 December 2015).

87 'Chinese Forces Kill 28 People "Responsible for Xinjiang Mine Attack,"' *BBC* (20 November 2015).

NOTES

88 Forsythe, 'Suspect in Xinjiang Mine Attack Spoke of Jihad, Chinese News Reports Say'.

89 'Xinjiang: The Race Card,' *Economist* (3 September 2016).

90 Andrew Jacobs, 'Xinjiang Seethes Under Chinese Crackdown,' *The New York Times* (2 January 2016).

91 Michael Martina, '"Violent Terrorism" in China's Xinjiang Has Dropped: Party Official,' *Reuters* (8 March 2016).

92 Byler, 'Spirit Breaking,' p. 124.

93 Ibid., p. 50.

94 UHRP, *UHRP Briefing: Refusal of Passports to Uyghurs and Confiscation of Passports Held by Uyghurs Indicator of Second-Class Citizen Status in China* (7 February 2013).

95 HRW, 'China: Passports Arbitrarily Recalled in Xinjiang' (21 November 2016).

96 'Life Sentence for Asylum Seekers,' *RFA* (26 January 2012).

97 Kendrick Kuo and Kyle Spriger, 'Illegal Uighur Immigration in Southeast Asia,' *cogitASIA* (24 April 2014).

98 Parameswaran Ponnudurai, 'Malaysia Hit for Deporting Uyghurs,' *RFA* (4 February 2013).

99 Catherine Putz, 'Thailand Deports 100 Uyghurs to China,' *The Diplomat* (11 July 2015).

100 Ibid.

101 WUC, 'Seeking A Place to Breathe Freely' (2 June 2016).

102 Ibid., pp. 18–20.

103 Ibid., pp. 8–9.

104 Chelsea Sheasley, 'Chinese Official: Train Station Attackers Were Trying to "Participate in Jihad,"' *The Christian Science Monitor* (5 March 2014); Nadia Usaeva, 'Chinese Authorities Kill "Religious Extremist," Detain 21 Others,' *RFA* (24 December 2014).

105 'China Claims 109 Uighur Refugees Deported From Thailand Planned "To Join Jihad"' *VICE News* (12 July 2015).

106 See Nodirbek Soliev, 'Uyghur Militancy in and Beyond Southeast Asia: An Assessment,' *Counter Terrorist Trends and Analyses*, 9:2 (2017), 14–20.

107 See 'Explaining Indonesia's Silence On The Uyghur Issue,' *Institute for Policy Analysis of Conflict* (20 June 2019).

108 'China "Breaks Turkish-Uighur Passport Plot,"' *BBC* (14 January 2014).

109 Ibid.

110 Feliz Solomon, 'China Orders Everyone in One Province to Hand Their Passports Over to Police,' *TIME* (25 November 2016).

111 Qiu Yongzheng and Liu Chang, 'Xinjiang Jihad Hits Syria,' *Global Times* (29 October 2012).

112 Lin Mellian, 'Xinjiang Terrorists Finding Training, Support in Syria, Turkey,' *Global Times* (1 July 2013).

113 Jacob Zenn, 'China Claims Uyghur Militants Trained in Syria,' *Jamestown Foundation Terrorism Monitor*, 11:14 (2013), 1–7.

114 See TIP, *Gheriblirgha Jännät Bolsun #1* (May 2014), TIP, *Gheriblirgha Jännät Bolsun #2* (May 2014); TIP, *Nadir Surätlär Albumi #3* (June 2014).

115 See TIP, *Jisir Shughur Fäthisi* (April 2015), TIP, *Qarqur Fäthisi* (August 2015), and TIP, *Äbu Zohur Härbiy Ayrodrom Fäthisi* (September 2015).

116 Dima Nassif, 'The Syrian Village of Zanbaqi is Closer to China than to Damascus' (Arabic), *Al Mayadeen TV* (3 September 2015); Mohanad Hage Ali, 'China's Proxy War in Syria: Revealing the Role of Uighur Fighters,' *Al Arabiya* (2 March 2016).

117 'Islamist Group Claims Syria Bombs "to Avenge Sunnis,"' *Al Arabiya* (12 March 2012).

118 Zenn, 'China Claims Uyghur Militants Trained in Syria.'

119 See TIP, *Jisir Shughur Fäthisi*; TIP, *Qarqur Fäthisi*; TIP, *Äbu Zohur Härbiy Ayrodrom Fäthisi*; *Sahil Gaptiki Yeqinqi Jänglär Nos. 1–4* (October 2015).

120 TIP, *Bugun* (July 2015); TIP, *Oyghan* (September 2015); TIP, *Fidayi* (October 2015); TIP, *Ehdimiz* (July 2015); TIP, *Diniga Qayt* (August 2015); TIP, *Hush Mubarak Gheriblar* (June 2015).

121 TIP, *Aslima* (November 2015); TIP, *Bizning Ghayimiz* (November 2015); TIP, *Tosmighin* (February 2015); TIP, *Nadir Suretlar Albomi, 7–9* (May 2015).

122 See TIP, *Bizler Bu Davanin Ordulariyiz* (Turkish) (July 2015); TIP, *Gharip* (Kazakh) (May 2015); TIP, *Jenhisttin Sebepteri* (Kyrgyz) (2015).

123 Gerry Shih, 'AP Exclusive: China's Uighurs Grapple With pull of Extremism,' *Associated Press* (29 December 2017).

124 Ibid.

125 Nassif, 'The Syrian Village of Zanbaqi is Closer to China than to Damascus'; Christina Lin, 'Will Turkey's Invasion of Syria Draw China into the War?' *Times of Israel* (4 July 2015).

126 Emrullah Ulus, 'Jihadist Highway to Jihadist Haven: Turkey's Jihadi Policies and Western Security,' *Studies in Conflict and Terrorism*, 39:9 (2016), 781–802.

127 Colin P. Clarke and Paul Rexton Kan, 'Uighur Foreign Fighters: An Underexamined Jihadist Challenge,' *The International Centre for Counter-Terrorism – The Hague*, 8:5 (2017), p. 3.

128 Itamar Eichner, 'Israeli Report: Thousands of Chinese Jihadists are Fighting in Syria,' *YNet News* (27 March 2017).

129 Mohanad Hage Ali, 'A Different Type of Jihadi,' *Carnegie Middle East Center* (30 August 2017).

130 Ibid.

131 The schools appear to be well-resourced, and one can access a variety of the textbooks used in TIP schools at the TIP website; see: www.muhsinlar.net/ug/muslim_php.php?muslim_kitap_tur=15&bat=1, last accessed 26 February 2020.

132 Sheena Chestnut Greitens, Myunghee Lee and Emir Yazici, 'Counter-terrorism and Preventive Repression: China's Changing Strategy in Xinjiang, *International Security* 44:3 (2020).

NOTES

6 CULTURAL GENOCIDE, 2017–2020

1 Raphael Lemkin, *Axis Rule in Occupied Europe: Laws of Occupation, Analysis of Government, Proposals for Redress* (New York: Columbia University Press, 1944) p. 79.
2 Ibid.
3 Ibid.
4 Leora Bilsky and Rachel Klagbrun, 'The Return of Cultural Genocide?' *European Journal of International Law*, 29:2 (2018), 373–396; Robert Van Krieken (2004) 'Rethinking Cultural Genocide: Aboriginal Child Removal and Settler-Colonial State Formation,' *Oceania*, 75:2 (2004), 125–151; Damien Short, 'Cultural Genocide and Indigenous Peoples: A Sociological Approach,' *International Journal of Human Rights*, 14:6 (2010), 833–848; Lindsey Kingston, 'The Destruction of Identity: Cultural Genocide and Indigenous Peoples,' *Journal of Human Rights*, 14:1 (2015), 63–83.
5 Shai Oster, 'China Tries Its Hand at Pre-crime,' *Bloomberg Businessweek* (3 March 2016).
6 Adrian Zenz, '"Thoroughly Reforming Them Towards a Healthy Heart Attitude": China's Political Re-education Campaign in Xinjiang,' *Central Asian Survey*, 38:1 (2019), 102–128, p. 105.
7 Ibid., pp. 113–114.
8 Ibid., pp. 114–115.
9 Ibid.
10 Ibid., p. 115.
11 Adrain Zenz and James Leibold, 'Chen Quanguo: The Strongman Behind Beijing's Securitization Strategy in Tibet and Xinjiang,' *Jamestown Foundation Chine Brief*, 17:12 (2017) 16–24.
12 Ibid.
13 Wu Qiang, 'Urban Grid Management and Police State in China: A Brief Overview,' *ChinaChange.org* (12 August 2014).
14 Ivan Nechepurenko, 'Suicide Bomber Attacks Chinese Embassy in Kyrgyzstan,' *The New York Times* (31 August 2016).
15 Olga Dzyubenko, 'Kyrgyzstan Says Uighur Militant Groups Behind Attack on China's Embassy,' *Reuters* (6 September 2016).
16 'Kyrgyzstan: Chinese Embassy Attack Still Mired in Mystery,' *Eurasianet* (5 October 2016).
17 Te-Ping Chen, 'China Vows to Strike Back Over Embassy Attack in Neighboring Kyrgyzstan,' *The Wall Street Journal* (7 September 2016).
18 Adrian Zenz and James Leibold, 'Securitizing Xinjiang: Police Recruitment, Informal Policing and Ethnic Minority Co-optation,' *The China Quarterly* (12 July 2019) p. 10.
19 Ibid., p. 11.
20 James Leibold, 'Surveillance in China's Xinjiang Region: Ethnic Sorting, Coercion, and Inducement,' *Journal of Contemporary China* (2019) p. 5.
21 Daren Byler, 'Ghost World,' *LOGIC*, No.7 (1 May 2019).
22 Ibid.

23 Edward Wong, 'Xinjiang, Tense Chinese Region, Adopts Strict Internet Controls,' *The New York Times* (10 December 2016).

24 Oiwan Lam, 'Leaked Xinjiang Police Report Describes Circumvention Tools as "Terrorist Software"' *Global Voices* (29 October 2016).

25 HRW, 'China: Big Data Fuels Crackdown in Minority Region' (26 February 2018).

26 Ibid.

27 Leibold, 'Surveillance in China's Xinjiang Region' p. 2.

28 Ibid.

29 'Xinjiang Attack: Four "Terrorists" and One Bystander Killed, Says China,' *Reuters* (28 December 2016).

30 'Chinese Police Kill Attackers After Xinjiang Explosion' *Reuters/Agence France-Press* (29 December 2016).

31 Stephen Chen, 'Chinese Police Out in Full Force After Xinjiang Terror Attack,' *The Star* (15 February 2017).

32 Ibid.

33 Nectar Gan, 'Censure of Officials Sheds Light on Sweeping Surveillance Measures in China's Restive Xinjiang,' *South China Morning Post* (7 April 2017).

34 'Xinjiang's "Open Letter" Drive Forces Uighurs to put Loyalty to China in Writing,' *RFA* (2017).

35 Philip Wen, 'Fellow Uighurs Should Beware of "Two-Faced" People in Separatism Fight, Official Says,' *Reuters* (10 April 2017).

36 Eva Li, 'Show of Force in Xinjiang Sends Hardline Message,' *South China Morning Post* (3 January 2017).

37 Ibid.

38 Philip Wen, 'China Holds "Anti-Terrorism" Mass Rally in Xinjiang's Uighur Heartland,' *Reuters* (17 February 2017).

39 Tom Phillips, 'In China's Far West the "Perfect Police State" is Emerging,' *The Guardian* (22 June 2017).

40 Ibid.

41 'Xinjiang Uyghur Autonomous Region Regulation on De-extremification,' *China Law Translate* (30 March 2017).

42 Ibid.

43 Ibid. Emphasis added.

44 Ibid.

45 Ibid.

46 Zenz, '"Thoroughly Reforming Them Towards a Healthy Heart Attitude,"' pp. 106–112.

47 Ibid. p. 117.

48 Ibid., p. 116.

49 Cf: Zenz, '"Thoroughly Reforming Them Towards a Healthy Heart Attitude"'; Megha Rajagopalan, 'This is What A 21st-Century Police State Really Looks Like,' *Buzzfeed News* (17 October 2017); Tom Phillips, 'China "Holding at least 120,000 Uighurs in Re-education Camps,"' *The Guardian* (25 January 2018).

50 Nathan VanderKlippe, 'Frontier Injustice: Inside China's Campaign to

"Re-educate" Uyghurs,' *The Globe and Mail* (9 September 2017); HRW, 'China: Free Xinjiang "Political Education" Detainees'; Eset Sulaiman, 'China Runs Region-wide Re-education Camps in Xinjiang for Uyghurs And Other Muslims,' *RFA* (11 September 2017).

51 HRW, 'China: Free Xinjiang "Political Education" Detainees.'

52 Ibid.

53 Sulaiman, 'China Runs Region-wide Re-education Camps in Xinjiang for Uyghurs And Other Muslims.'

54 Ibid.

55 Zenz, '"Thoroughly Reforming Them Towards a Healthy Heart Attitude,"' p. 118.

56 Shawn Zhang, 'List of Re-education Camps in Xinjiang,' *Medium* (20 May 2018).

57 Zenz, '"Thoroughly Reforming Them Towards a Healthy Heart Attitude,"' p. 122.

58 Nick Cumming-Bruce, '"No Such Thing": China Denies U.N. Reports of Uighur Detention Camps,' *The New York Times* (13 August 2018).

59 'Inside the Camps Where China Tries to Brainwash Muslims Until They Love the Party and Hate Their Own Culture'.

60 Nectar Gan, 'Xinjiang Camps: Top Chinese Official in First Detailed Admission of "Training and Boarding" Centres,' *South China Morning Post* (16 October 2018).

61 Shohret Hoshur, 'Xinjiang Authorities Up Detentions in Uyghur Majority Areas of Ghulja City,' *RFA* (19 March 2018).

62 Tenner Greer, '48 Ways to Get Sent to a Chinese Concentration Camp,' *Foreign Policy* (13 September 2018).

63 Cf: 'Inside the Camps Where China Tries to Brainwash Muslims Until They Love the Party and Hate Their Own Culture'; David Stavrou, 'A Million People Are Jailed at China's Gulags. I Managed to Escape. Here's What Really Goes on Inside,' *Haaretz* (17 October 2019); Chang Xin, 'Xinjiang Camp Survivor Exposes CCP's Fake News,' *BitterWinter* (28 August 2019); Ferris-Rotman, 'Abortions, IUDs and Sexual Humiliation'; Eli Meixler, '"I Begged Them to Kill Me." Uighur Woman Tells Congress of Torture in Chinese Internment Camps,' *TIME* (30 November 2018); Ben Mauk, 'Untold Stories from China's Gulag State,' *The Believer* (1 October 2019).

64 See Roberts, 'Fear and Loathing in Xinjiang'; Stavrou, 'A Million People Are Jailed at China's Gulags.'

65 Roberts, 'Fear and Loathing in Xinjiang.'

66 Ibid.

67 Stavrou, 'A Million People Are Jailed at China's Gulags.'

68 'Inside the camps.'

69 Erkin Azat, 'A Letter From a Prison Guard in the Newly Built Concentration Camp in Dawanching,' *Medium* (18 May 2019).

70 Stavrou, 'A Million People Are Jailed at China's Gulags.'

71 Roberts, 'Fear and Loathing in Xinjiang.'

72 Azat, 'A Letter From a Prison Guard.'

73 See Ferris-Rotman, 'Abortions, IUDs and Sexual Humiliation'; Meixler, '"I Begged Them to Kill Me."'

74 'Inside the Camps Where China Tries to Brainwash Muslims Until They Love the Party and Hate Their Own Culture'; Stavrou, 'A Million People Are Jailed at China's Gulags'; Meixler, '"I Begged Them to Kill Me."'; Mauk, 'Untold Stories from China's Gulag State.'

75 Meixler, '"I Begged Them to Kill Me."'

76 See Ferris-Rotman, 'Abortions, IUDs and Sexual Humiliation.'

77 Mauk, 'Untold Stories from China's Gulag State.'

78 Azat, 'A Letter From a Prison Guard.'

79 Ibid.

80 Adrian Zenz, 'Beyond the Camps: Beijing's Grand Scheme of Forced Labor, Poverty Alleviation and Social Control in Xinjiang,' *SocArxiv Papers* (12 July 2019), 9–10.

81 Ibid., pp. 9, 11.

82 See: Vicky Xiuzhong Xu (with Danielle Cave, Dr. James Leibold, Kelsey Munro, and Nathan Raser), 'Uyghurs for Sale: "Re-education," Forced Labour and Surveillance Beyond Xinjiang' (Policy Brief, Report No.26/2020), *Australian Strategic Policy Institute* (March 2020) and Dake Kang and Yanan Wang, 'Gadgets for tech giants made with coerced Uighur labor,' *Associated Press* (7 March 2020).

83 'Journalists from 24 countries visit Xinjiang,' *Xinhua* (23 July 2019).

84 Zenz, 'Beyond the Camps,' p. 12.

85 Ibid., p. 12.

86 Ibid., p. 3.

87 Zenz, 'Beyond the Camps,' pp. 16–18.

88 Xiuzhong Xu, 'Uyghurs for Sale.'

89 Zenz, 'Beyond the camps,' p. 8.

90 Chris Buckley, 'China's Prisons Swell After Deluge of Arrests Engulfs Muslims,' *The New York Times* (31 August 2019).

91 See Shohret Hoshur, 'Xinjiang Authorities Secretly Transferring Uyghur Detainees to Jails Throughout China,' *RFA* (2 October 2018); Holly Robertson, 'China Reportedly Begins Mass Transfers of Uighur Detainees from Xinjiang to Prisons Nationwide,' *ABC News* (9 October 2018).

92 Phillips, 'In China's Far West the "Perfect Police State" is Emerging.'

93 For a particularly good account of this system, see Josh Chin and Clément Bürge, 'Twelve Days in Xinjiang: How China's Surveillance State Overwhelms Daily Life,' *The Wall Street Journal* (19 December 2017).

94 'China Uighurs: Detained for Beards, Veils, and Internet Browsing,' *BBC* (17 February 2020); Adrian Zenz, 'The Karakax List: Dissecting the Anatomy of Beijing's Internment Drive in Xinjiang,' *Journal of Political Risk*, 8:2 (February 2020).

95 Darren Byler, 'China's Nightmare Homestay,' *Foreign Policy* (26 October 2018).

96 Timothy Grose, '"Once Their Mental State is Healthy, They Will Be Able to Live Happily in Society,"' *ChinaFile* (2 August 2019).

97 Steven Jiang, 'Chinese Uyghurs Forced to Welcome Communist Party into their Homes,' *CNN* (14 May 2018).

98 Ibid.

99 Lily Kuo, 'Revealed: New Evidence of China's Mission to Raze the Mosques of Xinjiang,' *The Guardian* (6 May 2019).

100 Bahram Sintash and UHRP, 'Demolishing Faith: The Destruction and Desecration of Uyghur Mosques and Shrines' (28 October 2019).

101 Kuo, 'Revealed: New Evidence of China's Mission to Raze the Mosques of Xinjiang.'

102 Grose, '"Once Their Mental State is Healthy, They Will Be Able to Live Happily in Society."'

103 Ibid.

104 Ibid.

105 'Millions Attend Flag Raising Ceremonies Across Xinjiang,' *Global Times* (16 April 2018).

106 Darren Byler, 'The Future of Uyghur Cultural – And Halal – Life in The Year of The Pig,' *SupChina* (6 February 2019).

107 Byler, 'Xinjiang Education Reform and the Eradication Of Uyghur-Language Books.'

108 Ibid.

109 Adrian Zenz, 'Break Their Roots: Evidence for China's Parent-Child Separation Campaign in Xinjiang,' *The Journal of Political Risk*, 7:7 (July 2019).

110 Ibid.

111 Ibid.

112 Wong, 'To Temper Unrest in Western China, Officials Offer Money for Intermarriage.'

113 Eva Xiao, 'China Pushes Inter-ethnic Marriage in Xinjiang Assimilation Drive,' *Agence France-Press* (17 May 2019).

114 See Darren Byler, 'Uyghur Love in a Time of Interethnic Marriage,' *SupChina* (7 August 2019).

115 Ben Dooley, 'Tear Gas, Tasers and Textbooks: Inside China's Xinjiang Internment Camps,' *Agence France-Press* (25 October 2018).

Conclusion

1 Chris Buckey and Stephen Lee Myers, 'China Says it Closed Muslim Detention Camps; There is Reason to Doubt that,' *The New York Times* (9 August 2019)

2 Eva Dou and Philip Wen, 'Admit Your Mistakes, Repent: China Shifts its Campaign to Control Xinjiang's Muslims,' *The Wall Street Journal* (7 February 2020)

3 See Ellen Halliday, 'Uighurs Can't Escape Chinese Repression, Even in Europe,' *The Atlantic* (20 August 2019); Ondrej Kilmes, *China's Xinjiang Work in Turkey: The Uyghur factor in Sino-Turkish Relations*, Paper

presented at the workshop "Mapping China's footprint in the world II," organised by Sinopsis and the Oriental Institute of the Czech Academy of Sciences (2019).

4 Kilmes, *China's Xinjiang Work in Turkey.*
5 TIP, *Abdulhäq Damollam Bilän Sûhbät* (August 2019)
6 Ben Westcott and Robert Roth, 'UN Members Issue Dueling Statements over China's Treatment of Uyghurs in Xinjiang,' *CNN* (29 October 2019)
7 Ibid
8 Shoshana Zuboff, *The Age of Surveillance Capitalism: The Fight for a Human Future at the New Frontier of Power* (New York: PublicAffairs, 2019)

A NOTE ON METHODOLOGY

1 S. Frederick Starr (ed.), *Xinjiang: China's Muslim Borderland* (New York: M.E. Sharpe, 2004).
2 See Daniel de Vise, 'US Scholars Say Their Book on China Led to Travel Ban,' *The Washington Post* (20 August 2011).

INDEX

John R. Bowen, *Can Islam Be French? Pluralism and Pragmatism in a Secularist State*

Roxanne L. Euben and Muhammad Qasim Zaman, eds., *Princeton Readings in Islamist Thought: Texts and Contexts from al-Banna to Bin Laden*

Irfan Ahmad, *Islamism and Democracy in India: The Transformation of Jamaat-e-Islami*

Thomas Barfield, *Afghanistan: A Cultural and Political History*

Sara Roy, *Hamas and Civil Society in Gaza: Engaging the Islamist Social Sector*

Michael Laffan, *The Makings of Indonesian Islam: Orientalism and the Narration of a Sufi Past*

Jonathan Laurence, *The Emancipation of Europe's Muslims: The State's Role in Minority Integration*

Jenny White, *Muslim Nationalism and the New Turks*

Lara Deeb and Mona Harb, *Leisurely Islam: Negotiating Geography and Morality in Shi'ite South Beirut*

Esra Özyürek, *Being German, Becoming Muslim: Race, Religion, and Conversion in the New Europe*

Ellen Anne McLarney, *Soft Force: Women in Egypt's Islamic Awakening*

Avi Max Spiegel, *Young Islam: The New Politics of Religion in Morocco and the Arab World*

Nadav Samin, *Of Sand or Soil: Genealogy and Tribal Belonging in Saudi Arabia*

Bernard Rougier, *The Sunni Tragedy in the Middle East: North Lebanon from al-Qaeda to ISIS*

Lihi Ben Shitrit, *Righteous Transgressions: Women's Activism on the Israeli and Palestinian Religious Right*

John R. Bowen, *On British Islam: Religion, Law, and Everyday Practice in Shari'a Councils*

Gilles Kepel, with Antoine Jardin, *Terror in France: The Rise of Jihad in the West*

Alexander Thurston, *Boko Haram: The History of an African Jihadist Movement*

David Kloos, *Becoming Better Muslims: Religious Authority and Ethical Improvement in Aceh, Indonesia*

Muhammad Qasim Zaman, *Islam in Pakistan: A History*

Walter Armbrust, *Martyrs and Tricksters: An Ethnography of the Egyptian Revolution*

Sean Roberts, *The War on the Uyghurs: China's Internal Campaign against a Muslim Minority*

Ismail Farjie Alatas, *What Is Religious Authority? Cultivating Islamic Community in Indonesia*

Printed in the USA
CPSIA information can be obtained
at www.ICGtesting.com
LVHW092008181223
766777LV00003B/334